W9-BNN-581

Praise for Karen Hering's Writing to Wake the Soul

"In this powerful, lovely, practical, and provocative book, Karen Hering offers the world both a new form of ministry that transcends multiple traditional boundaries and profound evidence that the asking of unanswerable questions brings forth wide-open spiritual narratives of astonishing depth."

Mary Farrell Bednarowski, professor emerita of religious studies, United Theological Seminary of the Twin Cities

"So many of us want to write! Writing satisfies some profound longing— to become more fully ourselves, to connect more deeply to loved ones, to help transform our hurting world. In *Writing to Wake the Soul*, Karen Hering gives us the tools to act; our faith in writing can lead to a trustworthy spiritual practice."

Elizabeth Jarrett Andrew, author of *Writing the Sacred Journey* and *On the Threshold*

"My soul yearns for a time when I can do contemplative writing. Having a guide to engage in such writing is an immensely precious gift that Karen Hering has given us. Elegant, accessible, and poetically imaginative, *Writing to Wake the Soul* is a great companion to have in one's spiritual journey. Don't go without it!"

Eleazar S. Fernandez, author of *Burning Center, Porous Borders*

"This is one of the best books ever written about the relationship between writing and spirituality. Karen Hering offers readers a wise and generous guide to mining essential material and transforming it into writing that is authentic and revelatory. Those who approach this book with open heart and mind will discover much about themselves."

Bart Schneider, author of *Blue Bossa* and *Beautiful Inez*

"Karen Hering's invaluable guide, *Writing to Wake the Soul*, brings alive the venerable art of writing as a spiritual practice for our time and place. It will awaken you to your own spiritual inclinations, as well as introduce you to a wealth of wisdom handed on by pilgrims who have preceded you on the way."

Donald Ottenhoff, executive director of Collegeville Institute for Ecumenical and Cultural Research

"Profound in its clarity and completeness, here is a contemplative guide to awaken the nurturing spirit in each of us. Like a good guide, this book will take you by the hand as you journey, but only long enough to help you discover the compass and spiritual grounding you already carry within."

William C. Moyers, author of *Broken*

"In *Writing to Wake the Soul*, Karen Hering has given us a spiritual practice that helps us tell our own stories while listening more deeply to those of others. This is important and healing work, and Hering's book invites and equips us to participate in it. It's a book I plan to use myself, alone, and with others. Will be especially helpful in respectfully addressing sensitive issues such as sexism and racism."

Jonathan Odell, author of *The Healing*

"Karen Hering is a wise and welcome spirit guide. From hints on quieting the inner critic to generous insistence that everyone is a writer, *Writing to Wake the Soul* invites private devotional practice. It will also awaken discussion between people of various faith backgrounds and those with no formal tradition at all."

Rev. Victoria Safford, senior minister, White Bear UU Church and author of *Walking Toward Morning*

WRITING
TO WAKE
THE SOUL

WRITING TO WAKE THE SOUL

Opening the Sacred Conversation Within

KAREN HERING

ATRIA BOOKS
New York London Toronto Sydney New Delhi

BEYOND WORDS
Hillsboro, Oregon

ATRIA BOOKS

A Division of Simon & Schuster, Inc.
1230 Avenue of the Americas
New York, NY 10020

BEYOND WORDS

20827 N.W. Cornell Road, Suite 500
Hillsboro, Oregon 97124-9808
503-531-8700 / 503-531-8773 fax
www.beyondword.com

Names have been changed to protect identity in some instances.

Managing editor: Lindsay S. Brown
Editor: Gretchen Stelter, Anna Noak
Copyeditor: Linda M. Meyer
Proofreader: Meadowlark Publishing Services
Permissions: Sheri Gilbert
Interior Design: Devon Smith
Composition: William H. Brunson Typography Services

First Atria Books/Beyond Words hardcover edition November 2013

For more information about special discounts for bulk purchases, please contact
Simon & Schuster Special Sales at 1-866-506-1949 or business@simonandschuster.com.

The Simon & Schuster Speakers Bureau can bring authors to your live event. For more
information or to book an event, contact the Simon & Schuster Speakers Bureau at
1-866-248-3049 or visit our website at www.simonspeakers.com.

Manufactured in the United States of America

10 9 8 7 6 5 4 3 2 1

Library of Congress Cataloging-in-Publication Data

Hering, Karen.
　Writing to wake the soul : opening the sacred conversation within / Karen Hering.
　pages　cm
　Includes bibliographical references.
　1. Spiritual journals—Authorship.　I. Title.
　BL628.5.H47　2013
　204′.46—dc23

　　　　　　　　　　　　　　　　　　　　　　　　　2013019108

ISBN 978-1-58270-412-8
ISBN 978-1-4767-0661-0 (ebook)

The corporate mission of Beyond Words Publishing, Inc.: *Inspire to Integrity*

For David and Cat:
you have added to my life's unfinished sentences
in beautifully surprising ways.

--- ∞∞ ---

What is this precious love and laughter
Budding in our hearts?
It is the glorious sound
Of a soul waking up!

Hafiz

--- ∞∞ ---

CONTENTS

PREFACE

This is a book of sentences, some incomplete . . .
a book of narratives left open,
questions unanswered,
of theology still being written . . .

It is a book about words
but mostly about what pulses beneath them,
what stretches beyond all naming—
between the lines,
off the page,
in the ellipses trailing after . . .

When I was a child, I wanted to be a missionary. Not a mission-ary's wife, I would explain with a four-year-old's insistence on being understood. I wanted to be the missionary. Years later, after my confirmation in a church where women were neither ordained nor present on the chancel during worship, I announced that I wished to serve as an acolyte, donning a white frock and cer-emonially lighting the altar candles at the beginning of worship. It was 1972. The church elders took a vote on whether to permit my request and reported back to me that, like my sisters before me, I was welcome to serve in the nursery instead. Acolytes were male, they reiterated, their edict pinching off the possibilities of my story in the church—and the church's narrative too.

The elders' decision was a formative moment for me, though perhaps not in the way it was intended, for it revealed to me the inadequacy of closed narratives, of stories bound in predetermined endings and lacking in imagination and surprise. Their denial of my request marked the beginning of a personal practice of questioning that has served both my faith and my life well, for I soon discovered that closed narratives do not just occur in communities of faith nor are they only a matter of gender. We seal our narratives in tombs of expected outcomes all the time. We do this whenever we presume to know what can and cannot happen from the gridlocked standpoint of what is without ever asking what might be.

In my own story, the germ of my religious interests and vocation remained buried for many years—for decades, in fact, well into my adulthood and even after I joined a community of faith that had been ordaining women to the ministry for over a hundred years. Finally, in my forties, I enrolled in seminary. At first, I said I was a writer wanting to steep my words in theology. Then, as my studies continued, I realized I was a minister too. I wanted to be ordained but not to any form of ministry I had already seen or experienced. I wanted to bring writing and ministry together in a new way, and I was blessed to have a spiritual director (and a few seminary professors too) who patiently told me, as often as I needed to hear it, that perhaps the work I was called to did not yet exist and would not exist until I named it and brought it into being.

Slowly, I grew into that possibility. I came to understand that my vocation might best be described with a sentence not yet written. By the end of my seminary training, I realized I was not going to pursue a typical congregational ministry. Rather, I made up a job description for "literary minister" as a sketch of the ministry I thought I was meant to do. I knew I would be asked to describe and possibly defend it in the rigorous ordination examinations ahead of me, so I took the job description to the co-ministers of a large urban congregation in my denomination and asked them to help me find the faults in it. Instead, they asked how we might together find a way to develop such a ministry in their congregation. They too held the narrative open, as did the national foundation that funded the literary ministry's start-up; the individual donors who later supplemented the foundation's grant; the congregation that housed and encouraged the new ministry of words and story; my husband and family, my ministerial mentor, my committee on ministry; and dozens of colleagues, friends, and other supporters who kept assuring me it was not folly to keep moving forward even though I could not say exactly where I was headed or whether the path would prove entirely passable.

This is how it happened that I became a "literary minister," inviting others to explore their own faith and their questions about faith in a contemplative practice of writing that took shape along the way—and this is what I offer in this book. It is no wonder that both this practice and this book are based on keeping narratives open; both are the result of an open-ended narrative—as are each of our lives and the larger story we are all writing together.

INTRODUCTION

Sitting over words
very late I have heard a kind of whispered sighing
—W. S. Merwin[1]

M y mother lived with a terminal neuromuscular illness for two
years before it began to steal her ability to speak. Then, as
her breath and pronunciation waned, she acquired a communica-
tions device—a state-of-the-art computer designed to serve as her
voice. By touch screen and eventually, as her hands weakened too,
by movement of her eyes, she could select words, phrases, and whole
sentences, and command the communicator to speak them.

Making this remarkable device useful and efficient required
stocking it with a ready supply of phrases my mother might need
as her illness progressed. One day, as she was becoming acquainted
with the computer, we sat together reviewing the phrases already pro-
grammed into it, deleting the ones she would not need and adding
others she might wish to have readily available. At first this was easy.
Long retired and now confined to her nurse-assisted apartment, she

quickly charged me with deleting all phrases about going to work or to the mall. Then, as a lifelong Christian without close acquaintances from other faiths, she went on to remove references to going to the mosque and the synagogue. Finally, we came to a new group of questions, and as we scrolled through them, she stopped on one and said flatly with her diminishing breath, "Delete that."

I could not help feeling the long shadow cast by the question's six simple words: "Why is this happening to me?" I studied my mom's face. Confined to a wheelchair for a year and a half, she had lost a lot of weight but still looked beautiful to me and younger than her eighty-two years. Turning from the words on the computer screen to read the emotions written across her features, I recognized a familiar flash of impatience. She was a doer, a teacher by profession, a taskmaster by inclination, with a quick mind that leaned toward the literal and pragmatic. When I asked her why she wanted to delete it, she explained with a slight wave of her thinning hand, "It's unanswerable. Who needs it?"

My finger hovered over the delete command. "You know," I observed, "in the Bible, in the middle of all his troubles, Job asked a lot of unanswerable questions."

Our eyes met and lingered in a wordless exchange.

"Sometimes it helps to ask a question even if it is unanswerable," I said. "Sometimes the answer isn't the point."

I don't know what she was thinking in the silence that followed. But I do know what the gaze we shared meant to me. It was an embrace between souls, wordless and timeless, bottomless as love can be—big enough and strong enough to hold a question, even an unanswerable one.

"Keep it," she said quietly, and we moved on to the rest.

The task, it turned out, was harder than we'd thought it would be. She was entering a stage of terrific and unpredictable decline in her illness. Who could possibly know what words, phrases, and expressions she might need as her losses mounted? What questions would ever be sufficient? What vocabulary could speak the prayers she might wish to utter? What could possibly name the unimaginable experiences to come?

These questions have stayed with me ever since, not only in the final months of my mother's life, but also in the larger context of the world and our times. We don't often fully grapple with the many losses of this century, but if you want a hint of it, try reading out loud the list of animals that have already gone extinct in recent years. Read it slowly, as the solemn tribute that it is, naming those unique beings that will never walk the earth or swim the seas or fly the skies again: there's the sea mink and the short-tailed hopping-mouse, the Toolache wallaby and the pristine mustached bat, just to name a few; the Mascarene parrot, the silver trout, and the desert bandicoot; the Atlantic gray whale and the broad-faced potoroo. We don't often stop to name and count them, but all of these—and many more—are gone forever.

If this memorial list wanders too far from home, think of some favorite natural place you once enjoyed—a stretch of coastline, a northern lake, a swath of prairie or forest—that no longer glistens or grows in the same way it once did. You might check out photographs of the earth's shrinking glaciers, or simply look up into the night sky and let yourself wonder over the many stars now invisible to the eye as the lights of our cities veil more and more of the cosmos beyond.

The natural world is full of examples of loss these days, but for all the time we spend debating how long our natural resources will last and how best to preserve them, beneath these debates there sits a sorrow that is often left unspoken. What words, after all, could be adequate to the magnitude of these losses—not only the loss of species and wilderness but of the lifestyle we have grown accustomed to and which we are rapidly learning will not be possible to continue? Our grief, displacement, and disillusionment are real if often unnamable; and the joy, love, and wild appreciation that sometimes arise in the midst of deep grief can feel just as unspeakable. What words, which phrases, and which expressions will we need? What questions will we want to ask—answerable or unanswerable—in the years ahead?

The most universal language has always been that of image and metaphor, an ancient tongue that speaks in poetry and parable, in memory and imagination. It is a language spoken by each of us nightly in our dreams and by all of us collectively in the mythology that shapes our world and our understanding of it. These metaphors are capable of carrying what dream practitioner Jeremy Taylor calls our "not-yet-speech-ripe" awareness. He imagines, playfully but with some seriousness too, early hominids dreaming of strange noises that would turn out to be the first words ever spoken.[2]

What awareness might be stirring in the collective unconscious today, waiting to emerge in our words? What are the strange noises waking us at night not yet formed into speech, and what might they teach us if we learn to listen to them and decipher their larger meaning?

Today, ours is a vocabulary much enlarged by science, technology, and the accumulated knowledge of history. Even so, if we find ourselves at a loss for language strong, pliable, and generative enough to express our experience, we might well ask if the Western mindset so dominant in the twenty-first century has perhaps diminished our access to the language of myth, metaphor, and imagination that we need. Have we unwittingly forgotten or deleted the unanswerable questions we need to be asking, or the words, metaphorical phrases, and stories that might give us the language to ask them?

I prize hard facts at least as much as the next person. First trained as a journalist, I crave the clarity and clean lines of good facts. But their literalism does set limits. Our culture's emphasis on the veracity of facts has a shadow side—a discomfort with mystery, myth, and metaphor that sometimes borders on disdain. *Myth or fact?* we repeatedly ask, as if truth could be threshed in this way, one being grain and the other chaff. Can we instead weave them together, warp and weft, making a stronger fabric of more intricate pattern, a poetic narrative tenacious and timeless enough to make use of both?

This book, and the spiritual practice of writing it describes, is about reclaiming our vocabularies of faith and restoring our capacity for metaphorical thinking. It explores how we might wake what Hebrew scripture calls the "still, small voice within"[3] by engaging in contemplative correspondence with our inner self, soul, and wisdom. In the pages that follow, you'll find poetry and story, myth and meditation, etymologies and images, history and hard science—as well as a plentitude of questions, many of them ultimately unanswerable but all of them richly ponderable. In the sixty reflections and writing prompts provided in Part 2, you'll find an invitation to add your own stories, words, and images to the conversation. The larger story of the universe is still being written, and each of us has a part to play in how that story ultimately turns out.

I have written this book out of my lifelong passion not only for words but also for their transformative power. It is rooted in my personal experience and a longstanding, if not always daily, practice of writing that has saved me time and again from despair, depression, defeat, cynicism, and countless other unwanted conditions that appear more often than I'd like. Now, several years into a literary ministry in which I have led hundreds of guided writing sessions for people of different faiths and worldviews, I have been privileged to witness how words have saved others as well, both on the page and as they share them with one another. In these sessions, I've watched writers and non-writers alike gaining fluency in their own languages of faith (for they are not one but wondrously many) and becoming more adept at translating into and from the faith languages of others; and I have seen firsthand how this has been empowering and healing beyond anything I had expected.

THE PRACTICE OF CONTEMPLATIVE CORRESPONDENCE

Contemplative correspondence is a spiritual practice of writing rooted in theology and story; drawn to the surface by questions, prompts, and ellipses; and most fully experienced when its words are accepted as invitations into conversations and relationships with others. It is also an invitation to keep our language pliable and our narratives open, and to let our questions lead toward something more, something beautiful and whole, beyond all naming.

Contemplative correspondence combines a number of spiritual practices and writing methods with the intention of sacred connection, spiritual growth, and creative flow. Its lineage is long and its sister practices are many. Like *lectio divina*, a practice of reading and meditating on scripture, it turns our ear toward truths found in poetic language and imagery, and like prayer, it is a practice of both speaking and deep listening. Like guided meditation, it invites participants to sit in stillness, present in the current moment, while being attentive to the gifts of memory and imagination; like journal writing, it reflects on our daily lives; and like Tai Chi (also called Tai Ji by many practitioners) and yoga, it directs our awareness both inward and outward, to the energy flowing through us and stirring just beyond our senses and our movement. None of its components are new. It is less a matter of reinventing the wheel than it is a new way of hitching the wheels to a cart, which is really what all writing is about—giving new arrangement and assembly to words and meanings that are already on hand.

Like prayer, this practice is doctrinally neutral. It claims no allegiance to a specific faith or even to a particular position on the theological spectrum, insisting only that life holds more than meets the eye and that spiritual practices can help connect us to that more. It can be used by the theist, agnostic, and atheist alike. Some say this kind of writing is the most basic work of creating meaning—a human effort of ordering the chaotic nature of our experience. Others say it's a matter of opening oneself to revelation and to meaning already embedded in the world, whether it's been placed there by nature and evolution, by a holy Creator, or by some combination of these working together. From any perspective, this spiritual practice of writing can be described as our creative participation in a universe still unfolding.

Of course, the practice of contemplative correspondence does have its own story of origin. It was developed at Unity Church-Unitarian, an urban congregation in Saint Paul, Minnesota, where each month the worship services focus on a different theological theme such as faith, brokenness, incarnation, or blessing. As the congregation's consulting literary minister, I was charged with creating opportunities for members to reflect on worship themes in their own words. Each month, I offered a guided writing session that corresponded to the worship theme, and the members' reflections that had begun in worship were deepened in the writing sessions as they drew from their own life stories to flesh out the theme in their own words. Members also shared their writing—in the sessions, in a literary journal the church began to publish, and sometimes in worship services—and this further enriched and expanded the congregation's collective understanding of the themes.

In time, the guided writing sessions attracted people from beyond the congregation, and I began offering sessions in other settings as well—in other communities of faith, in spiritual or value-based organizations, at a local literary center and a seminary, and in personal and workplace retreats. I discovered that this particular approach to writing was fruitful in a wide variety of contexts, helping people of different faiths, and those of no faith affiliation, to listen to their own inner wisdom and to share that wisdom with one another.

At its essence, whether practiced in groups or alone, contemplative correspondence focuses on theological themes or words, and involves personal writing that is informed and inspired by religious teachings, poetry, stories, visual images, physical objects, memory, imagination, science, history, and wordplay. The practice is reflective and the writing is associative, often beginning from prompts or half-written sentences that trail off in ellipses. It is not abstract but concrete and experiential writing, drawing from what we see, hear, smell, taste, and touch, and reflecting on what we sense and feel. Finally, in the spirit of correspondence, the writing invites participants into dialogue not only with their inner voice and the holy but also with others, whether it is other participants in a group writing session or other voices present in the religious teachings, stories, poetry, and images that precede each prompt. In this way, the writing invites reflection on our personal experiences but always in the context of a larger, shared narrative and with encouragement to keep the narrative open to new possibilities as well as new voices.

FOR WRITERS AND NON-WRITERS ALIKE

When I started leading guided writing sessions, I thought the programs would appeal mostly to those with a strong interest in writing, either as a hobby or a profession. But I quickly discovered that many participants had not previously identified themselves as writers and that this practice can be as appealing and fruitful for those who consider themselves writers as for those who do not.

Of course, it is not for everyone; no spiritual practice is, and any practice that involves writing will send some people running in the other direction. Because writing is often regarded as requiring a gift or a particular skill set, some fear the writing in the sessions might be measured by the rules of grammar, spelling, and style. But contemplative correspondence intentionally steers clear of critique, leveling the ground between writers and non-writers. Many participants who have had difficulty writing in other settings or with other approaches have been happily surprised to find their words flowing easily and prolifically in this practice.

HOW TO USE THIS BOOK

This book is written in two parts. Part 1 offers a reflection on writing, metaphor, and spiritual practice, as well as a practical guide to contemplative correspondence. Part 2 explores ten theological themes with material that can be used in contemplative correspondence, alone or in groups, or by readers who wish to reflect on the themes without writing. Because it is my hope that the book will be useful to readers with and without pen in hand, I offer a few suggestions for different approaches to the pages that follow.

If you wish to learn about and practice contemplative correspondence, I suggest reading Part 1 from the beginning before giving the writing sessions a try in Part 2. However, if you are short on time and eager to begin, you could learn enough to start your practice by reading chapter 5, then jumping in and trying the writing explorations in Part 2. In Part 2, you can start your practice with any of the ten themes, but whichever theme you choose, it's best to follow the prompts from the first to the last within that theme because often they build on one another, directly or indirectly. After you've done the practice for a while, you'll likely have a sense of how it works for you and whether you wish to modify it. You might also supplement the writing explorations with additional readings and teachings from your own wisdom sources or by creating your own prompts. Eventually, you might choose other words and themes, developing your own explorations and prompts as you go.

If you are reading this book without desire for a writing practice, you might use it in several ways. You can read the reflections in Part 2 without any of the earlier chapters and without doing any writing. They can be used as daily meditations; as material for religious education, retreat planning, or creative writing classes; to spur conversation with a spiritual director or mentor; or to spark sermon writing or other creative compositions.

Still other readers might enjoy the opening chapters of the book as an exploration of writing and spiritual practice, and as an invitation to consider the role of language and metaphor in shaping our future possibilities, both personal and collective. Whether or not we undertake writing as a spiritual practice, expanding our capacity for metaphorical thinking will help us bridge the gaps currently widening in our public discourse and rhetoric. Not coincidentally, it also supports creativity, coaxing the muse to speak, and helping us each discover our own way of seeing things.

However you read and use this book, I hope you will find in it an antidote to the way words sometimes harden like wedges that drive us apart. This book and this practice of writing remind us that the first purpose of language is connective, to relate, and that, in the midst of all our differences and divisions, we still belong to and with one another.

PART I

THE SPIRITUAL PRACTICE OF WRITING

What
Is the
Root of all these
Words?
One thing: love.
—HAFIZ[1]

The human gift of language is born of the desire to connect, to share our experience with each other. Our words are bridges built between one person and the next while also crossing time, from the moment they are written down to the moment they are lifted from the page by a reader.

Religion too, in the root of the word and in its best practice, is about what binds us together, one person and one moment to the next. The human religious impulse toward love and compassion connects the spark of the sacred within each of us to the shining wholeness of life embracing all of us.

The spiritual practice of writing brings these two gifts together and invites us to heed the age-old human calling to seek the meaning of our lives.

1

WHY WE WRITE

> *I have been wakeful at night*
> *and words have come to me*
> *out of their deep caves*
> *needing to be remembered.*
> —**WENDELL BERRY**[1]

Why do we write? Not just those of us who call ourselves writers, but all of us. Whether we wear the writer label or not, most of us know what it's like to wake up reaching for words. We all have stories that are uniquely ours to share, and we know the feeling of searching for the right words to recount the events of our lives and to articulate the underlying meanings they carry—what makes them funny or sad, assuring or infuriating, inspiring or disturbing—which is to say, what makes them worth telling and listening to in the first place.

If we are literate and enjoy the rights of free speech, it can be easy to forget that to tell one's story is a basic human need, and to put it down in writing is a way of being seen that can have profound implications. Around the world and throughout history, naming our human experience is often a first step in transforming it, on personal levels and more broadly. As Nigerian writer Ben Okri put it, "[C]hange the stories individuals and nations live by and tell themselves, and you change the individuals and nations."[2]

The Afghan Women's Writing Project is a program based on this premise, supporting women's voices with the belief that to tell one's story is a human right. For many writers, but especially for those writing in times and places that seek to silence them, this is more than a matter of personal expression. Anyone who has read *The Thousand and One Nights* knows that storytelling sometimes involves great risk but can also wield tremendous power—over the one doing the telling and over those on the receiving end too. Like Scheherazade, every storyteller holds the possibility of turning expected endings into new beginnings. One of the participants in the Afghan Women's Writing Project noted that her writing has not only made her life visible but has also empowered her with a new sense of possibilities. She said, "I took my pen to write and at first I was afraid: what to write? about what? But [. . .] I took the pen; I didn't write from outside of my heart, I began to write about whatever was in my heart [. . .] I took the pen and I wrote and everything changed. I learned if I stand, everyone will stand, other women in my country will stand."[3]

In my own exchanges with writers in Nicaragua, I have heard countless examples of how stories, words, and poetry have brought about great change, personally and nationally. After the national literacy campaign reduced Nicaragua's illiteracy rate from 51 percent to 12 percent in the early 1980s, one person described the impact dramatically, saying, "Not knowing how to read and write is like walking with your eyes closed and with a cane." Another wrote, "The power of knowing how to read and write makes me bigger, more human."[4] Twenty-five years after that campaign, I sat at a table in Managua with a small group of visiting writers as Nicaraguan journalist and poet María López Vigil vehemently declared, "All lives are stories. If we know how to tell a life's story, we can understand it. We can be transformed by it."[5]

Closer to home, in the ordinary challenges of daily living, nothing has brought the power of words and stories into full, gut-level awareness for me as clearly as my experiences parenting in the middle of the night. My son, Charlie, was an easy child. A delightful, responsive young companion of few fits and tears, he rarely had tantrums or outbursts by day.

But at night, when he was about eighteen months old, it was another matter. Sometimes, just an hour or so after his father and I had fallen asleep, Charlie would cry out in a terrified scream that catapulted us from bed and sent us running into his room, adrenaline coursing through our veins. There, we would find him still asleep in his own bed, caught in the grip of a fear so fierce it would not allow him to waken. Instead, he would cry loudly and inconsolably, experiencing what we eventually learned were night terrors. He would not rouse even when we picked him up. In his sleep, he would push away from our embrace or any attempted comfort, resisting all efforts to draw him from his terrifying dream.

After much experimentation, we discovered the only thing that worked in these nights was to tell a story. Not just any story, though. You could not just say "Pete and Judy were walking through the park one day." It had to be fresh and not too predictable. You had to have a real plot told in poetic narrative, bringing events together in a new or surprising arrangement and making something happen. Because what would finally loosen the grip of Charlie's terror as we kept talking right through his tears and his screams would be the compelling detail, the ironic plot twist, or the unusual pairing of images. Only when the story caught Charlie's attention with the hook of a new possibility and then reeled him in with a line strong enough to hold him and all his thrashing resistance too, only then would he leave the fearful dream behind and awaken, sniffling but no longer sobbing, listening attentively to hear how the story would turn out.

We may never know, empirically speaking, why these stories worked the way they did. Was Charlie listening through his dream state, in the way that sleepwalkers often do, bringing what they see and hear into conversation with the dream world that still grips them? Was he waiting, with the tentative ear most of us lend to the stories we encounter, only offering full attention when the story delivers something of interest, something beautiful or curious or otherwise enticing? Or was it us, the storytellers, who changed as we turned ourselves over to the stories we told? Perhaps as David or I walked the bedroom floor on those sleepless nights, holding Charlie's wailing resistance in our arms, our own breathing became deeper, our presence more calm, and our heartbeat more steady as we entered the rhythms of the story unfolding, as we let its sequence and turn of events take shape in our imagination, find words, and be told.

Either way, it was during those late nights in Charlie's bedroom, reaching for words and images, characters and sounds, and tying them all together in the net of a plot, that I gained new respect for the way in which stories can catch hold of us, hauling us in from our fears and resistance, pulling us into wakeful and comforting relationship with one another.

"*Homo fabula*," Okri calls our species. "We are storytelling beings. We are part human, part stories."[6] For it's not just that we need to hear stories, but we all, each in our own way, need to tell them as well.

It is an urge that develops early, side by side with the human gift of language, and stays with us all our life long. Not long after Charlie began talking, he told his first story. One warm spring evening, we were in the backyard playing basketball with our beloved neighbor Laurie, and we all paused at one point to admire the sun setting in the west while the full moon rose majestically on the opposite horizon. Later, as we changed Charlie into his pajamas for the night, his first story came tumbling out, composed entirely of three words and not a verb among them. "Sun. Moon. Lau—rie," he said, drawing the last word out with long and lingering awe, as if realizing for the first time that a moment of delight and beauty could be reassembled by naming its parts and carried forward by telling its story again. "Sun. Moon. Lau—rie." He repeated the words over and over like a mantra, as if astounded to discover he now had the power to evoke a moment of wonder gone by, with nothing more than a few words.

In his book *Poetry as Survival*, Gregory Orr says our need to tell stories is a basic human impulse to create order out of chaos. Not only does this make the world more comprehensible, it also makes life, and its traumas, more bearable. Orr knows this firsthand. At the age of twelve, he caused his younger brother's death in a tragic hunting accident. After silently carrying the grief and guilt of this tragedy for years, he finally found relief in a high school English class where he learned to write poetry. "That first poem I wrote," he said, "[. . .] liberated the enormous energy of my despair and oppression as nothing before had ever done. I simultaneously felt revealed to myself and freed of myself by the images and actions of the poem."[7] Telling our stories, putting our experiences into words and poetic narrative, is more than an act of artistic expression; it can be the transformative and healing work of survival.

I once led a writing session on the topic of brokenness, and although I'd been leading similar sessions on different themes in the congregation for over a year at that time, none of the programs I had offered elicited as many advance inquiries from congregants as that one. One by one, people who were thinking about participating shared with me a few details from their own personal stories of brokenness, asking if I thought they should attend. Each person was drawn to the session as a chance for healing but was hesitant for fear the writing might be too painful.

One of these members, Neil Mikesell, attended the session, his own brokenheartedness tucked carefully out of sight as he did. He participated quietly and diligently, and at the end of the two-hour program, when I invited participants to share what they had written, I expected Neil would remain silent. Instead, he read a beautiful four-line poem he'd written about the brokenness of his relationship with his children inspired by a broken pocket watch he'd retrieved from the middle of the table during one of the writing prompts.

Afterward, Neil stopped in my office and told me, with visible relief, "Now I can finally begin my healing." Of course, it was not that quick. For a full year he worked on that poem. Though his healing began with the lines written in the session, it continued for months afterward until he combined that poem with another. The new poem paired a lament for his broken relationship with a redemptive connection to a larger love and to lasting time that cannot be measured in minutes or hours; and both the poem and poet were lifted into a new experience of wholeness. Neil told me later that although his pain remained, he knew his heart was mending.

old man
out of habit he looks at his watch
there's no change in the position of the hands
not that it matters
they won't be calling anyway
they're gone
the time has passed when he matters to them
he has become irrelevant
he has become inconvenient
he has become disposable
another throwaway
in a throwaway world
he looks at his watch again and knows

broken though this watch
time continues measured or not
broken though this heart
love continues returned or not[8]

It was beautiful—both the poem and the process Neil engaged in to make his healing possible. When he published the poem in the church's literary journal and read it at a church coffeehouse, the balm of its message spoke to many others as well, and that too was important, connecting him to the world outside his pain so that he no longer carried his brokenness alone.

Of course, it is not just brokenness but also the overspill of love and joy that begs for words. It can be any emotion that wakes us in the middle of the night or sends us reaching for words at any time of day. For it is in our need to both proclaim and lament, to protest and rejoice—our urge to share our experience of the world with one another—that we become who we are. Naming, after all, is an important way of bringing things into being, including ourselves. "For all [people] live by truth and stand in need of expression [. . .]," said Ralph Waldo Emerson. "The man is only half himself, the other half is his expression."[9]

2

WHY METAPHORS MATTER

We can so seldom declare what a thing is,
except by saying it is something else.
—GEORGE ELIOT[1]

The truth is, in the search for human expression, words often come up short. As T. S. Eliot famously put it, "Words strain, / Crack and sometimes break, under the burden."[2] Especially when reaching toward our biggest unanswered questions and life's deepest mysteries, words are almost never enough. And yet, they are all we have. So we do what we can with them, trying our best to express what we feel and what we experience, what we wonder and what we know. *or we talk about something else*

This is when and why we turn to metaphor—those words and phrases and even whole stories that carry a greater cache of meaning. With metaphor, we often find that language works like a fishing net drawing up deeper meanings that lie well below the surface of what our words describe. And we can use this knotted net to haul in from our unconscious what the poet Sam Hamill calls "the surprise / catch of the day, . . . something / just beyond what words can say."[3]

When we write as a spiritual practice, we are tying our words together in nets that allow us to trawl the deeper waters of consciousness and mystery—just as the poets do in Sam Hamill's description above. Because contemplative correspondence intentionally seeks to connect our unique experience of the world with the larger meanings beneath, behind, and beyond it, metaphor is an important tool in this spiritual practice.

The word metaphor, at its root, means to transfer. A good metaphor transfers our understanding of something known and near at hand, often a physical reality, to other concepts harder to grasp. (Using the word *grasp*, for instance, as something we might do with a concept, is itself a metaphor, helping us imagine that something intangible can be held in our hand.) In this way, metaphors engage us in what cognitive scientists George Lakoff and Mark Johnson call *imaginative rationality*, drawing on our dual capacity for imagination *and* rationality.[4] So, metaphors defy the notion that we must choose between these two human faculties. The great gift of human consciousness is that we are capable of engaging both at once; one might even say we are compelled to do just that. Virginia Woolf described this as the writer's work, using her own metaphor of fishing with hook and line to portray how the two work together:

> She was not thinking; she was not reasoning; she was not constructing a plot; she was letting her imagination down into the depths of her consciousness while she sat above holding on by a thin but quite necessary thread of reason.[5]

So it is, in contemplative correspondence: with metaphorical thinking we engage reason and imagination together, not to construct a plot or prove a hypothesis but to explore what is out of sight—the unknown or unnamed within us and beyond us. Like Woolf's fisherwoman writer, we let our imaginations down into the depths of memory and consciousness (individual and collective) and we hold on by a "thin but quite necessary thread of reason," hoping to haul our catch up to the shore. As we engage metaphor in this kind of writing, we not only increase our awareness of our own lives, we also gain or regain access to a wealth of religious myth and language, whether old or new, familiar or foreign; and we come to see our individual lives in the context of mystery and meaning so much larger.

For a long time in early adulthood, I had trouble appreciating the metaphorical truths of stories from the Bible. I had been raised in a religious tradition that read these accounts with a keen focus on the top layers of the stories' specific events, characters, and other details, often without drawing up and really wrestling with the weightier symbolic meanings below the surface. By my late teens, craving a different approach, I had turned away from both organized religion and its ancient stories as sources of wisdom. When I did, ironically if not surprisingly, I ran straight into the metaphor-shunning world of journalism, with its own infatuation with who-what-when-where surfaces and its own brand of fact-based literalism. As a journalist I was trained to look just for facts, as crisp and sure as the clatter of my Underwood typewriter.

But my youthful skepticism about the old Biblical stories and my resistance to religious words in general—words like *God* or *prayer, sin* or *redemption*—left me without metaphors and language that I have since found to be invaluable for exploring the meaning of my life and its connection to others. Contemplative correspondence is an invitation to visit and revisit religious stories, words, and images—including those we are still using, those we thought we'd left behind, and some that may be new to us—and to regard the metaphors they offer as nets we cast out into the waters of mystery. At times, this fishing might bring into our boats something beautiful or meaty, or even something large and dangerously thrashing. Other times, as poet Heid E. Erdrich notes in the final stanza of her "Origin of Poem," it might simply be a matter of finding and feeling our connection to what is deep and alive, well below the surface of things. In either case, it can require a lot of casting and long, patient waiting:

> *We fish our own waters*
> *green and layered*
> *weedy and warm—*
> *Nothing rises,*
> *no ripples, but we wait.*
> *All we want is the tug—*
> *something deep, alive, on the line.*[6]

The poet W. S. Merwin said, "A real metaphor and real image keeps bringing up new facets, new dimensions, new distances."[7] It also brings up new relationships. It opens perception. Every time we cross the bridges provided by good metaphors, we are able to look at the world from a different shore. From that new vantage point, we not only gain understanding of the distant shore; we also receive a fresh perspective on the shore we came from and how the two are related, connected not just by the metaphor's bridge but also by the gap it spans. This suggests what a growing body of empirical evidence confirms about how metaphors function—they are not just linguistic or literary tools but conceptual building blocks of abstract thought and reason.[8]

The desire for connection, which is at the root of all reaching for language, is what calls us back to stories and metaphor, over and over again, as we look for ways to explore what is shared in our human experience as well as what is unique. In the widening polarization of the twenty-first century, the poet Adrienne Rich memorably said that what we really need is to develop "the great muscle of metaphor, drawing strength from resemblance in difference." Speaking a few years after the September 11 attacks in 2001 and the United States's response to those attacks, Rich decried the claim that the world was irreparably divided between those who hold fiercely to religious beliefs and those who do not. She noted poignantly, "If there's a line to be drawn, it's not so much between secularism and belief as between those for whom language has metaphoric density and those for whom it is merely formulaic—to be used for repression, manipulation, empty certitudes to ensure obedience."[9]

Metaphors are meant to connect, not to divide. In religious teachings and in any realm where different worldviews come into play, when we explore truths as metaphorical, we open new possibilities for dialogue and understanding instead of insisting on conflict and breach. By reminding us of the unity beneath all things, metaphorical thinking not only helps us better understand our own experience and inner truths; it also equips us for religious and interfaith conversations with others and for discerning the larger meanings of current events.

About a year after I began my work as a literary minister, one of the congregation's senior members, an octogenarian and World War II captain of a German submarine chaser, a man with a quick and practical mind, told me candidly that my written reflections on the church's monthly worship themes were far too metaphorical for him. My writing might carry more weight, he suggested, if it were more concrete. I listened carefully. I liked Duncan. I wanted to know what kind of writing might reach him too. And then, as he continued, Duncan made his point by saying that metaphors were like "shingling in the fog." I asked what that meant, and by way of explanation, he told me a story about Paul Bunyan and how one foggy day he set his crew to the task of shingling a new roof. All day long, the men kept busy pounding nails into the shingles, but as the fog began to clear, the shingles all fell to the ground with a clatter, making the men aware they had just nailed them to the fog.

Clearly, metaphors will not work if not anchored in the ground of our experience and our rational understanding of it. But even for a concrete thinker like Duncan, when trying to communicate across different ways of seeing and understanding, the most effective tools are often found in metaphor, or in this case allegory, which is basically a metaphor extended in the form of story.

What might it mean to develop and flex "the great muscle of metaphor" in the twenty-first century? As author James Geary put it in his insightful book about the power of metaphors, "Metaphorical thinking half discovers and half invents the likenesses it describes."[10] And this is what contemplative correspondence does, taking note of how things are related and connected even, and especially, in the midst of difference. It is a way of paying attention that tells us meaning is multilayered and multifaceted, and that the sometimes ambling practices of correlation, correspondence, and conversation will be far more effective paths for exploring truth than heading out determinedly on the narrow passages of fact-finding or one-way absolutes.

WORDS AS METAPHORS

Every word is, in a sense, a metaphor, not only conveying its most obvious definitions but also other innuendos. If we think of words as the "fossil poems" Emerson dubbed them to be, we become more aware of the skeletons of old meanings pressed into them, whether visibly or invisibly. Even when we are unfamiliar with a word's etymology and earlier usage, we can be influenced by the old associations it carries like a tincture vaguely coloring the word today. Especially when a word is in flux, in the process of being reappropriated by a new context or by a particular group, the hints of old meanings can hold invisible sway. Becoming more aware of these fossil inferences, then, gives us greater understanding of the words we use and how we use them.

Consider, for example, the word *geek*, a word undergoing transition as its common usage increases and as new generations claim it with zeal and pride. As recently as the early 1990s, the word was defined by the *Oxford English Dictionary* of the day as "a simpleton, a dupe; a person who is socially inept or boringly conventional or studious."[11] It was a derogatory label still stained by its earliest and much more gauche meaning as the name for a carnival performer who bit the heads off live chickens.

In usage, by the midnineties the word had already begun its new association with specialized computer skills and savvy. As technology soon proliferated in our daily lives and elevated many "computer geeks" in visibility and status, the perception of geekiness also gained stature, until the word eventually became a kind of badge of knowledge and devotion while still carrying a slight taint of social awkwardness. A 2011 dictionary entry defined geek as an unfashionable or socially inept person but added that when used with a modifier, as in "computer geek" or "movie geek" or "word geek," it means "a knowledgeable and obsessive enthusiast."

Clearly, the word has come a long way in a relatively short time, and if you've ever embraced your "inner geek" or announced you are going to "get your geek on," you are part of a usage trend giving the word an increasingly positive spin. Even so, this might be as much about our growing willingness (and even desire) to embrace social awkwardness as it is a full rehabilitation of the word's meaning. Both the dictionary and current usage suggest that even in its modified and more positive meaning, a tincture of social gawkiness remains, like the faint echo of a ghoulish freak show years ago. Knowing the word's old story gives us a richer understanding of its innuendo when we use it.

More to the point of religious language, we might look at a word like *redemption*, which is considered at length in Part 2 of this book. Even a brief look at the word's fossil associations might help explain some of the mixed feelings we have about it now. For here is an old-fashioned word for salvation whose usage has waned in progressive religious conversation almost in proportion to its waxing in secular cultural reviews. How many times have you heard a book, a play, or a movie praised as "redemptive"? What's behind this shift from religious to secular usage? Why such discomfort in one realm, where the word once held strong currency, and such esteem for its message in another? We might find a clue in the root meaning of *redemption*, which is the repayment of something owed, a meaning that perhaps strikes too close to the nerve of our times. Riddled with debt as so many of us are, it's no wonder we meet the word with an uncomfortable combination of aversion and attraction.

THE WAY OUR BRAINS WORK

In my work as a minister and writer, I often depend on metaphor to point toward connections and openings not always immediately visible. But metaphorical linkage is not just a literary exercise, nor can it be dismissed as metaphysical or mystical. It is the way our brains work.

In recent decades, neuroscience has drawn a fascinating picture of how our brains process and rely upon metaphor, which Geary describes in lay terms in *I Is an Other*. As he explains, the human brain evolved to manage sensory information long before abstract concepts commanded as much attention as they do today. This means the brain's neural circuitry was first designed for the senses and the sensory world understood through them. As humans became increasingly occupied by abstract thinking, our brains developed a kind of scaffolding that runs alongside the original neural circuitry, allowing the original wiring to serve more than one purpose.[12] For instance, the circuitry that monitors environmental temperatures also serves to measure and process emotional temperatures. It turns out, one of the earliest metaphorical associations shared across cultures is the link between affection and warmth, a metaphorical understanding of affection derived from an infant's first physical experiences of being held.[13]

Metaphor's linkage between the physical and the psychological is called *embodied cognition*. Our capacity for embodied cognition grows under the shared influence of individual experience and cultural context, and as it does, each of us develops a storehouse of metaphors that allows us to understand abstract concepts in terms that are physiological—sensory, concrete, and measurable.[14] For instance, the abstraction of time becomes comprehensible in Western culture with the conceptual metaphor "Time is money." It's a saying that may sound familiar, but it lies mostly unspoken in comparison to other words that are used far more frequently to understand and communicate the concept of time. So we talk about *spending* our time, or we might say someone is *wasting* our time or that something will *save* us time. Is it *worth* your time, we might ask, or do you need to *budget* your time better? Lakoff and Johnson call these associations *entailments*, traits inferred or implied with a word's usage often without our awareness.[15] The entailments of the "time is money" metaphor provide a vernacular of time that we use freely, typically without conscious awareness of the conceptual metaphor on which it is based.

In another example, Lakoff and Johnson explore the abstraction of love as understood by numerous conceptual metaphors, some of them conflicting with one another. Consider "love is a journey." (We're either in step with each other, or we're going our own separate ways.) "Love is magic." (I've fallen under her spell, or he's dreamy.) And "love is a physical force." (We are attracted to one another, and there are sparks between us, and now my life revolves around you.)[16]

Often doing their work out of sight, the basic conceptual metaphors serve as frames that organize what we know. They can also function as filters that limit our new knowledge to those concepts for which we already have a frame or metaphor. Lakoff says when we encounter new knowledge—even in the form of new facts—if it doesn't fit the frames or metaphors at our disposal, the frames we have will stay and the facts will "bounce off," unabsorbed.[17] Conversely, when we acquire a new conceptual metaphor, it allows us to receive new varieties of information by providing the scaffolding with which we can connect the information to our brain's circuitry. Our neurons actually grow new extensions in our brains to handle this, causing a physical change that increases the number of thinking patterns available to us in our minds and increases our ability to imagine and establish new ways of being in the world.

Simply put, metaphors give us more options. Linking what we know in our bodies to what we wonder in our questions, metaphors tie one concept to another until we have a net, and nets in hand, we can begin to trawl through even the deepest waters of mystery and our unanswerable questions.

3

WRITING AS A
SPIRITUAL PRACTICE

The purpose of all prayer is to uplift the words,
to return them to their source above.
—LIQQUTIM YEQARIM[1]

It is one thing to acknowledge that we all reach for words and that metaphors help us understand the big questions, but as we reach for metaphors with pen in hand, when does that writing become a spiritual practice?

DEFINING SPIRITUAL PRACTICE

Spirit, like beauty, is best known in the eye—and the heart—of the beholder. One person's spiritual practice might be another's distraction—or even affliction. To define what makes a practice a spiritual one, we might do best to take note of its fruits. Anthony de Mello tells the story of a spiritual master who defined spirituality as that which brings us to inner transformation. When a seeker asked the master about following the traditional methods handed

21

down by spiritual leaders, the master replied that the old methods are only as true to spirituality as their function and results. "A blanket," said the master, "is no longer a blanket if it does not keep you warm."[2] Spiritual practices in the twenty-first century, whether ancient or new, are those that still keep us warm and bring us to inner transformation.

Spiritual practices are activities and postures that awaken us to the ground of our being and to the pulse of life within us and around us. A spiritual practice will deepen our relationship with the sacred source of life, by whatever name we know it—Enlightenment, God, Allah, Spirit of Life, or Truth itself. It will call us into a higher-quality relationship with ourselves and others, alerting us to the connectedness of life and our role within that connectedness. It might be as simple as focusing. And as anyone who has tried to focus knows, it can be as elusive as that too.

For the ancient Jews, when the temple was destroyed, it was their practices that helped them keep their faith and identity, whether they were wandering in wilderness or suffering conquest by others. For many of us today, the sacred structures, spaces, and traditions of earlier generations have been destroyed or desecrated, or they might have become inaccessible to us for any number of reasons. When this happens, it is our own spiritual practices that can help us keep our faith and our identity intact and alive.

We might count a number of familiar activities as spiritual practices. Prayer and silent meditation are common examples. Practices of the body and movement, such as yoga, Tai Chi, and walking meditation, are others. *Lectio divina* (holy or meditative reading) and *scriptio divina* (holy or meditative writing) are practices rooted in words. Each of these is, on one level, a simple practice. And yet it might be said of any of them that a lifetime is not long enough for learning them.

They don't have to be difficult or demanding. We don't need to give up our day jobs to do them, nor, I believe, do we need to do them every day. However, on some level, they do require a commit-ment. They must be cultivated with some regularity and intention. They are not accidental. Now and then, with some good fortune, you can experience the kind of awakening I'm talking about without adhering to a spiritual practice, just as you can happen upon a patch of wild blueberries and enjoy a trailside treat. But if you want to harvest enough berries for jam (and year-round enjoyment), you'll either want to cultivate your own blueberry patch or you'll need to know how and where to find the most plentiful ones growing near your home. And you'll want to bring a pail.

Because spiritual practices are essentially receptive—meant for listening, waiting, opening, seeing, apprehending—they require that we be prepared to reap their fruits. The main reason we call them *practices* is to acknowledge the necessity of this preparation. We are practicing and thus becoming more adept at what it takes to receive the abundance ripening all around us and within us.

The frequency and regularity of a spiritual practice can also be self-determined. When my son was young and learning to play the harp in the Suzuki method of instruction, his teacher said he didn't *have* to practice daily, but he should practice every day that he took time to eat. Spiritual practice is, I'm grateful to say, per-haps broader than that, but it is still based on hunger. Everyone's circadian rhythms are different, so why wouldn't our spiritual rhythms be different too? One person might need to do something daily to make it an active, salient, and nourishing part of his or her life. For the next person, it might be a weekly cycle. What's impor-tant is that it be frequent enough to become effortless, habitual, and reliable.

How often will you need to do it in order to miss it if you stop? How long can you go without it before you hunger for what it brings you? If you don't find yourself hungering for it when you give it up, you might ask yourself if you have ever fully tasted its fruits.

Some use the term *spiritual discipline*. Others, including many dedicated to one spiritual practice or another, eschew the word *discipline* for its connotations of correction and punishment. But the Latin root of the word *discipline*, meaning "instruction of disciples," strikes me as fitting. In a spiritual practice or discipline, we are all students learning lessons in paying attention and spiritual living. Not only that, but we are also *lifelong* learners, never finished but always practicing, not with a goal of perfection (as in "practice makes perfect"), but with the hope that over time, our spiritual growth and the activities that cultivate it will come more easily.

THE SPIRITUAL PRACTICE OF SEEING METAPHORS

In the spiritual practice of writing, especially the kind described here as contemplative correspondence, we become more adept at metaphorical thinking. As it becomes easier to think metaphorically, we begin to see more metaphors around us; and the more metaphors we see, the more bridges we have access to, inviting our connection to other people, to other perspectives, and to other possible outcomes.

Yannis Ritsos, a twentieth-century Greek poet active in the anti-Nazi resistance, beautifully describes the power of seeing through words and metaphors in his poem "The Meaning of Simplicity." He writes, "Every word is a doorway / to a meeting, one often cancelled."[3] The test of the word's truth, according to Ritsos, is whether it refuses our attempts to cancel the meeting and calls us into a meaningful encounter anyway.

Practicing contemplative correspondence makes it easier to spot the countless metaphors of daily living as doorways to the larger meanings often hidden behind, beneath, or beyond them. First we regard the world at hand, tangible and tantalizing, fragrant and fractal, describing its edges, its discord, and its harmonies. Then, as we do, even if we don't find the larger meanings, if we refocus our eyes on the possibility of larger meaning, we'll be looking through the particularities of our own lives, knowing there is more.

French anthropologist Claude Lévi-Strauss noted that the human brain develops its capacity according to the demands of our physical and cultural survival as well as our interests. He marveled over evidence of ancient cultures where people could see the planet Venus by day. After consulting with astronomers and European navigational history, he found additional references to sailors who could see Venus in broad daylight and concluded that it was made possible by two things—the need to navigate vast waters by day, and a knowledge of the stars and planetary patterns that helped the early sailors know where to look. Speaking in the 1970s, Lévi-Strauss said, "Today we use less and we use more of our mental capacity than we did in the past,"[4] suggesting that the demands of the twentieth century caused many people to develop their capacity for scientific and abstract thinking while losing some capacity for sensory perception. "[A]s scientific thinkers," he noted, "we use a very limited amount of our mental power."[5]

Is it possible to recover mental capacity that we've left behind thinking it is no longer needed? This is the question that I would pose to Lévi-Strauss if he showed up on my doorstep today, because it seems to me that in the twenty-first century, we could use a bit more capacity for mythic memory and metaphorical thinking than most of us currently have.

Curious about Lévi-Strauss's example of seeing Venus, I tested this out as best I could. One night, awakening about 4:30 AM and unable to return to sleep, I stepped outside to find the moonless sky filled with stars. In the east, Venus was just rising over the horizon, brightest of all. Sunrise was two hours away, so I bundled up in some warm clothes and sat on my deck in the autumn darkness, intently watching Venus as the sky gradually lightened. One by one the constellations were extinguished by the approaching dawn. The sky turned vaguely blue and the grass and trees emerged around me, first as forms and then with colors. I kept my eyes on the sky, though, staring intently at Venus as the tails of light that had made it appear as a star slowly retreated. Just before I lost sight of it altogether, it resembled the tiniest orb of a moon barely discernible against the brightening sky. Then, with my next blink, it was gone. Shifting my eyes to the horizon, I saw that the sun was already well above it. It was an hour past sunrise, and I had seen Venus by day!

Similarly, in contemplative correspondence, I have found that by focusing our attention on the surfaces of our daily lives as metaphors for something more, we train our inner eye to see what might otherwise remain unnoticed—what Thomas Merton called the "hidden wholeness." John Calvin once said, "Wherever you cast your eyes, there is no spot in the universe wherein you cannot discern at least some sparks of [God's] glory."[6] Learning to see this wholeness or these sparks of divinity—and to name them for what they are—is what a spiritual practice trains us to do. Spiritual practices increase our capacity for focusing, for paying attention, for noticing patterns. They train our vision so that we can see what has always been there—whether in the daytime sky or in the ground beneath our feet—but may have escaped our preoccupied minds and habits of distraction.

A spiritual practice also requires our internal consent, a willingness to sit still long enough to receive—and be changed by—what comes, which is what happens in creative work as well, as the poet William Stafford described in these lines from "When I Met My Muse":

> Her voice belled forth, and the
> sunlight bent. I felt the ceiling arch, and
> knew that nails up there took a new grip

on whatever they touched. "I am your own
way of looking at things," she said. "When
you allow me to live with you, every
glance at the world around you will be
a sort of salvation." And I took her hand.[7]

Like most forms of spiritual practice, accepting the invitation into creative work and living requires an openness to change—a surrender so complete it reveals a wide new view to us. But significantly, it is a surrender to our *own* way of seeing, as it is in spiritual practice. The muse, too, has a place—and a salvific role to play—in our lives and spiritual practices. Welcoming the muse is about seeing possibilities already here in this world that have gone unnoticed. As writer asha bandele said, "The world is so magnificent, the way it keeps rebirthing itself to you, if you're amenable."[8] When imagination is called upon and strengthened through the practice of a spiritual discipline—an intentional focus on truth and reality larger than oneself—it is less a matter of make-believe than it is one of seeing what already exists in the possibilities lying in wait beneath the surface of things. It is not unlike seeing Venus by day.

WRITING AS A SPIRITUAL PRACTICE

Writing can serve as a spiritual practice in many different forms, some of which you have likely experienced. Perhaps you've had a correspondence with a friend or loved one that verged on prayerful reflection, or your journal writing might serve that purpose. Maybe you write a haiku every morning, or a blog entry, as a way of paying attention. An early mentor of mine in the ministry often said her primary spiritual practice was writing weekly sermons, and I know many others who name the writing of their poetry, fiction, or essays as spiritual disciplines.

For much of my own life, journal writing has been an important act of soul centering. Initially unaware of my journal's spiritual purpose, I later fiercely claimed this writing as a spiritual practice when I realized my journal pages had become a kind of chapel for me, an intimate place that I frequented to whisper my gratitude, praise, and laments, and even, at times, a petition or two. I know many people who regard their journal writing similarly, and perhaps an equal number who consider it a spiritual practice to write daily "morning pages," a discipline of clearing the mind at the start of each day with three longhand pages of stream-of-consciousness writing advocated by Julia Cameron in her book *The Artist's Way*.[9]

Fundamentally, writing as a spiritual practice in most of its forms looks a lot like journal or letter writing. It involves sitting down with an open page, without outline, plan, or six points leading toward a predetermined conclusion. Writing as a spiritual practice is an invitation to wander and discover; it is an opportunity to take a step—or many steps—into the unknown. When you write as a spiritual practice, you are not following a charted trail; you are setting out to do a little bushwhacking on the open page, and where you'll end up is often as unknown as the route you will take to get there.

What makes some writing a spiritual practice and not others is less a matter of form than one of orientation and intention. Writing becomes a spiritual practice when it serves as a personal correspondence with "the still, small voice within,"[10] a way of listening to one's inner truth, and to the sacred source of that truth. Some might call this a correspondence with God, others with the soul. Still others describe it as a letter to and from oneself, a chance to open time and space for listening to the shy, inner voice that is quickly silenced by a busy pace or a noisy world. It is tuning in to the whisper that sometimes prods us awake in the middle of the night, because the night might be the only time quiet enough for it to be heard. Writing as a spiritual practice awakens our ear to the inner self and, in doing so, to the holy.

Thinking of this as a letter to and from ourselves might make it seem easy, but in fact, it describes an exchange that many of us have long avoided, whether because of the time, patience, and silence it requires, or because we might be reluctant to hear what our inner voice has to say. Each time we turn to our email inbox or our smartphones for the next newsfeed or text message, we are tuning out and turning away from our inner voice and the conversations we might have with it. One hundred fifty years ago, Henry David Thoreau noted the costs of shutting down this inner correspondence:

> When our life ceases to be inward and private, conversation degenerates into mere gossip. [. . .] In proportion as our inward life fails, we go more constantly and desperately to the post office. You may depend on it, that the poor fellow who walks away with the greatest number of letters proud of his extensive correspondence, has not heard from himself this long while.[11]

When was the last time you heard from yourself? When was the last time you wrote to yourself? Writing as a spiritual practice invites you into such a correspondence, with regularity and with intention.

Correspondence, of course, carries other meanings too, notably the connection between one thing and another. The practice of writing described in this book intentionally directs our attention to how things are hitched, one to another. It can be as basic as Charlie's three-word composition of awe and wonder at the close of a good day—"Sun, Moon, Lau—rie!"—a constellation of names that oriented him to the universe and to relationship. When writing serves as a spiritual practice, it connects the dots of our experience and opens our eyes to the connections already there, holding the world together.

Nature, of course, is replete with evidence of these connections, but they are increasingly out of sight to many of us as wilderness experiences become few and far apart. Emerson described it this way: "Nature offers all her creatures [. . .] as a picture-language [. . .] Here we find ourselves suddenly not in a critical speculation but in a holy place, and should go very warily and reverently. We stand before the secret of the world, there where Being passes into Appearance and Unity into Variety."[12]

Words matter not because of what they are or what they say but because of what they point toward: the sacred ground of unanswerable questions and unspeakable mysteries. My friend Bart Schneider, a lifelong writer and editor, says he first glimpsed the power of writing at the age of fifteen, when a poet visited his high school. He recalls the poet saying, "Science tells us what things are. Poetry tells us what things are like." It was a simple distinction that ignited his curiosity and launched him into a lifelong vocation of poetry and other forms of writing, telling "what things are like," which, he notes, "allows for many more imaginative opportunities than telling simply what things *are*."

Telling what things are like is a matter of seeking, discovering, and sometimes creating connections between this and that, between you and me. It is the muscle of metaphor Adrienne Rich was talking about. It doesn't ignore how things are different. It acknowledges there are (at least) two sides to every coin. The spiritual practice of writing, like other forms of prayer and meditation, simply helps us pay attention to both sides of life's currency. It wakes us up to the particulars of our own experience while always asking, "What is this *like*? How am I—and how is my experience—connected to others and to life as a whole? And what does that connection mean?"

It can be easy to forget in the present climate of religious divisiveness, but making connections is the root meaning of *religion*, a word tracing back to Latin origins meaning to "bind." Writing that

intentionally looks for sacred connections participates in the dialogue at the core of human existence, the dialogue between what is
fleeting and the eternal. It lifts up the way each one of us is a beautiful and unique conversation—an exchange at turns poignant and
simple, sorrowful and joyous, tremulous and bold—between our
physical, mortal bodies and the more lasting breath of life moving
through us.[13]

In contemplative correspondence, we record that exchange
between our particular experience and the larger meaning running
through our lives. We write about the world we see, hear, taste, smell,
and feel. Then, as the ancient Chinese poets described the writer's
task, we lift our eyes.

"[G]ood work / joins earth to heaven," wrote Lu Chi almost two
millennia ago,[14] having earlier advised, "Know when to lift your
eyes / and when to scrutinize."[15] As we put our own experience into
words, noticing its unique texture and scent, its sound, color, and
flavor, by lifting our eyes we begin to discover what transcends these
particulars. And in that discovery, our words will point toward a
larger experience of life where greater meaning—and connection to
others—dwells.

4

THE INVITATION OF
ELLIPSES ...

The whole sky is yours

to write on, blown open
to a blank page.

—RITA DOVE[1]

A s a particular spiritual practice of writing, contemplative correspondence is rooted in theological themes and words, and
is characterized by writing that comes about through open-ended
questions and half-written sentences trailed by ellipses.

An ellipsis is most simply—and visually—an omission from
a sentence marked by its namesake string of dots (. . .). The term
applies to unmarked omissions as well, an absence of words that
might be considered superfluous or could be understood from context. Sometimes it is used to avoid stating the obvious or unnecessary
repetition; in other cases, it purposely leaves meaning open and
invites the reader to supply it, making possible a rich conversation
between writer and reader. Louise Glück writes about the allure and
power of this invitation: "I am attracted to ellipsis, to the unsaid, to
suggestion, to eloquent, deliberate silence. The unsaid, for me, exerts

great power. [. . .] It is analogous to the unseen; for example, to the power of ruins, to works of art either damaged or incomplete."[2]

An ellipsis is about the unspoken, the deliberate silence, the unfinished sentence trailing off. It carries the power of suggestion and attracts us with our own desire to complete it, a kind of call-and-response. How satisfying it can be, when making a puzzle, to find the last piece in your hand and snap it in place, uniting the larger image. It is human nature to wish to make things whole.

As Glück points out, this is the compelling nature of any ruins. Consider the ancient Pueblo cliff dwellings in the desert canyons of the Southwest. If you visit the dwellings today, you can climb ladders to enter rooms that have not been occupied for seven hundred years and find yourself imagining the half-standing walls as if they were complete. A larger ghost image of the structure rises up in your mind's eye, and you might almost smell the smoke of a cooking fire in the air. As you conjure this image, you participate in it. No longer just a tourist, with the help of a little imagination, you experience the place from an older point in time, gaining access to history through the mind's habit of completing what is only half there in any twenty-first-century visit to the Pueblo village.

This happens in nature as well. In southern China, there is a saying that sightseeing in Yangshuo and Guilin is "70 percent imagination." It is a region known for the other 30 percent, the limestone peaks forming a landscape of tall mounds, overgrown, green, and often veiled by mist, their shapes as evocative as clouds. Many are named for the shape of their silhouettes: Elephant Trunk Hill. Five Fingers. Nine Horses. Camelback. Others without names look like heads turned back to the sky, mouths gaping, leaving me to wonder, when I saw them, were they hungry or howling or singing to the gods?

We do this participatory viewing, filling in the blanks, all the time. It's why optical illusions work. And rough sketches. Sentence fragments. Or syncopation. The human brain loves to string things together, to connect the dots, to draw upon previous knowledge to make things whole. We long to participate in making or uncovering meaning; it is what we are doing whenever we connect our interior landscape with the external, and the temporal and material with the eternal.

This idea also surfaces in an ancient Islamic teaching about the end times. Muslim scholar Mahmoud Mustafa Ayoub says the thirteenth-century Persian mystic Farid Ud-Din 'Attar predicted that the last days will be known by the appearance of two *Dajjal* ("evil one" or literally "one who lies"). Each of these apocalyptic liars, having only one eye, will speak the lie of a different perspective: one, who has only a right eye, will see the world as entirely consisting of spirit; the other, with only a left eye, will see the world as no more than matter and material things. The lies they tell will only be defeated by the restoration of stereoscopic sight, in which the spiritual and the material are joined, and reality can be seen as a whole.[3]

This is in no way to suggest that we are now in the end times, but we are living in a challenging time, one in which we would do well to remember our gift of binocular vision, and to further develop our capacity for seeing the world's material and spiritual traits, and how they are connected. At its core, this is what contemplative correspondence does.

Alfred Stieglitz's series of photographs "Equivalents" is a visual example that depends on the correlation between inner and outer realms, a correlation also made in spiritual writing. Taken in the 1920s and '30s, Stieglitz's series comprised over two hundred photos of clouds, most framed by nothing but sky and some entirely without orienting clues to what was up and what was down. They were some of the first photographs to be widely acclaimed even though they lacked any context pinning them to a literal meaning. Without these reference points, viewers were invited to interpret the photos according to the emotions stirring within them, matching the image to an inner equivalent. Of course, it is an invitation well known to any child lying flat on her back in a field, looking up at the clouds. But sometimes it takes the work of a boundary-pushing artist to return adult viewers to a state of mind common in their childhood. So, too, do metaphors engage our child's mind in the important lifelong task of delighted associations and of linking our emotional world within to the external physical world around us.

As gratifying and healing as this correspondence between inner and outer meaning can be, it is important to note that other, less healthy connections lurk in the unspoken and the unfinished sentence. Sadly, the power of suggestion also evokes the oppressive systems of racism, sexism, and other injustices that we have all internalized. Oppressive systems live most tenaciously in the unspoken. They thrive in innuendo. They depend upon the persistent grip of assumptions that decades ago became unmentionable in polite conversation but still hold court within all of us, shaped as we all are by racism and sexism and other systemic oppressions.[4]

Whole books—a few named as resources in the appendix—have been written about the unspoken nature of white identity, privilege, and framing, for instance. I mention it now to underscore the potency of ellipses and as an important reminder that this, like other forms of deliberate silence, can be used for good or ill ends. When we engage ellipses in writing as a spiritual practice, it is critical that we do so with every possible effort to counter the weight and pull of unspoken oppression. One basic step is to include a diversity of voices that we can converse with, on the page and in person.

Like any form of worship and prayer, contemplative correspondence depends upon creating a safe space, establishing a trustworthy environment in which the writer can explore inner and outer terrain with vulnerability as well as courage. This is especially important in groups and for those whose experiences and voices have been marginalized or silenced. When engaging in this practice alone, it is also helpful to bring our writing into conversation with others' poems and stories, especially those by people of different backgrounds and positions of privilege. Alone or in groups, grounding our writing practice in respectful conversation with others will make a difference in the transformation it makes possible.

AN INVITATION OF INCLUSION

The word *ellipsis* traces back to the Greek *elleipsis*, meaning to "leave out," and that is how this practice works—with words left out. In *Caring for Words in a Culture of Lies*, Marilyn Chandler McEntyre writes about words as trailheads. In this practice, we begin with a word, such as one of the ten featured in Part 2 of this book (*faith, prayer, sin, love, justice, hope, redemption, grace, hospitality*, and *reverence*), each serving as a trailhead into theological terrain, inviting our entry and exploration. As we begin our trek, our attention is drawn to wonders on all sides of the trail—stories and poems, images and etymologies, bits of history and science. Then, not too far along the way, we pause. The metaphors are then laid open, and an unfinished sentence or a question invites us to pick up where the sentence or question leaves off, continuing on the trail again—or bushwhacking in a whole new direction—with our own words and stories as a way to further explore the terrain.

In the years I have led groups in this process, I have noticed that the writing prompts serve as a kind of on-ramp. Some of the most intimidating words a person can write are the first words put down on an empty page, the ones that determine where the writing will go, at what pace, and in whose voice. The opening reflections, questions, and writing prompts used in contemplative correspondence offer a kind of running start to skip over the anxiety of choosing the page's first words. In order for the prompts to work well for different writers and different moments, though, they must be open-ended, written in a way that offers many options for the words that follow. Like a strategic word that opens up a clogged Scrabble board, a good writing prompt can often be as easily completed in one direction as in the opposite. It offers a boost while still letting each writer choose which direction he or she will go once up to speed. In addition, the poems, stories, and definitions provided in the reflection leading up to each writing prompt surround the writer with an ample supply of images and metaphors in the same way that a sous chef lines up recipe ingredients, all chopped and prepared, before the head chef steps in to do the cooking. This is why many of the writing prompts begin with making lists; listing helps us line up our words and images as ingredients kept close at hand before we begin to write.

Whether practiced in a small group or individually, the writing in contemplative correspondence is personal. Drawing from the particulars of our own experience, we fill in the omission, but the sentence is never truly completed. Rather, we regard it as a work in progress, an understanding unfolding over time through a conversation that strives to include an ever-growing number of voices, first completing the sentence for ourselves and then sharing the truth we've found there with one another. It addresses the concern raised by Nigerian writer Chimamanda Ngozi Adichie when she warned about "the danger of a single story" (whether it's ours or someone else's) in the way it hides the true variety of human experience. She said, "The single story creates stereotypes, and the problem with stereotypes is not that they are untrue, but that they are incomplete. They make one story become the only story."[5]

My nephew Joey spends a lot of time with a family of first-generation Polish Americans. Like many recent immigrants, his friends open their home and offer warm hospitality to a steady flow of others newly arriving in this country. Whenever they serve a large meal for special occasions, Joey tells me, the table is set with an extra place open, which they affectionately call the "traveler's chair." Sometimes it's filled with a drop-in newcomer. Other times it remains empty, a beautiful reminder of those who are not seated in body but are included in spirit. It is akin to the practices of the Jewish Passover Seder, in which the words of the Haggadah (the Seder readings) invite "all who are hungry to come and eat," and a glass of wine is poured for the prophet Elijah, and the door is ceremoniously opened with an invitation for the hungry and for Elijah to come, bringing the spirit of redemption to each family's Seder table.

Contemplative correspondence is a way of setting a "traveler's chair" at the table. It opens our shared human story with an invitation to those who may not have been welcomed to the table of our daily lives before—be they prophets of old, marginalized people of our own day, or our own inner voice, long banished from the busy land of our lives. Elliptical writing counters the assumption that the table is full and the story already complete or that meaning can be staked out, claimed, and controlled by those with the loudest voices and greatest power. Rather, this practice asserts that meaning is always unfolding and is woven of threads drawn from the deep pockets of every being and every place and every time.

For many of us, the beauty of this practice is its invitation and encouragement to tell our own story. It reminds us that each of us has a story with the power to reach and to move not only ourselves but others as well, and it affirms that the world needs our story to be more complete. But the practice does not stop there. It also insists that our story is only powerful and meaningful to the degree that we are willing and able to engage it in conversation with larger, open-ended narratives. It calls upon us to listen for the stories and the presence of others. Think of it this way: if the ellipses of the writing prompts in contemplative correspondence appear to you as a traveler's chair that welcomes you to the table, when you sit down to write, remember to pull up another traveler's chair next to you, so the next newcomer will find a place to sit as well. Their story too is needed.

Writer Howard Schwartz, a scholar of Jewish mythology, has written his own tale warning of the dangers of the closed language that befell the tenth, lost tribe of Israel that wandered in the wilderness. After many years of disagreement about where to seek the promised land, one day the people lost the word *open* and without it they were unable to unroll the scroll for their daily prayers.

Fearing the meaning of this fateful sign, the people withdrew from one another. Loving partners slept alone that night, and as they did, they also lost the word *hold*. For days, they remained alone in their separate tents, not packing up to move on with each new morning as they had been, and soon they realized their journeying had ended. And they lost the word *search*.

So it continued. Word after word was lost until the people and the creatures around them had all fallen silent. "Within a year," the story ends, "no one could speak the ancient tongue; its words were scattered through the desert like clouds of dust."[6]

The practice of contemplative correspondence strives to keep words like *open*, *hold*, and *search*—and the words of faith explored in this book, *prayer*, *sin*, *reverence*, and *redemption*—active in our vocabularies and dynamic in their meaning. It is a spiritual practice of reclaiming words, some left along the roadside and others worn out from misuse, and finding new meaning in their old stories, dusting them off so they might shine and be useful again.

This is also a practice that can be and has been used to unleash creativity, to overcome writer's block, to develop characters, and to plant the first seeds of an essay, a sermon, or a poem. Many participants in the sessions I lead have shared poems and other extraordinary writing developed from these writing prompts. But when engaging contemplative correspondence as a spiritual practice, this more polished writing is not the goal even if it may appear as welcome but incidental fruit. The true aim of this practice is to open us to something just beyond what words can say and something just beyond *us* and what we know and see from our particular place and our particular time.

5

A PRACTICAL GUIDE
TO CONTEMPLATIVE
CORRESPONDENCE

*But don't be satisfied with stories, how things
have gone with others. Unfold
your own myth, without complicated explanation,
so everyone will understand the passage,*
We have opened you.

—JALAL AL-DIN RUMI[1]

To create your own practice of contemplative correspondence, individually or in a group, start with the guidelines in this chapter, which are based on what participants have said makes this practice meaningful for them. (More specific tips for using this book in groups or alone are provided in the appendices.) Then, try it out using the sixty reflections and writing prompts on the ten different themes in Part 2. The prompts can be completed in separate sessions or grouped together, three or four from one theme at a time. As you become acquainted with how the practice works best for you, you can also use Part 2 as a model for developing your own material to write about these themes or other themes of your choosing.

None of this is carved in stone. The guidelines are intended only as a starting point, to be modified according to your own needs and situation. As you make this practice your own, however, you will want to consider several characteristics of contemplative correspondence:

- Making time and space
- Welcoming your inner writer to the page
- Connecting what is near and far
- Engaging imagination and memory

MAKING TIME AND SPACE

Cultivating an intentional approach for any spiritual practice requires clearing time and space for it, which is really a matter of paying attention to the thresholds that mark that clearing. This means being clear with ourselves about when, where, and how we are entering our practice, and when it is drawing to a close. This is especially evident in physical spiritual practices, such as yoga or Tai Chi, where a certain amount and type of space is required, whether it's rolling out a mat or clearing enough room. Also, in physical practices, our bodies will insist that we begin with warm-up exercises and will typically reward us with a quiet, lingering pose at the end, so that time is marked off at the start and finish. In practices such as meditation and prayer, liminal postures, gestures, sounds, and phrases commonly serve as thresholds, marking off the time in between as separate from our daily activities—and more focused and devoted.

Like these other practices, contemplative correspondence also benefits from creating thresholds in time and space, as we begin each session and then draw it to a close. This is a practical matter—preparing a space that will accommodate our writing and reflection, equipped with what we need to write and relatively free from distractions—and it is also qualitative—garnering the potent energy found on any threshold and making use of it in our practice.

In a general sense, thresholds are characterized by transition, whether they are physical doorways separating the interior space of our homes from the outside, or lines in time marking life passages such as marriage, graduation, or death. As such they are often accompanied by a sense of dynamic power and vitality, or even danger and thrill. They mark times and places where identity and understanding can undergo significant shifts. By tending to the thresholds of our spiritual practice in even the simplest ways, we can tap this dynamic and use it for transformative results. After all, the power of any spiritual practice comes when it takes us to the threshold of our usual awareness. It can open our eyes to the way things still shine beneath the dust of daily living. So we mark the beginning and ending of the time we've set aside for contemplative correspondence by some ritual action as an indication that we are stepping outside of ordinary time, moving into a time and space we have set aside as sacred.

This doesn't have to be elaborate. You can do it in any number of ways, often drawing from basic rituals of meditation or worship. For instance, you can light a candle, use a singing bowl or chime, read opening and closing words out loud, or begin and end with a word of prayer or silent meditation. If you already have an opening and closing ritual that you use individually or in your congregation or community, it may be good to incorporate this, letting your habits and familiar practices trigger a contemplative frame of mind. I typically begin a writing session by lighting a candle and reading a short poem. I hold the poem in a moment of silent centering that ends with the striking of my singing bowl. When the bowl stops singing, I begin the reading that sets up my first writing.

Creating thresholds also involves protecting the time and space devoted to your practice. This means closing the door and asking others not to disturb you. Whether you are at home or in a community building, look for a space that's not a thoroughfare or permeable to a lot of loud activities. Do what you can to avoid the interruption of phone and email tones telling you that messages are accumulating. In the twenty-first century, these beeps and ringtones are probably the most plentiful form of dust blowing across our thresholds. If it's difficult to go offline while you write, try starting with a shorter time. Better to give yourself ten minutes uninterrupted than an hour with your phone or children or competing activities in the next room tugging at your attention.

Finally, think about how you want to manage the time. Name a beginning and an end, and try to stick with it. Sometimes, when we become familiar with a spiritual practice, it can be so rewarding that we don't want to stop; but in order to make it sustainable in the context of a full life, it will need to be contained! If you're doing it individually, you might take half an hour for the entire session. Or, for a session using just one of the prompts in this book, you might decide you'll write for ten or fifteen minutes on the prompt, adding a little time on either side of that for the opening and closing ritual, and for reading the reflection that leads up to the prompt. If you don't like watching the clock, you can also set page goals. For instance, say you'll write two pages for each prompt. Whatever you set as the perimeter, though, try to maintain it with integrity but without rigidity. One of the first reasons people give for not continuing a spiritual practice is that it takes too much time, so disciplining ourselves to a manageable time limit might be the only way to make our practice feasible.

Once you've set your guidelines, in time or page length, try to keep writing for the full duration, even if you think you've finished early. Sometimes just by keeping the hand moving and the words coming, we unearth a surprising truth we hadn't known was awaiting our attention.

Tending to the space for your practice also involves paying attention to aesthetics. It doesn't take a lot. A small table or altar clear of clutter and appointed with a candle can be enough. I like to add something green or alive, like a plant or flower. You could incorporate a small photo, statue, or sculpture of significance. Arrange this with a singing bowl or chime if you wish to use one, and save room for the practical things you'll need—your writing tools (paper and pen or computer); any books, materials, or other objects needed for your prompts; and perhaps a glass of water or a cup of tea. As much as possible, set yourself up so that you can stay put for the duration of your writing time and choose your surroundings as you would for worship or meditation or prayer—they should be comfortable, visually appealing, separated from the interruptions and distractions of noise and traffic.

On a more philosophical note, thinking about the thresholds of our writing in time and space also serves to remind us that we are tending to thresholds in our awareness. Although this discipline is dependent upon words, the words are not the destination but the vantage point from which we might glimpse something further out. Each writing prompt with its ellipses trailing off asks us to lift our eyes toward the horizon and turn our ears toward the silence, listening for the "still, small voice within" that might complete the sentence.

I wrote the following poem (begun in one of my own practice sessions) as one expression of this reaching, the kind that occurs in my own practice as well as the reaching I experienced after my mother's death.

How We Carry On, Remembering
The singing bowl rings.
The clear chime grows thin,
one last thread trailing
like gossamer
dangling in the wind.
I cannot tell exactly where it ends.

My listening reaches into
the quietus
holding your last words
and the bowl's dimming note.
Silence shimmers clear.
Finally,
my ear
      rests
      deaf.

Still
the chime sounds
in bone and breast
buried there,
remembered
  and struck anew
every day
since your last breath.

Just as the singing bowl's note trails off and our ears reach into the silence for the last thread of sound, this writing practice is intended to take us to the threshold of awakening, opening our awareness to what the silence carries and to the vast world beyond our doorstep.

WELCOMING YOUR INNER WRITER
TO THE PAGE

When I lead a guided writing session, I always begin with a covenant for the group. My hope in offering the covenant is for all of us to start, as the saying goes, on the same page and to make the process as clear to the newcomer as it is to those who have participated before. The covenant I use comprises four statements that are explained in more detail in appendix A, the first one being simply that we are all equal as writers. For the duration of our time in the session, I tell participants we will consider all of us to be on equal standing as writers, no matter how much or how little writing we have done before or what kind and quality. All we need for this practice is something to write with, something to write on, and something to write about. Oh yes, and the intention to write. Even if you engage contemplative correspondence on your own, it may be helpful to begin by reminding yourself that you are ready to write and equal to any other writer in this way.

Another key to inviting your inner writer to come forward is to notify the inner critic that it is strictly off duty during this writing and spiritual practice. The second statement of the group covenant in my writing sessions is that we agree not to engage in critiquing— of each other's writing *and* of our own. Often the release of tension that follows this statement is almost palpable.

Most of us have an inner critic in some form or another, one who likes to speak up in our most vulnerable moments of risk and disclosure. When we write, the inner critic might carry the voice and the lessons of an early teacher or mentor—one who impressed upon us (usually with good cause and the best of intentions) the rules of proper punctuation, grammar, and spelling. These are lessons worth learning and ones that I often depend on when revising my writing for publication or public speaking. In fact, when we befriend our critical mind and get it to treat us with respect, the work of revision can itself become another form of spiritual practice with its own revelations and truths. But for *this* kind of writing, revision is not the point and the inner critic is not our friend. Judging our writing as good or bad, our grammar as proper or flawed, our spelling as right or wrong, our thinking as interesting or mundane will only serve to frighten off the voice of the soul, often as quick to retreat as a bird on a branch or a wolf in the wild. Before you start writing, then, go ahead and send your inner critic out for a stroll. Release it, pack it a lunch if need be, send it off with best wishes. No need to worry it will roam too long or too far. I have yet to meet anyone whose critic has left forever. It will return when you need it—if not well before.

A malady commonly known as writer's block will sometimes result from the presence of an inner critic who is too strong, sitting like a muscle-bound bouncer at the door of our thoughts and imagination. For years I have challenged my own writer's block with the well-known advice William Stafford frequently gave students when they struggled to put words on the page: "Lower your standards. And keep writing."

Lower your standards. It's a useful reminder of the way perfectionism can stifle expression, both soulful and creative. But it is also a plea to lay down our defenses, according to Stafford's son Kim, also a writer and a teacher of creative writing. Writer Luis Alberto Urrea said Kim once pointed out to him that "lowering your standards" is a phrase born of military meaning, a reference to dropping the flags of war intended to announce and provoke battle. Remembering his father's pacifism, Kim Stafford suggested that what his father was saying in this often-quoted phrase was that in our creative work, we will do well to invite peace, to befriend the creative spirit, to lower our battle standards, and to let the quiet, inner voice speak.[2] In writing as a spiritual practice, we are reminded to do the same.

CONNECTING WHAT IS NEAR AND FAR

The writing explorations in this spiritual practice ask us to notice the tangible world with all of our senses open, to describe our embodied responses, and then to connect our experiences and responses to a larger story. The prompts often issue an invitation to recall something that happened, someone you met, or somewhere you ended up, and then to consider: What did you see, hear, smell, taste, and touch? How did it make you feel? And how might the story your life tells be opened to new possibilities and outcomes, to greater connection with others, to a deeper sense of mystery? This is writing more concerned with posing questions than with answering them. As theologian Robert McAfee Brown once said, "Puzzles are meant to be solved. Mysteries are to be experienced."[3]

It is important to include all the components as we write, not only describing our experiences but also how we felt about them then and feel about them now, while exploring how our story connects us to others and how it can reveal new outcomes. Covering all of these bases is especially critical when writing to heal from emotional pain or injury. Louise DeSalvo's book *Writing as a Way of Healing* notes that when writing only recalls what we've experienced without exploring our feelings and the possibility of new endings, it can sometimes do more harm than good, causing us to re-experience old trauma without promoting the healing that comes when we envision and claim a new ending.[4] Other studies have shown that when our personal writing also draws upon our larger worldview or faith, connecting our personal story to a larger context of meaning, the chances of it having a healing effect become greater still.[5]

Not long ago, personal reflection like this was the stuff of letters written to our loved ones in scrawling penmanship, sometimes delivered a full week after they were posted. Now, we compose emails. We text or maybe we blog when feeling more wordy. But much of our online writing is done on the fly, fingers moving on keyboards and touch screens so hastily that we are developing whole new categories of repetitive motion injuries as we type and touch.

In contemplative correspondence, we write at an intentionally slower pace. We record our words within the margins of silence as a reminder that our writing, as poetry was once described, is born as the "orphan of silence,"[6] growing from the unspeakable as surely as it will return to it. In between, in the words that rise to express our questions and to complete our sentences, we enter the present fully with our senses and hearts flung wide open, recording our own story in the larger human narrative of history and place. It is the most important story we can tell—the story of what we see and know, what we experience and feel from wherever we stand and wherever we have been. *And* it is the smallest, most incremental chapter of the larger story in which we all belong. "Never again," wrote John Berger, describing the many-faceted truths of postmodernism, "will a single story be told as though it were the only one."[7]

Each of our stories matters—as a way of sharing our truth and experience and also as a way of preparing us to hear and understand the stories of others. Writer Dorianne Laux once said, "Your experience is not yours alone, but in some sense a metaphor for everyone's."[8] When we write and exchange our stories with each other, the common canon of our human narrative expands and the possibilities for our shared future grow with it. Neuroscientists studying the way our brains process stories have discovered that when we read an account of someone else's experience, fictionalized or not, it activates the same areas of our brains that would be involved if we were having that experience ourselves. It's a scientific explanation of a longstanding observation that reading enlarges our lives—our personal world, our range of experience, and our understanding. In so doing, reading or receiving the stories of others will increase our capacity for wonder, for compassion, and for curiosity by opening to us the view from others' windows. C. S. Lewis noted that reading teaches us "to see with other eyes, to imagine with other imaginations, to feel with other hearts." We turn to literature and stories, Lewis claimed, because we crave a larger view than our single perspective allows. "We demand windows."[9] The spiritual practice of writing from theological themes gives us more windows to look through, first by calling to our attention the view unveiled by various wisdom teachings and stories, and then by encouraging us to write our own words in correspondence with those teachings and stories.

Metaphysically, we might say this is a matter of connecting the material world with the transcendent, the particular with the universal, the inner landscape with a wider horizon. Psychologically, we might notice its similarity to Carl Jung's free association and what he called *active imagination*, a method of prompting patients to embellish their dream imagery through writing or other art forms, and thus bring the dream's deeper archetypes or universal human experiences to the surface.[10]

This is the purpose of focusing our writing on a theological theme. It keeps the writing aimed beyond the borders of our individual experience and connects it to other people, times, and places. Different writing practices, with good purpose and useful results, do not include this thematic focus and instead keep the writer's individual experience front and center. But contemplative correspondence is intended to connect the writer's particular story to something older, longer lasting, and more whole. Organizing the writing prompts around a theological theme is a way of zooming out from each writer's story to notice how it shines in a sky full of stars, and how it holds one point of many in a constellation made across time and space. It draws upon the ancient recognition of a unity or oneness beneath all particular beings and experience.

ENGAGING IMAGINATION AND MEMORY

One of the best tools for lifting our eyes from the particulars of our lives is our imagination—not just the imaginative powers that dream up fantastically fictional settings, people, and storylines, but the kind of imagination that sees through the surface of what is real and familiar, and then reassembles it in an astonishing and beautiful new order. Artful metaphors do this all the time, as did the prophets of old and the gods, goddesses, and tricksters of mythology. Artists, activists, and leaders of social change do it too. *What if?* is a question not just for children or idle daydreamers but for all of us involved in the necessary and important work of rearranging what we already know into a brand-new order, as yet unknown, as yet unseen. *What if?* is a question that beckons forward a brand-new story yet to be told.

This imaginative act is also the work of religion. Christian theologian Eugene Peterson notes that the Christian gospel story itself is both open to and opened by the imagination. He writes:

> As we enter and imaginatively participate, we find ourselves in a more spacious, freer, and more coherent world. We didn't know all this was going on! We had never noticed all this significance! [. . .] Story brings us into more reality, not less, expands horizons, sharpens both sight and insight. Story is the primary means we have for learning what the world is and what it means to be a human being in it.[11]

Consider the old Taoist story about Chuang Tzu's dream. The ancient Taoist master told his friend one day he had just dreamt he was a butterfly, fluttering about weightlessly, enjoying his freedom and flight, and utterly forgetting he had ever been anyone or anything else. When he awakened, again in his human body, recounting his dream to his friend, he could only wonder if that too—his existence as Chuang Tzu—was only a dream. "What if," he asked his friend, "I am really a butterfly dreaming of being Chuang Tzu?" Sometimes it takes a dream in which we experience new forms and ways of being to remind us that our waking hours carry the possibility of new identities as well.

At their best, religion, mythology, and art open up the story we have been telling ourselves, personally and collectively, and challenge our habit of premature closure. They usher us to the doors of mystery. They acknowledge our longings. They question our insistence that we already know, that we are certain, that we are in control. The imagination opens all of this up like the tilling of soil. So our creative mindset moves and thrives in the space trailing after each question and lingering before any answer.

Memory too plays a part. We are, after all, creatures that exist in time. Our individual and collective memory provides images, experiences, sensations, and awareness that our imaginations depend and draw upon when posing the question *What if?* For instance, if I consider the question *What if pigs could fly?* I conjure up my memories of all that I know about pigs and about flying, while imagining some way to put these together. This is the playful and profound task of the improvisational artist, whose performances are always created in the moment, composed onstage from a small set of givens. It might be a character, a line, an object, a setting, or a circumstance. Whatever is given, the performer accepts it as it is and builds the storyline from there. The saying used in improvisation is "Yes, and . . ." You receive whatever was given, saying yes; then, you build on it, saying "and . . . ," and you continue from there. So if you and I are onstage together and you hand me a plunger and ask that I use it to open the door, I don't argue. I don't complain. I don't even question. I say, "Yes. Of course," and I imagine a keyhole in the shape of a plunger. So the story moves on, and we move with it.

In the same spirit, contemplative correspondence receives what is given—a story, a poem, an object, an image, a bit of history or scientific information, a word's etymology or a family tree of its related words—and continues from there. By calling up old stories and parables, we arouse mythic memory. By adding new information or tales of current events, we equip ourselves with contemporary awareness. And by recalling our own memories, we open the vast storage inside each of us, holding our most personal inventory. Each of these givens can awaken us to memory's treasury of images and storylines. Then, our own writing, beginning where the prompt and our memories leave off, launches us imaginatively and evocatively into a new arrangement, understanding, or possibility.

As pleasant as this imaginative practice can be, the urge against it can be strong. Our culture's preference is for knowledge, for facts and the certainty trailing after them in the form of opinions. To help us break the habit of premature closure, contemplative correspondence sometimes makes use of surprise, which means it is best not to read ahead or to think through the writing prompts before taking in the stories, poems, or exercises that lead up to them. However you are able to, try to stay in the moment, writing from the prompts as if they were spoken to you by someone you care about, beginning a sentence and then trailing off and waiting for you to complete it. Follow wherever it leads, with your imagination fully present, perhaps sitting next to you in the spot recently vacated when your inner critic went out walking.

The third agreement in the covenant of my writing sessions is that we will consider all writing to be fiction until proven otherwise. This is just another way of saying that sometimes our imagination will offer the best, if not the most direct, road to the truth. Sometimes the facts, sitting like boulders in the middle of that road, will be obstacles we need to walk around, not in denial but not in submission either. In the yin-yang relationship of fact and fiction, it is important to know the line where one ends and the other begins, but it is equally significant to see how both stand side by side in the larger circle of truth.

BEFORE YOU BEGIN

Writing is a solitary activity. Whether we do it alone at home or at a table with others, the act of writing is an intimate one and the words we use when we do it are, at least initially, privately held between each writer and the page. It can be helpful, then, to remember that the feelings that arise in our writing need not be carried alone.

When we practice contemplative correspondence, we may be writing about great joy or deep sorrow. We may encounter our own vulnerability, perhaps our fears or our grief, our worries or our anger—any or all of these and many other feelings can surface when corresponding with our inner voice and truth, and this can make it difficult either to continue the writing or to re-enter our daily activities after the writing is done.

If, as you write, you experience resistance to the topic or the feelings it stirs, and if it is a time and a place in which you feel safe and supported in doing so, you might try leaning into your resistance. Sometimes knots are tied around our more closely guarded truths, and our willingness to explore the knotted resistance can be illuminating. If, however, you experience sorrow, anger, or other difficult emotions as you write, I encourage you not to carry the emotional weight of your writing and your story alone. Awakening to our own experience and feelings should also reveal our connection to others, reminding us that whatever we write, whatever story we are living through, whatever feelings we are experiencing or have experienced, all of it is held in a story larger still, in a narrative in which many companions are present, offering both guidance and help with the burdens we carry.

As a spiritual practice that increases awareness of self and the sacred, contemplative correspondence has been used by some as a starting point for conversations with their spiritual directors. It has fed conversations with friends and loved ones, trusted mentors and teachers, and therapists or counselors. It also provides a record of thoughts, feelings, and insights that you can return to over time, remembering the period in your life when it was written and often discovering new meaning that you might not have seen on the day it was written. It serves as a correspondence across time as well as an epistolary novel that we write and then read on another day.

In physical forms of spiritual practice, such as yoga or Tai Chi, teachers leading their groups from one position into another frequently remind those practicing to listen to their bodies, modifying the positions as they need to, taking into account their strengths as well as their limits. In contemplative correspondence, we are wise to follow the same advice. On any given day of writing, we should listen to our body and our soul, modifying the prompts and our response to them as needed to honor both our strengths and our limits.

Both life and art are born of limitations as well as inspiration, so learning to regard our limitations with generosity and patience is a good starting point for any endeavor. No need to put off writing until another day when the words might flow better, when we might be more confident or witty, less grief-stricken or better focused. When we acknowledge that who we are and how we are today is the only possible place from which to begin anything, the open page will be there, waiting for our words.

PART II

IN YOUR OWN WORDS

I would give all metaphors
in return for one word
drawn out of my breast like a rib
—ZBIGNIEW HERBERT[1]

Nothing resonates as deeply as a single word drawn from our experience to speak our truth boldly in the language of our own lives.

Each chapter that follows focuses on one word, such as *faith*, *hope*, or *grace*. First, we consider the old stories and metaphors pressed into the word over time. Then we explore the word in the light of our own headlamps, mining it for new veins of meaning in the context of our lives. We might uncover an old meaning that we hadn't known before. Or we might chisel out a new understanding revealed by our unique approach. As we enter a correspondence with the word's fossil wisdom and its expanded possibilities, we emerge with greater fluency to speak our own truths and to hear the truths of others.

So each chapter ends with the simple instruction: Begin writing whenever you are ready and follow wherever it leads.

6

WRITING ABOUT FAITH

FAITH AS A VERB

Faith is a dynamic, multifaceted activity,
an active dialogue with promise.
—SHARON DALOZ PARKS[1]

In the early teachings of many world religions, the word *faith* appears not as a noun but as a verb. It is a way that we live, a loyalty that we grow into over time. In the original Buddhist texts, the Pali word for faith meant "to place the heart upon." Our own English word *faith* derives from the Latin word *fides*, also the root of *fidelity*, meaning trust or trustworthy and implying something or someone we can rely on.

What do you trust most deeply? What do you know to be reliable? Is it science or society, the common good or the human conscience? Do you place your heart upon God, Nature, Love, Life, or the holy ground of Being? This doesn't usually mean choosing just one. For many of us, navigating life's challenging currents requires that we come to trust some combination of the above. Like white-water rafters who learn different strokes for different conditions, faithful living can be a matter of learning when to rely on each of the loyalties engraved upon our hearts, and what those loyalties will require of us. It is not static but an agile discovery of how faith moves and acts in our lives.

Religious historian Wilfred Cantwell Smith claims we might understand faith better if we considered it as a verb, rediscovering "what it means to have faith, to be faithful, to care, to trust, to cherish, to be loyal, to commit oneself: to rediscover what 'believe' *used to mean*."[2] He explains that *believe* stems from the Old German word *belieben*, a relational act of love meaning "to hold dear." Its early Modern English equivalent, unfortunately as extinct today as the Carolina parakeet, is the extraordinary verb "to belove." Faith, or belief, in this sense meant orienting oneself toward another in loyalty and commitment, and with affection, trust, and what Smith describes as "self-giving endearment."[3]

It can be difficult to grasp this older, relational understanding of faith. Today we are more likely to locate faith in institutional structures that we regard as nouns—religions, religious buildings or icons, or doctrine itself. If we trace the meaning of faith back to its earlier manifestations, though, we find something much more participatory. Faith as an act of placing one's heart suggests a give and take that requires movement. It is more akin to dancing than to doctrine. Not only is it made of motion, never sitting still, as life itself does not, but it also sets other things in motion. We might try, if we can bear it grammatically and sonically, to think of "faithing" and ask ourselves what motion and action might characterize it.

"To offer the heart," Buddhist writer Sharon Salzberg says, "is not like offering a fingernail or a lock of hair we were ready to discard anyway; it is to offer the core, most essential part of our being."[4] This is an offering we make not once but on an ongoing basis. Each day, we surrender anew our life's energy and focus to whatever we have named as our life's deepest meaning or purpose (or whatever, even without naming, claims our attention most fiercely). This is, after all, a pretty good way to figure out what or whom we regard as God or as sacred. Consciously or unconsciously, with each day's living, we are choosing where, to whom, and to what we will offer our heart. In this way faith emerges from our daily choices, whether quietly or boldly, joyfully bounding, mindfully marching, or gradually growing.

In Your Own Words

What are some of the verbs that describe faith's action or movement in your life? Does it leap? Take root? Cradle? Embrace? Grow? Climb? Dance? Brainstorm a list of action verbs—words about physical movement or activity—that might describe what faith does or feels like. The words can represent movements or actions vastly different from one another. They might describe your own experience of faith or the way someone else has described it to you. After you've listed a good number of words, choose one and place it in the following prompt (for example, "Faith leaps . . ."), continuing to write wherever it leads.

Faith _____ . . .

Save your list of "faithing" verbs. Keep it on your personal altar if you have one. Tape it near your desk if you're writing about faith. Add to it over time. Keep your eyes open for photographs that depict your "faithing" verbs. If this is fruitful for you, make a writing prompt with a different verb every day for a week, or use any of the verbs on your list to add muscle and movement to your future writing about faith.

AT HOME WITH FAITH

You, estranged from yourself,
short-sighted turtle looking for home,
be home to yourself.
  —NORITA DITTBERNER-JAX[5]

Ironically, although faith is a living, moving thing, it also involves an inner belonging that can look and feel a lot like settling in. It's what Sharon Salzberg calls "a homing instinct"[6] and Wilfred Cantwell Smith describes as "a quiet confidence and joy which enable one to feel at home in the universe [. . .]"[7]

In a way, faith is about coming home to ourselves. Sufi poet Hafiz put it beautifully in his poem "No More Leaving":

> *At*
> *Some point*
> *Your relationship*
> *With God*
> *Will*
> *Become like this:*
> . . . .
> *God will climb into*
> *Your pocket.*
>
> *You will simply just take*
>
> *Yourself*
>
> *Along!*[8]

Some of us were raised in faith traditions that fit us about as well as a glass slipper meant for someone else's foot. We know too well the pain of trying to walk in a faith that contradicts who we are, whom we love, what we know, or what we do and do not trust. Obedience can—with force and a strong shoehorn—be compelled from the outside, but not faith. If faith is truly a matter of trust, it requires a better fit with our inner self and soul. In my own religious journey, from the fundamentalist church of my childhood to Unitarian Universalism where I now place my heart, I can remember the relief of finally sitting in a church and realizing I'd found my spiritual home. It was as if my whole self sighed, for the first time relaxing inside and out in the middle of worship—at last, a trustworthy place for my searching soul.

Of course, the beautiful thing about faith as a verb is that once we find home, faith helps us carry our home within, which is where any true sense of home must begin. When you find something so trustworthy that you are at home in the universe, journey and destination get a little intertwined. Home can be found in a much wider set of possibilities when carried within, and this is what makes it possible for people of different faiths to converse, to pray, or to worship with one another.

In Your Own Words

Think back to a house or apartment where you felt at home as a child. It might be a place you lived in while growing up, or it might be a grandparent's house or that of another relative, friend, or teacher who helped you feel at home with them and with yourself. If a house or apartment does not come to mind, perhaps there was a school or church or another place where you felt at home as a child. Choose one place, and briefly sketch its floor plan and furnishings as you remember them.[9] Take your time. Let your memory fill it in. When you have it roughly drawn, put a star in the places where you remember feeling most at home—at the kitchen table, in a living room chair, in a favorite corner of the attic, in (or perhaps under!) your bed.

Choose one of the places with a star and describe what it felt like to be there. Describe the surroundings and furnishings, what happened there, what you did, how you felt, who was with you. Describe who you were when you were there. Begin with:

I was at home in . . .

WHAT WE TRUST

We all have major questions of faith. . . . The goal is to come to see uncertainties as the spots in our life where God enters in. It is trust that counts—not questions, not answers.
—JOAN CHITTISTER[10]

I grew up in a family that camped. In a feat just short of a miracle, we fit six of us into a canvas-topped tent trailer meant for four. One night, bedded down in a campsite on the edge of a high river bluff, we awoke to the sound of rain pelting our tent top and rivulets streaming beneath the camper, cascading over the nearby cliff. The wind caught the edges of the trailer's canvas until it billowed and snapped with percussive warning. My parents exchanged urgent, undecipherable whispers. A flashlight beam briefly cut the darkness, the zippered doorway whined open and closed, and my father disappeared into the storm.

A few minutes later he returned, soaked to the skin, reporting that we were now secured for the night. Using the fat ropes from his old Navy hammock, he'd tied the camper to a nearby tree with a sailor's expert knots. We could all go back to sleep, he said; and we did. Powerless as we felt in the gales of the storm, those thick ropes and the strong knots we knew my father could tie tethered us to something larger and unseen that we trusted.

But how do we know what is trustworthy? How do we know where to put our faith, and what we can rely on in the middle of a storm? As the morning light would tell us, the tree we were tied to likely had a root system too shallow to hold us securely had the wind blown much harder that night. How do we determine where and when, in what and in whom to place our faith? When I look back on this now, I realize that more than the rope and the tree, we had placed our faith in my father—and his rain-soaked assessment of the storm and our position in it.

In an often-told story from seventeenth-century Europe, an architect whose engineering pushed the boundaries of current thinking designed a public structure that included a large, covered open space on the ground level for a market. When the town leaders reviewed the architect's plans for the building, they protested that the weight-bearing supports were too far apart. Fearing that the structure was unsound, they insisted that more columns be added to support the beams overhead.

The architect assured them the design did not require the extra columns but was unable to convince them. In the end, he acquiesced and added four interior columns. Unbeknownst to the others, though, he made each of the four new columns two inches too short, giving the appearance of supporting the beams while leaving just enough space for his own convictions to stand. Over time, the story says, the original design was proven trustworthy, but in its conception, it was not the design but the columns that provided a visible symbol in which the townspeople could place their faith.

Does it matter whether our own columns of faith in the architecture of our lives provide weight-bearing support themselves or simply give us the confidence we need to keep going in times of doubt? The shortened columns in the story sound innocent enough, but only because the architect's engineering, though unprecedented at the time, was trustworthy. Because faith is ultimately a matter of surrender, we ought not take too lightly the decision of where to place it.

Theologian Paul Tillich said, "Faith is the most centered act of the human mind."[11] One way to determine whether we have placed our faith idolatrously, he noted, is by asking whether it leads to a loss of center or more deeply regains it in a larger context. For instance, placing one's faith in individual success, as many do, may work for a while. It may even result in commendable and visible accomplishment. But, Tillich observed, eventually this is likely to produce the hollow existence that often haunts achievements or affluence ungrounded in greater meaning or a larger cause.

A different danger can arise when faith is placed in nationalism or rigid religious dogma. Both offer greater meaning and cause, but in their most extreme and demanding forms, they sometimes dangerously deny our personal centers of conscience, will, and empathy, especially when they deny concern for those not included in their boundaries or their creeds. If faith is a relationship, it is meant to reach not only toward the divine but also toward self and other. Faith must incline our hearts toward life and the way life hitches each of us to all of us. Faith must serve life over time in the widest sustainable sense, if it is to prove trustworthy. This is not the same as saying faith assures our safety. To the contrary, we each know countless stories of how faithful living can cause people to risk their own well-being or to put their lives at stake. What faithful living *does* assure us, if not personal security, is the survival of what gives our lives meaning and the endurance of life as a whole over a time frame longer than our individual life span can reach.

If this seems too large a call, we are reminded by poet Thomas R. Smith that our lives are made of countless small acts of trust, the simple repairs and deliveries that give us daily practice in faithful living.

Trust

It's like so many other things in life
to which you must say no or yes.

So you take your car to the new mechanic.
Sometimes the best thing to do is trust.

The package left with the disreputable-looking
clerk, the check gulped by the night deposit,
the envelope passed by dozens of strangers—
all show up at their intended destinations.

The theft that could have happened doesn't.
Wind finally gets where it was going
through the snowy trees, and the river, even
when frozen, arrives at the right place.

And sometimes you sense how faithfully your life
is delivered, even though you can't read the address.[12]

In Your Own Words

Materials needed: For this exploration, you'll want to write the first part on paper that can be cut apart in a future prompt, and you'll want to use either colored paper or a colored pen or pencil that will distinguish it from the writing you do in the next prompt.

What do you trust? What specific objects or activities, places or practices come to mind when you consider what you have found to be trustworthy? What are the wisdom teachings, stories, traditions, or communities that you trust? Who are the people, contemporary or ancient, known personally or through their teachings, that you count on? Using a colored sheet of paper or writing with a differently colored pen or pencil, make a list of things, people, teachings, and practices that you trust. Your brainstorming list can draw from science, nature, religion, your personal life, and any combination of the above. It can be made of single words, phrases, or brief sentences, written in lines spaced loosely enough that you will be able to cut them apart.

Keep the list on hand for another writing exercise. For now, briefly scan what you've jotted down. Pick one thing that you remember trusting in a particular incident. Recall an occasion when you depended on it. What happened in that experience? How did it feel to trust this person, place, community, idea, practice, or teaching? How did you know it was trustworthy? Where did you feel your trust—in your mind, your heart, or your body? Begin writing with the prompt:

I trusted . . .

FAITH'S TWIN, DOUBT

Doubt is a pain too lonely to know that faith
is his twin brother.
—KAHLIL GIBRAN[13]

Few of us today would have trouble trusting Wren's guildhall market space. But each day has its wonders. What about the Endless Bridge built as part of the new Guthrie Theater in Minneapolis in 2006? The evocatively named structure is a heavy cantilever appendage jutting from the theater toward the Mississippi River, with no visible supports beneath it despite the obvious weight of the wide cement steps offering outdoor seating at its open end. Farther west, the glass-bottomed Grand Canyon Skywalk hangs four thousand feet over the Colorado River with a similar absence of undergirding. Some people will not venture onto these platforms. But the many who do walk out on them without hesitation are able to because of their faith in modern engineering—or perhaps in the building codes that verify the structural soundness of that engineering.

Faith is sometimes juxtaposed with reason, as if the two repel each other. In our scientific age, this dualism says the only thing we can really trust is reason. But many who have considered faith at great length propose instead that faith and reason, and doubt as well, must all coexist. "For faith to become mature," developmental psychologist Sharon Daloz Parks writes, "it must be able to doubt itself."[14] And in many cases, it survives that doubt by being anchored in reason. "Reason," Paul Tillich says, "is the precondition of faith; faith is the act in which reason reaches ecstatically beyond itself."[15]

When I consider the Endless Bridge, I imagine reason as the engineering that makes it possible, while the cantilever beams, like faith, reach out beyond the building's walls with their own inner strength and integrity. Both are needed for the bridge to bear its load and offer its stunning and reliable thrust into open space, where it presents a panoramic view of river and cityscape unrivaled from other vantage points.

What vistas are revealed to you when you walk to the farthest reaches of your faith?

We can always find plenty to stir our doubts and challenge our faith. The dimensions of greed, the persistence of poverty, the terror of war and violence (much of it ignited by religion itself), all have the capacity to pull the rug out from under faith's feet. The sheer size and weight of these challenges can send us searching for answers we can easily grasp. But if we look too quickly past life's questions, grabbing for an answer, we will have missed faith's more enthralling promise. Without patience for the doubting and sometimes dangerous ways of our questions, we send faith on the run, knowingly or not, and are left clutching only hollow certitude instead. "[O]ne part of me has always been eager to pin faith down, [. . .]" confesses the poet Luci Shaw, before adding tellingly, "another part of me is restless, creative, shaking at the reins."[16]

Recovering a wider view of truth often requires letting go of certainty, asking an open question, and making room for a larger (possibly unknowable) answer. That's when faith shows up, reaching out to meet that truth, while bearing the full weight of our doubts and all the rest that we carry.

In Your Own Words

Materials needed: Like the previous prompt, you'll want to write the first part of this one on paper that can be cut apart in a future prompt, and you'll want to use either colored paper or a colored pen or pencil that will distinguish it from the list you made in the last prompt.

What challenges your faith? What are some of the doubts that make it hard to have faith? They might take the shape of fears or skepticism. It might be something that rises from a contradiction, from a belief itself, or from experiences you've had, things you have learned, events you have observed. It might be the state of the world or the behavior of people in it. Your brainstorming can draw from history, nature, religion, science, personal experiences, or any combination of the above. On a sheet of paper you will later cut apart—and using a different color of paper or ink from what you used in the last prompt—make a list of things that challenge your faith today. They can be single words, phrases, or brief sentences written in lines spaced loosely enough that you will be able to cut them apart.

Save this page for the next writing exercise. If you wish to write more now, after making your list, write from the prompt below, continuing on one topic from your list or naming the many challenges to your faith. (Note: If you are writing this prompt as a daily practice, you might wish to end your writing session by going back and reading what you wrote in the previous prompt about what you trust.)

It's hard to have faith when . . .

OPENING OUR STORY

The world is before you and you need not take it or leave it
as it was when you came in.
—James Baldwin[17]

Buddhist monk Pema Chödrön says there is "no true story." This might seem to be merely a statement of postmodern skepticism, but on a deeper level, Chödrön is challenging the way we sometimes cling to personal perspectives and the one-sided stories we construct from them. She says that when we weave our opinions, prejudices, strategies, and emotions into a story, the story can come to claim its own reality. "But," Chödrön insists, "things are not as solid predictable, or seamless as they seem."[18]

When we regard our personal stories as if they were made of rock-hard reality, we get pinned down or walled off by them. This can happen with religious and historical narratives as well. If we let them take on a form too solid, we forget they are actually, like everything, woven of perceptions that are constantly changing. We piece these perceptions together into a story all the time because that gives us a compact way to carry them and we need that. But once we have a story, we can easily be tricked into thinking it is true in a fixed sort of way, and there is no room for faith in a story as tightly constructed as that. When everything is known, there is no room for possibility. Our identity, happiness, pain, and problems become fixed and immutable when we think the story we tell ourselves—about ourselves and the rest of the world—is fully composed and complete.

Faith, and the possibilities it generates, requires a more generous weave and a gentler grasp of ourselves and the stories we're made of. How else can we write a different ending than the one foretold by what we might dread or by the dreadful events of our times? Only when we hold our stories loosely enough that they can grow, reach, bend, and be changed do we invite into our lives the power and movement of faith. Only then do we discover that "the ordinary, or even oppressive, facts of our lives can become alive with prospect," as Sharon Salzberg puts it.[19]

An account about the French surrealist poet Robert Desnos during his imprisonment in a Nazi concentration camp shows how this works.[20] Desnos was part of a large group of prisoners corralled one day into the bed of a truck headed to the gas chambers. When the truck stopped and the prisoners descended, somberly forming a line, no one spoke, not even the guards. Then Desnos broke the silence, jumping in with wild and foolish energy. He grabbed the hand of a fellow prisoner palm up. Looking at it closely, he announced joyfully that he saw the man had a very long lifeline and was going to have three children.

The poet's excitement became contagious. One prisoner after another extended his hand to Desnos, and he gazed into each palm and proclaimed his improbable predictions of longevity, countless children, and abundant joy. The story of impending death they had all carried so heavily as they descended from the truck bed broke wide open, and before anyone knew what was happening, the entire mood began to change. The poet's audacious fortune-telling, so contrary to the circumstances of the moment, created a new opening, and they all began to slip through it, including the guards. The men's death, which had seemed inevitable, became almost absurd in the face of the fortunes being told. Eventually, the disorientation became so great, the guards were unable to go through with the executions and instead loaded all the prisoners back onto the truck and returned them to the barracks.

A story can be opened by bold acts like this, breaking assumptions apart with loud or ridiculous contradiction and imagination; or it can be more gently coaxed to simply breathe a little instead. Sometimes a quiet pause or a few softly spoken words can be enough to invite us into a new ending that no one saw coming. We should note, though, that this is no guarantee of a happy ending. In the story of Desnos's imaginative act of resistance, he did not survive the camps but died of typhus just days after the war's end. Even a story that successfully takes a new turn doesn't always end the way you want it to. Still, his poetic act of courage demonstrates the power of faithfully unshuttering a story and allowing the light of different possibilities to shine in.

In the Christian resurrection story, the boulder rolled away from Jesus's tomb turns the entire story of his capture and crucifixion in a new direction. In Judaism, the Exodus begins a new chapter in the ancient story of slavery and a long trajectory of liberation still unfolding today. In Buddhist teachings, the warrior Bodhisattva sees that everything is really a dream and is able to then let go long enough that a larger truth can emerge. "Belief clings, but faith lets go," said philosopher Alan Watts.[21] When we make openings in our own story, we let faith move between our tightly woven beliefs and doubts; we let faith reach through them toward something new, as yet unseen but trustworthy beyond belief.

In Your Own Words

Materials needed: For this writing session you'll need the writing you completed in the two preceding prompts on differently colored paper or written in two different colors of ink; a pair of scissors; and a glue stick or equivalent.

With your scissors, cut the list from your last writing exercise (things that challenge your faith) into horizontal strips of sentences or phrases of your own choosing. Next, in similar fashion, cut into pieces the other sheet of paper on which you listed things you trust. Arrange the differently colored paper/differently colored ink pieces together on a third sheet of paper, alternating or interspersing the two colors as the lines of a poem, making a collage, or even gluing or taping them together as a paper sculpture. Follow your impulses.

What emerges? What reaches out reassembled from your words and the faith they describe? What do you find in this new rearrangement? After considering what your reassembled words are saying, begin writing with the prompt:

The story my faith is telling me . . .

FAITH CALLS US FORWARD

Faith hasnt got no eyes, but she's long-legged.
—ZORA NEALE HURSTON[22]

Unfortunately, there are countless ways a person can lose faith. Sometimes the simple need for solid ground can work against us. Years ago, I was traversing a mountainside in the Julian Alps with my husband, David, when the path we were on disappeared beneath a swath of loose rocks about twenty feet wide. The scree originated far above us and stretched equally far below us before disappearing over a precipice. David moved across without hesitating. In seven rapid strides, he easily reached the other side where the path continued. Hesitating behind him, though, I saw the loose rocks shifting beneath his feet with each step. I watched wide eyed as the rocks clattered down the mountainside and tumbled out of sight, over the edge below.

Slowly, I followed, but by lingering too long on the loose rocks, I began slipping down with them. The more I slipped, the more rocks I heard bouncing over the edge below and the harder it was to keep myself moving forward. Finally, in the middle of the scree and sliding slowly toward the precipice, I stopped walking altogether. I was paralyzed by fear.

"Keep moving!" David shouted, his voice finally jolting me from my paralysis and pulling me forward like a lifeline until I finally reached the other side several yards below him but safely above the mountain's edge.

In Buddhist teachings, faith requires the acknowledgment that everything is changing. The ground beneath our feet is always shifting, and yet we must learn to faithfully keep moving across it. We long for stability and certainty, but when it comes right down to it, life and faith are both about growth and the change that growth requires. As Quaker philosopher Douglas Steere put it, "God is always revising our boundaries outward."[23] How will we muster the faith required by this constant growth and outward movement?

The Buddha once told a story about a herd of cows crossing a wide stream. The stream represents ignorance and suffering, and the older, wiser cows see it for what it is and cross without hesitation. The younger cows, stumbling and less certain, observe the older cows and eventually follow. Last of all, even the newest, smallest calves that have just learned to stand will risk the unknown terrain of the streambed because they hear their mothers on the other side. Their mothers' lowing inspires the young calves' trust, so they overcome their timid reluctance and cross the stream too. That trust is how faith works, according to the Buddha, tethering us to something reliable that beckons us to grow and keep going, even when we are afraid.[24]

Faith is about loyalty and trust. It is not a solitary condition but an act of relationship that turns our attention to those crossing the stream ahead of us and calling us forward as well as to those trailing behind, listening for our call. These roles will change from one day to the next. Like other relationships, faith deepens over time and has its own overspill. As our faith matures and we move through new stages, its influence in our lives naturally widens, strengthening our relationship with a growing circle of others, including those who have gone before and those who will come after us. In time, with encouragement from those who have gone before us, the circle stretches to encompass more. Eventually, even what we do not see or know becomes trustworthy and reliable enough for us to keep walking in faith, to keep moving, bringing a new possibility into being as we do.

"Now faith is the assurance of things hoped for," says the Christian scripture passage, "the conviction of things not seen."[25] As the text continues, it lists a long sequence of faithful exemplars from Hebrew scripture: Abel and Enoch; Noah and Abraham; Isaac,

Jacob, and Esau; Moses and Rahab; Gideon, David, and Samuel; and still others. All are commended for their faith, yet as the passage notes, not one of them received what was promised in his or her lifetime. Instead, we are told, they were given a greater inheritance, a deeper peace, a mutual love, and we their spiritual descendants have received these too as the legacy of their faith and ours to carry forward.

We, standing on the shore of the widening stream, can hear them, what the scripture calls a "cloud of witnesses," those who have gone before us and now call to us from the other side, encouraging us on by their example. They beckon us into a promise we are asked to trust even if it might not be fulfilled in our lifetime. So faith calls us forward, and when we respond, a greater inheritance awaits us. A deeper peace. A mutual love. An arc that reaches beyond what we can see, beyond what we can know.

In Your Own Words

What is the stream you are now crossing and how might your faith in those on the other side be calling you forward? Who has gone before you as your "cloud of witnesses," and how do they beckon you into and across life's many unknowns? As you muster the faith to cross into new terrain, who might be following behind you, and how will you call to them with encouragement? How might your own faithful living bid them forward too? Begin writing with this prompt, following wherever it leads:

Surrounded by so great a cloud of witnesses, I step into the stream . . .

7

Writing about Prayer

HUNDREDS OF WAYS TO KNEEL AND KISS THE GROUND

Let the beauty we love be what we do.
There are hundreds of ways to kneel and kiss the ground.
—JALAL AL-DIN RUMI[1]

I had come to the hospital chapel in grief after visiting a patient who was dying. I was sitting in the back of the room, tears rolling silently down my cheeks, when a woman entered behind me, passed to the front of the room and, facing eastward, unrolled her rug. She kneeled and her prayer tumbled out in words foreign to my ear but familiar to my heart. When she had finished, she stood, rolled her rug, and passed by me again on her way out. Our eyes met as she walked by. "Thank you," I said. "Your prayer gave me strength."

Some of my friends, like the woman in the chapel, have very specific practices of prayer, and each one can be very different from the next. Others take an open approach without particular forms. But each of our ways of praying can open holy space for others if we let it. In my own church, we follow no prescribed practices dictating when to pray or how, nor do we even agree about whether to name it as prayer. Sitting side by side on Sunday mornings, we may not be in the habit of kneeling, but we do make room for hundreds of ways to pray, respecting the diverse beliefs and practices present among us and with deep awareness of the many different needs and experiences that call us to prayer.

Still, questions about prayer hover. What does it *mean* to pray? And to *whom* are we praying? Is it prayer if it's delivered in an envelope that bears no address? Is it prayer if the message has no words? Is it prayer if it's lifted up on the currents of our doubts and questions instead of being carried off by the sturdy messenger of belief?

If we listed all the forms that prayer can take—petitions and gratitude, praise and lamentation, confessions and indictments, wailing words and silent breath, bended knees and wakeful walking, a listening ear, an open heart, a quiet space, a widening circle—we would find no shortage of ways to pray. What is it, then, within or beyond the hundred ways of praying, that makes them all prayer?

With or without speech, prayer is born of breath and bones, and hearts held open to ancient connection. It is the deepest song of the sea sounding through us. It is the oldest trace of living starlight that is buried in us and cannot be contained.

In Your Own Words

What is prayer for you? What opens your heart to ancient connection and lets the deepest songs sing through you or reveals the light within you? Of the "hundreds of ways to kneel and kiss the ground," what are your ways? Begin writing with these two words, repeating them as many times as you like in a series of statements, or just writing them once and following wherever they lead:

Prayer is . . .

KNOWING THERE IS MORE

The most blessed result of prayer would be to rise thinking,
"But I never knew before. I never dreamed."
—C. S. LEWIS[2]

A common assumption about prayer—especially, it seems, among many who resist it—is that it involves a request. Etymologically, we have good reason to assume this; after all, the root of the word *pray* means to ask earnestly. One could go so far as to call it a plea. In addition, many of us have experienced prayer as a request. For whether we name it as prayer or not, it would be difficult to find the person who has not, in some moment of need, or pain, or concern, whispered a plea for recovery or safety, for peace or relief.

Beneath these petitions, though, is a condition that is worth considering. A state of heart, you might call it, suggesting something more may be going on than the utterance of a request. Many religious teachings point out that the purpose of prayer is not to ask for things but to get to know God or, we might say, to know the sacred ground of one's being and to know one's true self in relation to that ground of being. As Leonard Cohen put it in his novel *Beautiful Losers*, "Prayer is translation. A man translates himself into a child asking for all there is in a language he has barely mastered."[3]

With this in mind, looking again at the etymology of the word *prayer*, we see that it also shares a common root with the word *precarious*. Perhaps its petitions are as much acknowledgments of vulnerability, of uncertainty, of need and interdependence, as they are specific requests to be filled. We could say that a prayer is a way of honoring the limits of our control and our knowing. No wonder it can be hard to begin.

Prayer is not a rational proposition, and this can make it difficult in our age of reason. As twentieth-century theologian James Luther Adams warned, we must be wary of rationalism and moralism that are unaccompanied by an open heart. "They give us a 'poise' that freezes the knees and keeps us erect [. . .] in the face of the divine demand for repentance, for change of heart and mind."[4]

So prayer might best be understood more as a posture than a plea. Whether standing or prostrate, it is a position of humility and receptivity, a posture of the heart as it acknowledges and leans toward what we do not know or understand. It is a willingness to be changed by our relationship to something larger than ourselves, opening our hearts and our awareness to the largest circles of life itself.

One summer day, while I was fishing with friends on a small lake, a bald eagle circled overhead as we cast our lines and waited. We watched the eagle rise, becoming smaller and smaller against the summer's wide blue sky. Finally, as we sat in the canoe, our faces turned up like baby birds in a nest, the tiny speck of an eagle circled one last time and then simply vanished, leaving us with the giddy sense that we'd been drawn right to the limits of our awareness and even a step beyond. The blue dome stretched seamlessly over our heads, and though we knew somewhere up there the eagle was still circling, likely looking down on us with its sharp, focused vision, we saw only a cerulean expanse of sky garnished by a few wispy clouds along the horizon.

I remember this sometimes when looking at what appears to be an empty sky, or when whatever I can see is not enough to reveal all that I know to be true.

Prayer can be like the eagle circling, rising higher and higher until that one instant, with one more push of its wings, when it simply disappears—we know it's there although we cannot see it. Blue sky closes in around it, and our hearts follow after.

In Your Own Words

How might prayer help you reach toward what you cannot see? How does it invite you to make room for what you do not know or what you cannot control? If you have a mantra or a brief prayer or meditation that you recite regularly or know by heart, say it out loud, or close your eyes and recall it in your mind's ear, once or twice. Or you can use the words of a meditation I whisper every morning and every night:

> *May you [or I or we] be safe,*
> *May you be well.*
> *May your heart be filled with peace, joy, love, and compassion.*
> *May you always feel Love's embrace, wherever you are, wherever you go.*

Whatever words you use, say them once or twice out loud or in your mind; then sit in silence for four slow breaths, in and out, paying attention to what trails after the words, in your heart, in your mind, in your body. Do the words—or the silence following after—in any way point you toward what you cannot see or do not know? Begin writing with the prompt, repeating it to begin a series of sentences or paragraphs, or just using it once and following wherever it leads:

What I do not know . . .

POSTURES OF PRAYER

> *[T]he longing for God*
> *is a prayer said in the bones.*
> —MARY ROSE O'REILLEY[5]

Like many religious practices, prayer is not an abstract idea. Prayer lives in the embodied world and is practiced with our senses. We experience it with prayer beads in the hand, with the vibration of om in our bones, with the scent of incense burning, the rhythm of drums thrumming, and the last trailing note from the singing bowl ringing. The first word in any prayer is spoken with our bodies, through posture, gesture, or stillness and the opening of our senses as an invitation into praise, grief, gratitude, or silence.

This opening of the senses is a preparation that takes many forms, and only the practitioner can determine which form to use and how. What matters is less about how prayer is done than whether it works—which is to say, whether we become still and fully attentive; whether we are able to listen well enough to hear; and whether we are willing to be changed. An old Buddhist story brings this truth home.

A devoted meditator who had used the same mantra for many years visited an old hermit who lived alone on an island in the middle of a lake, hoping to learn from the hermit's meditation practices. The meditator hired a man to row him out to the island, where he met with the hermit, had tea, and was delighted to learn that he and the hermit used the same mantra. When the hermit recited the mantra out loud, though, the meditator was shocked to discover he was mispronouncing it. He corrected the hermit and, returning across the lake, he considered how fortunate it was that he had visited so the hermit could learn to recite his mantra correctly before he died.

Then the boatman unexpectedly stopped rowing and stared. The meditator turned to find the hermit standing beside the boat on the surface of the water, asking again for the correct pronunciation of the mantra as he had forgotten it already.

"Clearly," the meditator said, full of humility, "no correction is needed." But the hermit insisted and after the meditator reluctantly recited the mantra again, he watched as the hermit turned around and carefully practiced the mantra as he walked back across the water, from the boat to the island's shore.[6]

Prayer positions us. If it is a spoken prayer, it is not as much about the words as it is about whether they orient us toward the holy. And we do well to remember this is not always an orientation or posture that is supine or silent. Prayer is often a joyful song and sound, an inner dance that might make a whirling dervish laugh with delight.

José Hobday describes what she calls the Four-Way Resurrection Prayer,[7] referring not only to the Christian resurrection of her own religious path but also to the ordinary resurrections we all experience in everyday living and exuberance and transformation. I describe it here as an invitation. After you've read it through, go ahead and try doing it. Then move on to the writing prompt that follows.

You begin this embodied prayer in a sitting position, paying attention to the wonder of your own body. Then, in the first step of the prayer, called *Standing Up*, Hobday instructs you to "get up," to stand if you are able. If not, you might lift your head, sit up a little straighter, or find some way to physically rise up. As you do, she invites you to think about other upward movements in your life. Whether it's learning or doing something yourself, or being lifted or assisted by someone else, she asks you to think of these as you stand, naming the "little resurrections" occurring in your life.

The second step is *Lifting the Spirit*. "Lift your mind, lift your heart," Hobday instructs, "as you have lifted your body." She reminds you to feel your love of family and others and how it lifts your spirits and your heart.

The third step is *Reaching for the Sky*. Now that you've risen in body and spirit, she tells you to let your body stretch even higher. Lift your arms if you're able, as high as they reach, turn your face up to the sky or the ceiling if you're able, or find some way to stretch and raise your body as high as possible. In Tai Chi, one of the forms of movements called "the Fan" expresses this as you stretch your arms above your head, fingers spread wide and reaching like the branches of a tree. With any movement like this, let your body stretch itself and feel its connection to the sky.

The final step in Hobday's practice is *Lifting Your Voice.* Go ahead. Let it out. Don't be shy. Shout something joyful, in any way you have of accessing your "voice." "Yahoo!" "Hallelujah!" "Amen!" "All right now!" or simply "Uh-huh!" This will be hard for many of us. With my buttoned-up German upbringing, it makes me self-conscious when I do this outside. It makes my dog jump when I do it in the house. But it can also feel amazingly good. It reminds me, when I get over my fears and just do it, that my body is meant not only to stand, to rise, and to reach, but also to joyfully exclaim. We are meant to experience each of these small resurrections to claim our full height and full voice. These too can be postures for praise and for prayer.

In Your Own Words

What are the sounds and gestures, the rituals or postures that serve as your prayerful reorienting? What signals to your mind, body, and heart that it is time for deep listening, for humble attention, for lifted praise?

Make a list of any feelings you noticed when doing the resurrection prayer exercises above. Add to this any feelings you have noticed in your own practices of prayer. Now make a second list of postures you have taken or might take when in prayer. Consider the different kinds of prayer—that of praise, of lamentation, of confession or petition—and the different postures you might use in each. Finally, make a list of the parts of your body that these postures depend on, parts of your body that make prayer possible for you, or might make it possible for others. Don't overthink your word choices. Jot down whatever words occur to you, as quickly as they come.

Scan your lists and circle any words that attract your eye or your interest. Choose one of the body parts and use it to fill in the blank in the prompt below. Begin writing from there, incorporating as many of your circled words as you can. If you've circled multiple body parts, you can repeat the opening prompt as many times as you like, substituting a different part of the body each time. (For example, if the body parts you've circled are "hands" and "eyes" and "knees," you would have three prompts, beginning with the words, When my hands pray . . . ; When my eyes pray . . . ; and When my knees pray . . .)

When my _____ **pray . . .**

PRAYER AS LISTENING

Whether you like it or no, read and pray daily. It is for your life; there is no other way . . . Do justice to your own soul; give it time and means to grow. Do not starve yourself any longer.
—**JOHN WESLEY**[8]

Although prayer has many different purposes and postures, some of the most familiar practices share a common approach: *Take off your shoes. Bend your knees. Fold your hands. Bow down.* These simple instructions are not meant for making speeches, claiming ground, commanding attention, or standing tall. No. Around the world, in so many religions, the practice of prayer calls upon us to fold our egos away and to make ourselves quiet and small. They remind us to pause from busy schedules and personal agendas and to point ourselves humbly in the direction of the holy. *Take off your shoes. Bend your knees. Fold your hands. Bow down.*

We are instructed to listen. When Mother Teresa was asked by a journalist what she said when she prayed, she replied, "I listen." Then asked what God said to her, she said simply that God listens too.[9]

It can be harder than you'd think to listen. It is much easier to listen only as a way of waiting for opportunities that will allow us to speak, to hear only the stories that will invite us to act—especially in our work for justice and peace, when there is so much that needs to be said, so much that desperately needs to be done.

Some years ago, I was traveling in Nicaragua with a group of North Americans and we heard a lot of talk about how much was broken in that nation's growing poverty. Our inclination was to ask, "What can we do? How can we help to fix the problems?" Whether it was a road washed out or a hospital placing patients two to a bed, or the lakes thick with pollution, over and over again, we asked, "What can we do?"

Then one evening, while staying on a small farm in the northern mountains, I felt a new answer stirring in my heart. I had just spent the day with my host, Elena, hauling water in heavy, string-handled buckets and patting out tortillas with our hands and frying them over a fire. After eating dinner together by the light of a single candle, we lingered at the simple wooden table in the dirt-floored room, singing songs to each other. I listened as Elena shared her hopes and her fears, and when I retired that night, for the first time on that trip, I knew what to do. Or at least I thought I had discovered where to begin—not with roads or hospitals or wells or waterways, as necessary as all of those are. No. The first step I needed to take as a North American was in taking the time to listen with my whole heart, with a patient ear, and the awareness that would allow me to discern another's story and to let my life be changed by it.

The journey of a thousand miles begins with the first step, Lao Tzu said in the Tao. But a better translation of this familiar passage is to say the journey begins beneath our feet—not in the first step but in the stillness that precedes it, in the place where we stand before we move, in the very ground of our being.

So we take off our shoes, standing on the holy ground of this earth. We fold our hands, pausing their habit of doing, doing, doing. And when we bow our heads, we can begin to listen for a story larger than our own, waiting first for a holy word, a sacred connection and understanding in which to root our lives and our work for peace and justice. May our listening be our prayer. May our prayer be our deep listening.

In Your Own Words

Materials needed: For this writing session you'll need a small supply of random photographs of faces (they can be people or any other living being), including at least a few you are not already familiar with. A magazine or two with human-interest photos can be a good source, or a computer with online access to a news website that collects "photos of the day or week" can be another. If you have a photograph of someone you know, still living or not, you might put that into the mix as well.

When have you recently paused to listen to a story not your own? When have you quieted your own voice (and the voices that support what you already know) long enough to hear something new, something that perhaps changed you or your understandings in a small or large way?

Look through the supply of photos you've gathered in advance and choose one that beckons you, without asking yourself why. Look at the photo for a few minutes, considering what that person might tell you if you paused to listen. Try to be open to the difficult things they might tell you as well as the ones you might be eager to hear. Begin writing with the words below, and follow wherever they lead you:

Bowing my head to listen, I hear (or heard) . . .

I'M THAT TOO

If a man wants God to hear his prayer quickly, then before he prays for anything else, even his own soul, when he stands and stretches out his hands towards God, he must pray with all his heart for his enemies. Through this action, God will hear everything that he asks.
—ABBA ZENO[10]

If prayer often seeks to change the way things are in our lives, the change that prayer is most likely to bring about is in us as the ones praying. The point of entering a posture of listening is to understand our connectedness, not only to the divine or to the universe, but also to other beings.

A prayer exercise found in Buddhism and Hinduism is one way to begin. The practice tells us to repeat a Sanskrit phrase that means literally "I am that"—or in a modified translation suggested by Ram Dass, "I'm that too"—whenever we are particularly drawn to or repelled by someone or something we encounter.[11] The phrase reminds us of the Jungian proposition that the people, beings, behaviors, or emotions that capture our attention do so because we already know them as some part of ourselves. It may be an aspect of ourselves that we shun or deny, consciously or unconsciously, or a part of us that we like and wish to bring forward, but the idea is that if we have noticed something with either strong attachment or resistance, we are likely already familiar with it from the inside out.

Some years ago, when I went to a teacher for advice about a difficult relationship with a supervisor at work, I received a similar gift of wisdom I am still using today. My teacher listened for a while and then simply asked what I saw in my supervisor that reminded me of myself. Was there some part of myself, he asked, that I'd left behind or wanted to leave behind, that in some way resembled my supervisor's behavior? He might as well have sent me off with instructions to recite "I'm that too."

I was recently reminded of this prayer after a day of technological problems with my computer's internet connection. It was late at night. I had already been on the phone for an hour and a half with a series of well-meaning technical support people, but there was no sign of progress. My husband had gone to bed, and the dog had long abandoned me to sleep as well. I didn't dare hang up, but I confess, I was beginning to think unkind thoughts when my call was transferred to yet another person who asked me to describe, for the umpteenth time, what was wrong and how it had happened. Then, with my impatience rising, I asked her name to add it to my list of all the others, and she said, "Karen." She likely had no idea what the brief pause after that meant, but on my end of the phone, I will tell you that hearing that she and I shared the same name had the same effect as saying "I'm that too." *I'm her and she's me and we're all in this together*, I reminded myself. I took a deep breath and smiled, imagining her under the fluorescent lights of a distant call center, trying to fix a problem in my little computer plugged in on the opposite side of the globe. As she took remote control of my computer, and I watched the cursor move around on my screen under her command, not mine, I marveled at the miracles of technology but also of more spiritual connections.

Prayer is not for the timid in any form, but this one especially requires courage. It causes us to see others and ourselves more candidly and with all our kinship intact. The honesty part, in particular, can be painful but also useful in mending personal relationships that become tattered. It is also a necessary step in seeing and understanding racism, sexism, or any oppressive system that depends on our participation as we, often unwittingly, project unwanted aspects of ourselves on those whom we regard as "other." It is worth noting, though, that this prayer will not bring healing in ourselves and in society unless it is combined with self-compassion. It is helpful only when it stirs enough compassion for ourselves that it then spills over to others. When that happens, this prayer can be as powerful a tool for healing as any you will find.

In Your Own Words

Think of a person, behavior, or incident you encountered recently that strongly moved you—either because it attracted you or caused you to pull away. What was it in the person or the incident that caused your strong reaction? Can you recognize yourself in that other person or being or behavior? How might your own desired or rejected traits be present in that person or that encounter?

As you recall this encounter, begin with the words of the Hindu prayer, and keep writing, following wherever it leads.

I'm that too . . .

SPACE FOR ALL WE CANNOT HOLD

Near that threshold where all words fail
is where prayer and poetry often converge.
—MARILYN CHANDLER MCENTYRE[12]

Prayer, though often shaped into words, is ultimately a way of reaching toward what lies beyond our language and our grasp.

Many years ago, after visiting a Buddhist *gompa* high in the Himalayas along India's contested northern border with China, David and I sat down on a hard-packed mound of earth overlooking the town and valley below. The dry and dusty view stretched out for miles around us. The outermost houses of the town of Leh blended into the brown dirt from which they'd been built, and frayed and faded prayer flags flapped on nearly every roof. The military-only road to China wound its way out of sight to the north, and a brick wall being built by a small crew of Ladakhi workers also pointed toward China. The sun was warm on our backs and the barren, brown mountain peaks across the valley cut a striking silhouette against the pure blue sky. The distant, slow pounding of a single mallet working on the wall below was the only sound breaking the silence.

Then, as we sat there without speaking, a wind came around the mountain and brushed our cheeks with sudden and intimate arrival. *Maybe this*, I thought, *was the reason so many Buddhist monks had settled there—the unfathomable touch of spirit rushing in to accompany those who stop to rest in that boundless sacred solitude.* It was for me an experience in the wide geography of prayer and a reminder of the way we turn to prayer when facing the enormity of life's events, for it is often only prayer that can reach across and around the greatest expanses.

In traditional Tibetan practice, prayers are sent into the world through prayer flags and prayer wheels that scatter blessings the way a farmer throws seeds. A typical prayer wheel has the words of a mantra such as "om mani padme hum" incorporated in the design of the outside surface, and inside it carries another copy of the mantra written by the person who made the wheel. As prayer wheels are spun, they release these prayers into the world.

Similarly, when the five-colored Tibetan prayer flags hang in the open air, fading and fraying with time, the mantras written on them are said to be lifted and carried away by the wind. In this way, writer Tad Wise explains, the wind blowing through the flags creates "blessed air [. . .] that has a calming effect"[13] and the prayers "'rub off' on the material world, constantly purifying it, bit by bit, over time."[14] Tibetan scholar Robert Thurman calls these practices "small acts of devotion" that "plant the seeds of greater spiritual accomplishment."[15]

What are the small acts of devotion that plant hope in your world? What are the gestures of prayer that stir a blessed wind in your life, or awaken you to its touch? Surely we don't need to travel to the Himalayas to know the longing for blessed wind or for scattered seeds of calm. The unknowns in our own lives can stretch out before us every bit as wide and unfathomable as the mountain valleys of northern India.

Sitting in a waiting room one day while her child was undergoing outpatient surgery, my sister Susan endured the wait by writing me a letter. It was a time she would have prayed, she explained, but that wasn't something she was accustomed to doing. So she wrote a letter instead, describing her feelings, naming her fears and hopes, seeking connection, crossing that vast stretch of waiting in which the minutes can drag on like hours. When the procedure was over, her child's surgery a success, and her fears allayed, she signed off. The next day, she mailed the letter; but as I later read it, it seemed to be addressed well beyond me, sending its story out into the wind, releasing its hopes like a prayer wheel still in motion.

Prayer is our reaching out, across the wide terrain of events beyond our control and sometimes even beyond the circumference of our questions. It draws us to the rim of a wider circle, making room, as the poet Jeanne Lohmann says, for all that is too big, too difficult, or too unknown for us to hold alone.

> *Prayer is*
> *circumference*
> *we may not*
> *reach around,*
>
> *space for all we cannot hold,*
> *the rim of Love toward which we lean.*[16]

In Your Own Words

Choose someone to write a letter or an email to about a concern, a dream, a hope, or a joy of yours. It can be addressed to a person real or fictional, contemporary or historical, someone you know or don't know; it can be addressed to God or the divine by any name, or yourself now or in another time; you might write to your deceased loved one or your child not yet conceived or not yet born. When you've chosen someone, write a letter to that person sharing something present in your heart right now, something that feels big, solid, or significant. Cut right to the chase and speak your truth as you write. Tell the person what you feel. Tell how it is for you in your life now.

Begin with the words below:

Dear _____,

Here I am . . .

When you finish your letter, hold it in your lap or on the table in front of you. Close your eyes or lift your gaze. Imagine a light wind blowing across the page before you, lifting your words and carrying them away. Notice the touch of blessed air on your skin. Take three slow breaths, in and out, and if the word feels right, end by saying Amen.

8

WRITING ABOUT SIN

BEGINNING WITH THE HISS

[S]tart with the talking snake.
Children like to hear what animals have to say.
—DAVID SHUMATE[1]

It can be difficult to find a good starting place when it comes to sin. Do we start in the Garden of Eden, with the tree of knowledge and human free will? Or with the forbidden fruit and the choice to taste it? Maybe we keep it simple and begin with the talking snake. Maybe we start by listening for the hissing of sin while also watching for the gentle presence of forgiveness shining like a full moon on our lives. Maybe we set out by remembering how sin and forgiveness give shape to one another, how the waxing of one invites the waning of the other. Because maybe we cannot really know forgiveness without first noticing how sin slithers within and among us. And maybe we won't see how we commit sin ourselves if we haven't already known the blessing of forgiveness and how it allows us to aspire once again to our better selves.

Maybe we have to be able to think—and write—about sin to lower our resistance to the gift of forgiveness.

So maybe we begin with the hissing of sin.

In Your Own Words

Thinking or writing about sin isn't easy. It calls up all kinds of difficult experiences and unwanted feelings. But naming these associations and feelings can be a necessary beginning in any earnest quest for grace or forgiveness. What do you experience when you think about sin? What do you hear when you consider sin's hiss? What coils quietly, rises coyly, or strikes unbidden, when you hear or utter the word *sin*?

When I hear the word sin . . .

I KNOW SIN WHEN I SEE IT

You already know enough. So do I. It is not knowledge we lack.
What is missing is the courage to understand what we know
and to draw conclusions.

—Sven Lindqvist[2]

Near the end of his life, John Steinbeck traveled around the United States noticing the way Americans live. After visiting a church in Vermont one Sunday morning and hearing a fire-and-brimstone sermon, he wrote:

For some years now God has been a pal to us, practicing togetherness. [. . .] But this Vermont God cared enough about me to go to a lot of trouble kicking the hell out of me. He put my sins in a new perspective. Whereas they had been small and mean and nasty and best forgotten, this minister gave them some size and bloom and dignity.[3]

Steinbeck's preacher offers an unflinching look at sin that might be even less common now in the twenty-first century than it was in 1960, when Steinbeck wrote this passage. Religious teachings from earlier times have been even less hesitant to name or tabulate the many forms of sin. I haven't counted them myself but I've read that Mosaic Law identifies 613 behaviors defining the difference between sinful and honorable living, of which 365 are prohibited activities or behaviors. With more manageable math, we might consider the Ten Commandments or, in a smaller number yet, the seven deadly sins named by Pope Gregory in the late sixth century:

1. Lust
2. Gluttony
3. Greed
4. Sloth
5. Wrath
6. Envy
7. Pride

Mohandas Gandhi created his own list, which he called the "Seven Blunders of the World," jotting them down on a note given to his grandson Arun not long before his assassination:

1. Wealth without Work
2. Pleasure without Conscience
3. Science without Humanity
4. Knowledge without Character
5. Commerce without Morality

6. Worship without Sacrifice

7. Politics without Principle

Gandhi named these as forms of passive violence that were likely to cause active violence, and his grandson Arun later added an eighth that seems especially important in the twenty-first century: Rights without Responsibilities.[4]

If these lists are helpful in prompting us to think about sin and its many forms and faces, still we are left with the question of how to recognize the sins themselves, whether we commit them ourselves or experience their impact when they're committed by others. It can be harder than you'd think. For instance, in a time when self-esteem is so highly touted, what does the sin of pride really look like? In a free-market world, what's the difference between greed and simply getting ahead? And in confronting injustices, is wrath always a sinful thing?

In a now-famous 1964 judicial ruling on a film charged with obscenity, Supreme Court Justice Potter Stewart insisted that obscenity was knowable although difficult to define. "I shall not today attempt further to define [obscenity . . .]," he wrote. "But I know it when I see it [. . .]"[5] For years, his measure stood, resulting in a strange practice called "movie day" in which many of the Supreme Court justices and their clerks, popcorn in hand, screened movies that had been charged with being pornographic, declaring as they did that they would know it when they saw it.

In Your Own Words

How do you know a sin when you see it? What does wrath look like? What does greed smell like? What is the sound made by sloth? What is the taste of envy, the texture of lust, or the shape of gluttony?

Choose one of the deadly sins or one of Gandhi's "seven blunders" to which you have a strong reaction—positive or negative. List any associations or descriptions of it that come to mind, in as many of the categories listed below as you can. Add any other descriptive associations that occur to you. Be specific. Use metaphors if you like (e.g., it tastes sour, not like a lemon but like old milk):

- Color
- Taste (be specific: what food is it like?)
- Smell (be specific)
- Texture or temperature
- Sound
- Machine
- Animal
- Motion

Looking over your list of associations and descriptors, circle a few that are especially evocative and use them to write about the deadly sin you've chosen. Begin with the sentence below, filling in the blank with the name of the sin and then describing that sin with the words you have circled from your list of associations, embellishing as you go (e.g., I know greed when I see it. Greed lurks like a cat waiting to pounce. Greed takes over like the stench of a dead fish in the weeds, stealing the joys of my spot at the beach). Keep writing, following wherever it leads.

I know _____ when I see it . . .

SIN VERSUS SINS

To find the origin,
trace back the manifestations.
When you recognize the children
and find the mother,
you will be free of sorrow.

—LAO TZU[6]

Despite all the listing and counting that have gone on over the millennia, and go on still today, in matters of sin, many contemporary theologians are less prone to such a numerical approach. Instead, they take a wider view using a variety of measures. There are barometers of brokenness, of missing the mark, of the absence of faith, of living a lie. There's the plumb line of self-centeredness, alienation, despair, rebellion, or refusing help from God. And there's the balance measuring our relationship to creation and others, or idolatry as the fierce attachment of our hearts to things that are not lasting.

Twentieth-century theologian Paul Tillich warned against using the word sin in the plural at all. He said we get distracted when we define sin as individual actions and suggested instead that we consider it with a capital S, regarding it as the condition or state of being that precedes any action we might label as sinful. The root of the word sin, he pointed out, may be linked to the root of the word *asunder*, meaning that the sinful state—or the condition that causes sin—is best understood as a separation from God. Or in other words, our alienation from the sacred ground of our being.[7]

When we think of sin in the plural, naming and counting its many variations, we quickly discover the reason for Tillich's warning. Definitions of sin change over time, giving rise both to conflicting interpretations and countless schisms in doctrine and in practice. Many contemporary sins today were considered acceptable in biblical times (slavery being one), while other things named as biblical sins are widely accepted today, even among the most faithful biblical adherents (wearing clothing woven of two kinds of material, for instance). "Sin and evil are not static concepts," says theologian Sallie McFague. "They change according to the attitudes and accompanying institutions that undermine flourishing in different times."[8] The definitions of sin themselves have been used as tools for control, to support the status quo, and to gain and maintain oppressive power over women, slaves, people of color, people of different sexual orientation, other species, and nature itself. We have good reason to be suspicious of defining sin.

In addition, old definitions of sin frequently perpetuated dualistic thinking that labeled the earth and our bodies themselves as sinful while elevating rational, disembodied experience as righteous. The results have been devastating to women, to indigenous peoples, to countless exterminated species, and to the earth and our ecosystem. Clearly, the kind of sorting invited by counting sins can itself become a sinful way of being.

So, Tillich advises, when trying to know what is sinful and what is not, we might trace the alleged sin back, looking for the condition in which it is rooted.[9] What might we learn about sin if we turned in the abacus and exchanged our judgmental counting for a wider question: what are the conditions of the heart and the systems of society that cause us to deny or sever our connection to the earth, to others, or to the holy?

In Your Own Words

Think of an act or behavior that some have labeled as sinful, something that you do not consider to be a sin. Or think of something that was called a sin years ago that is now acceptable or even encouraged. What does it mean to say this is not sinful? What do you learn about Sin with a capital S when you do? Write about this not being a sin, beginning with the prompt below, and let your writing then move to something you do regard as a sin.

There is no sin in . . .
But it is a sin when . . .

TOO TALL OR TOO SMALL

"Curiouser and curiouser!" cried Alice . . . ; "now I'm opening out like the largest telescope that ever was! Good-bye, feet!"
—LEWIS CARROLL[10]

In the adventures of Lewis Carroll's character Alice, she found herself growing so tall that she could hardly see her own feet. It's an image that comes to mind when I read ecological theologian Sallie McFague describing what may be the greatest sin of middle-class North Americans, of which I am one, as "living a lie" or "living falsely," out of proportion to our place in the natural world. "Selfishness," she says, "is the one-word definition of sin—at least for us first-world types."[11]

It is a concept reinforced daily in news stories about depleted or defiled natural resources and the devastation wrought by a changing climate, bearing plentiful reminders that we have all, to some degree, been living just such a lie, taking more than our fair share. Here in the United States, we have, as a nation and most of us as individuals, been living well beyond our means—whether financially, ecologically, or both.

So we try to do better. We try to cut our consumption, our cost of living, and our dependence on nonrenewables. Like Alice, we may have grown so tall we cannot see our own feet any longer, but we are learning how to measure and reduce our carbon footprint. It is clear that our future, and the future of our planet, depends on it—this rightsizing of our lives.

And yet, as in Alice's adventures, we know there is more than one way to deny our proper size. We can judge ourselves too small as well. When Alice was not growing too large, she was often shrinking to an almost invisibly small scale, at one point fearing she "might just go out altogether, like a candle."

Have you ever felt so small it was as if you had disappeared? Have you ever *made* yourself small by saying it doesn't matter what you do as just one person? Have you ever held back, saying your vote, your phone call, or your comment will not change anything? I know I have too often snuffed out my own power like a candle by not adding my voice to those speaking up and speaking out for the earth, for the poor, for those who are suffering—or even for myself and my conscience. There are so many ways, some of our own choosing, whether consciously or not in which we can become smaller than our proper size, especially in a supersized culture.

As Alice put it, "being so many different sizes in a day is very confusing."[12]

In Your Own Words

Materials needed: You'll need a rock or stone that fits in your hand. (Keep this on hand for the next writing exercise as well.)

Take a rock and place it on the floor near you. Stand up next to it and make yourself tall. Look down at the rock, aware of how you tower over it.

Then, if you can, squat down next to it or raise it up to eye level. Imagine that you are an ant standing beside it. What would this rock look like then? How would you feel standing in its shadow, looking up and maybe not even seeing its top edge?

Think of a time when you have experienced the feeling of being too large in a way that could be understood as sinful. Perhaps you claimed more than you needed in possessions, in time, in attention, or in space. What did that feel like? How did it grow from or influence your connection or lack of connection to others and to God or that which is holy?

Now think of a time when you felt too small in a way that might have sinfully diminished the sacred spark within you. Perhaps you felt too unimportant, too powerless to make a difference in the world, too helpless to speak up for yourself or for others. What did that feel like? How did it grow from or create a lack of connection to others and God or that which is holy?

Begin writing with the prompt below (writing about being either small or large, or writing about both, though still one at a time).

Being so many sizes can be confusing. I remember being so small (or large) . . .

THE HARDENED HEART

There are times when life seems little more than a matter of struggle and endurance, when difficulty and disappointment form a crust around the heart. Because it can be deeply hurt, the heart hardens.
—John O'Donohue[13]

Our disconnect from God and others is often described in the Bible as the condition of a "hardened heart." A hardened heart signifies those who will not heed the holy, those who deny God's help, or those whose flintlike hearts no longer feel a connection to others. A heart can harden by closing our eyes and ears to God or to our neighbor, whether it's a neighbor we know or a stranger we do not. Or the heart can become hardened under the tough shell of opinions that sit like armor over our capacity for compassion or even conversation. In each of these cases, the hardened heart represents a loss of perception, perhaps the most basic sin—a break in our connection to the world around us, which is also a breach of our kinship with the sacred whole of life. As Jesus explained, this was why he often spoke in parables, trying to break through the calloused surface of the people's dull and inattentive hearts. He said:

> For this people's heart has grown dull,
> and their ears are hard of hearing,
> and they have shut their eyes;[14]

A hardened heart is what makes it possible to turn away from one another and from the sacred; to pull into protected, private worlds— the spiritual equivalent of a gated community; to deny relationships and responsibility; and to deny one's own deepest needs and longings, which are, after all, one of the key ways the holy speaks to us.

Often our hearts are hardened by judgment. Even though judgment is one of the tools used to know sin when we see it, it can also be a sin itself. In a story about Jesus in the temple courts, several religious teachers brought in a woman accused of adultery, asking Jesus if they were not commanded by Mosaic Law to stone her. To which Jesus replied by inviting all without their own sin to be the first to throw a stone at her. As the story continues, the crowd dispersed, one at a time, beginning with the oldest, leaving only Jesus and the woman. "Go your way," he said to her. "And from now on do not sin again."[15]

Have you ever felt your heart harden and lose its capacity for compassion because you've judged another person to be wrong, foolish, cruel, thoughtless, or just plain unworthy? Have you ever lost compassion for yourself in the same way?

Of course, sometimes a heart gets hardened from being hurt. We might harden our hearts to protect them and to protect ourselves from the bruising blows of life, of love, and of the losses involved in both. It's as natural a reaction as pulling your hand from a flame that has burned it. And yet, every world religion advises us to keep our hearts open. We are instructed not to pull or turn away from life's suffering, whether it is our own or that of another.

Removing the heart's armor is risky. Beneath that armor is the *bodhichitta*, according to Buddhist teachings, a soft spot in the heart that is vulnerable and easily wounded. But it is precisely that vulnerability, says Buddhist monk Pema Chödrön, that offers us a link to all living beings. By touching the soft spot of our own suffering and sorrow, she continues, we open a doorway through which we can find and restore our connection to others.[16]

In Your Own Words

Materials needed: You'll need a rock or stone that fits in your hand. It can be the same one used for the last prompt, but it doesn't have to be.

Pick up your rock or stone and hold it in your palm. Feel its weight and density. Notice how hard it is to the touch—impermeable, impenetrable, inflexible. We can think of this hardness in terms of how it seals off what is inside from anything that is outside. We can also think of it in terms of the hurtful impact it would have if we threw it at others.

As you consider the heft of the stone in your hand, think of it as a stone of judgment. It might be your judgment of others, or theirs of you. It could also be your judgment of yourself or even of God. Pay attention to the surface of the stone, considering its hardness, as the severity of judgment. Has a harsh sense of judgment ever distorted your perceptions of yourself or others? Have you ever felt such certainty in the virtue of your opinions or actions that it was hard to see or hear another way of thinking, believing, or being?

Holding the stone in one hand, write about this, beginning with one of these prompts.

I feel my heart harden when . . .

or

A heavy stone of judgment that I carry is . . .

After writing for a while with the stone in your hand, ask yourself: *Where or how might I set this stone down?* Continue writing, answering this question.

THE FALL FROM BELONGING

One longs not only to help, to be of use, but to participate,
to be defined by the largest arcs of meaning that connect flesh and river,
sky and word, revery and the least act of survival.
                                        —SUSAN GRIFFIN[17]

In the biblical story of the Fall that takes place in the Garden of Eden, we hear about that fateful decision to eat the forbidden apple, to taste knowledge, to test the meaning of free will—and the harsh consequences and expulsion that follow. And many teachings drawn from this story tell us humans are all fallen and cast out, each of us born into a state of original sin and separation, a statement that arouses no small amount of resistance in our twenty-first-century insistence on self-esteem, self-empowerment, and self-improvement.

But our resistance is perhaps unfair to the larger narrative in which the story of Adam and Eve in Eden is told. We miss the full meaning of being "fallen" and expelled from the garden if we try to understand it apart from the state of wholeness from which Eve and Adam fell, or without considering the profound and given belonging that was lost in their banishment. For unless we have first felt a deep sense of belonging, wholly unearned by anything we have done or claimed or purchased, we will not be able to recognize the most substantial consequences of sin and alienation. Which is to say, if we have not experienced that kind of belonging, we actually may not know sin when we see it.

One condition of sin common today is the way many of us have of convincing ourselves that we do not belong. This can be a matter of hubris—the habit of putting ourselves above others, whether it's our fellow humans or other living beings, because of how much we know or have or do. But it can also occur without reference to power or stature, or even when what makes us different puts us in a position of *less* power. Of course, we need to know how we are unique in order to know who we are in relation to others. But whenever we exaggerate our differences, we may be expelling ourselves from the garden of belonging before others have a chance to cast us out for their own reasons. Consider the many ways we sort ourselves by identity: by money or education, race or nation, orientation, gender, creed, looks, intelligence, age, physique, or language. These can be important aspects of who we are, but we can also cling to any of them so fiercely that we forget how much we have in common with *every* living being. And that forgetting can be a condition of sin.

I don't want to diminish for a moment the excruciating pain of being excluded by others for our differences and the necessity of sometimes guarding ourselves from that experience by not entering realms where we are unwelcome. In some cases, it is necessary to hold back for our safety or even our survival. However, there are also times when our emphasis on distinct identities can get in the way of our belonging to and with one another across our differences.

I had the joy of attending a seminary that was inclusive on many levels. My fellow students came from many different denominations and some were of different faiths. The student handbook and classroom culture both taught and required us to use inclusive language and references in terms of gender, sexual orientation, and global perspectives. This was great in theory, commendable in educational value, and critical for training religious leaders in the twenty-first century. However, in practice, it could make it hard to know whether you really belonged and when and where and how you did. In my student orientation session, the seminary chaplain told us a story about a recent class discussion related to sexual orientation. One student later told the chaplain how hard it was to be one of the only gay students in that discussion. Not long after, another student expressed the challenge of being one of the only heterosexuals in the conversation. Could it be both ways? Or do we sometimes exaggerate how different we are and how much it matters?

Nature gives us a beautiful model for belonging that not only bridges differences but depends on them. If we built our communities as similar webs of connection, fully engaging the best purposes of diversity, we might begin to experience belonging in a profound way that could be traced right back to the garden. We also might begin to heal the breach of relationship between humans and nature, finding what theologian Sallie McFague calls our "proper size" in the forest and in the web of life.[18]

In Your Own Words

Imagine arriving someplace where you are very aware of your differences as soon as you walk through the door. You look around the room anxiously. Maybe others are dressed more formally or more casually than you, or perhaps they are all speaking a different language. By whatever difference that comes to your mind, imagine a room full of people who are not hostile but whose first appearance makes you feel acutely aware that you do not belong.

As you hesitate in the doorway, someone approaches as if to greet and welcome you. Your first inclination is to leave without a word, but as you turn to go, the person catches your eye and asks, "Leaving? Already?" It occurs to you that leaving now would underscore the sense of separation you felt looking into the room. Remembering the definition of sin as a state of alienation from others, you wonder what it would feel like to discover a point of connection with those gathered there. The person smiles and says, "We've been hoping you would come."

What response rises silently in your heart? By what inner conversation do you choose to stay and seek connection or consider whether to turn and leave?

If I stay . . .

9

WRITING ABOUT LOVE

LOVE IS A ROSE, A RIVER, A FRUIT

Love is a fruit, in season at all times and within the reach of every hand.
Anyone may gather it and no limit is set.
—MOTHER TERESA[1]

As common as it is to try to express love in words, it often proves
difficult to categorize or define it. In writing about love, many have
turned to metaphors to tell the tale. Love is an ocean, a pearl, a key,
a battle, a flame, a tree. Love is a river, a journey, a guiding star, or as
Shakespeare put it, an "ever-fixed mark."[2] Writer Diane Ackerman
says love is both ever present and ever evasive, infusing our lives
as "the great intangible"[3] even as it begs for the legs, arms, lips, and
touch by which we know it best. Although the virtue of love calls us
into relationship, both with those we know and those we don't, the

truth is that it begins as an embodied experience with the tangible world around us. Our first knowledge of love is born in the particular relationships we have with those close at hand, those within range of our touch, our glance, or our words.

In Your Own Words

Materials needed: If including this prompt in a group writing session, you might wish to assemble a collection of diverse objects, photographs, or both, for participants to use for this prompt. If writing on your own, simply make sure you have within view a plentiful diversity of objects.

Look around you. Make a list of random objects you see and some of the things you associate with them. If you see an unlit candle, for instance, you might list candle, wick, wax, flame, fire, spark, match, torch, etc. Challenge yourself to include basic items you wouldn't normally notice—window, piano key, painting frame, table legs, door hinge. When you have a reasonable list of diverse items, write a top-of-the-mind sentence for each word as a metaphor for love. Write down whatever comes to mind without screening. For instance, Love is a key on the piano that we strike many times to keep its note sounding. Or Love is a window that I sometimes slam shut.

You can also expand the metaphor beyond its limits, as Mother Teresa did when describing love as a fruit "in season at all times."[4] If nothing comes to mind for a word, go ahead and skip it. Or if you find yourself writing a common metaphor, try writing its opposite to branch into a different association. For instance, *Love is not a rose; it is the ground on which the rose's petals will fall in time*. Challenge yourself to explore metaphors you haven't heard or seen before.

When you've written metaphors for about five minutes, if you feel you're done listing but want to keep writing, look back at your sentences and phrases, choose one, and keep writing about that metaphor, beginning with the words:

Love is . . .

EXPLORING THE LAND OF LOVE

We love because it's the only true adventure.
—NIKKI GIOVANNI[5]

I grew up in the Midwest, amidst farmland studded by boulders left behind when the last glaciers retreated, many of them long ago stacked into fences that mark borders. Perhaps because of this, I often suffer from a prairie farmer's mindset when it comes to large rocks and other obstacles. Like the early European settlers intent upon their straight-row plowing, I tend to see a boulder as something that should be moved, and I have to remind myself that it is not always so. Patrick O'Donohue, brother to Irish poet John O'Donohue, offered another take on the large stones embedded in their family's land in western Ireland:

> Here in the Burren you are befriended by rocks and stones wherever you go. They only become obstacles if you can't find your way around them. [. . .] The rows of vegetables never seemed perturbed as they continued around the possible obstacle like the flow of the river meandering on its way further down the valley. In fact, the fruits of the garden often flourished in the vicinity of this rock. The heat of the limestone warmed the seed and its size sheltered the tender young blossom. [. . .] In a mysterious kind of way it seemed beneficial, if not necessary, to have a "could be" obstacle on your path.[6]

If we sometimes experience love as a journey, it is one that crosses a wide variety of terrain and one that beckons even while presenting us with many barriers—massive boulders and other "could-be" obstacles that might befriend us if we can find our way around them. The barriers can take many forms. Crossing the wide plains of the heart's journey, at some point we might come to the canyons of judgment, where we stand on the edge for a very long time, looking warily at others on the far side. Or traveling along the shore, as the tide wets our feet and then retreats, we might feel the shifting ground of love's give-and-take. In truth, the land of love is as interrupted by "could-be" obstacles as it is blessed by the stone outcroppings that shelter young shoots from the wind. The question is, how will we respond to these? How will we make our way through the varied terrain of the land of love?

In Your Own Words

What beckons you into the land of love, and what challenges you as you enter and traverse it or dwell within it? In the land of love, what breathtaking landscapes have you encountered and what barriers have you scaled or skirted or been diverted by?

Sketch a simple map showing the land of love you have known, or the geography of love you have not yet entered but might wish to explore. Does it have rivers, forests, fields, mountains, valleys, or plains? Lakes, oceans, islands, peninsulas? Go ahead and name them, playfully if you like. (Note: If you prefer not to make a map, you might just describe in words the geography of love you have known.)

After sketching a rough map of your land of love, consider how its characteristics have shaped your experience or understanding of love. Is there an obstacle on your map that you might yet befriend? Begin writing with the prompt and keep writing.

Traveling through the land of love, I have known . . .

AN ATTRACTION TO WHOLENESS

Love makes your soul crawl out from its hiding place.
—ZORA NEALE HURSTON[7]

I like to think of love as an inner leaning, a kind of magnetic pull not only toward another person but also into a larger wholeness in which we all belong. Love is a longing to return to our original connectedness and oneness, a calling to remember the shared stardust of which we are all made.

This is no fuzzy proposition ungrounded in science. In recent decades, scientists researching the human brain have found that love is more than a counterbalance to the seat of our cherished reason. It is hardwired into the human brain as a natural and necessary connection to one another, a physical and emotional interdependence that has evolved within the human limbic brain as a necessity of survival.

This is the part of our brain system that evolved after the reptilian brain stem, which directs basic bodily functions and instinctive responses, and before the cortex, with its capacity for abstract thinking and problem solving. As such, the limbic brain is the seat of our emotions and our dreams. It is responsible for gathering sensory information from our environment and our bodies. Based on this input, it directs our bodies' emotional and physical responses, calling for anxiety or aggression or compassion, and presenting the specific emotions on our faces, the only place in the human body where our muscles are directly attached to the skin to allow for quick and distinct expression.

Even more fascinating is the limbic brain's capacity for synchronizing its response with that of others. In their engaging book *A General Theory of Love*, three physicians describe the limbic brain as not just active but *interactive*, with the power to calibrate its responses to the limbic activity of another person.[8] When we look at another person's face, we are reading the outward signals of that person's limbic brain at the same time he or she is reading ours. In a mutual exchange that is as scientific as it is spiritual, each influences the other. Facial expressions of compassion and love, as well as fear and anger, will elicit similar emotions in others.

During my ministerial training, I worked for a time as a hospital chaplain, and one day I was asked to visit a cognitively disabled patient who was distressed by the repeated seizures he was having. It happened that I didn't have my book of prayers with me that afternoon, or my book of various scriptures I could read to him, so I entered the patient's room empty-handed, feeling ill equipped and inadequate but knowing it was my job to show up anyway and be present. As I sat down, I encountered this person I'd never met before, different from me in some of the most basic ways we humans divide up demographically: gender, age, race, and religion. So I asked simply how it was for him on that day, and he told me. In short, simple words, he talked about his seizures and his fears and his hopes, until his voice trailed off and we looked into each other's eyes in a profound silence. Then he beamed at me with a broad, exuberant smile. I smiled back. And we grinned at each other in this kind of goofy way for a long moment without speaking. Finally he said, "You see me."

"I see the sparkle in your eyes when you smile," I replied. "Your joy runs deep."

"You *know* me," he exclaimed then, more seriously but wide eyed with joy and gratitude that I felt resonating inside me as he said it.

"You know me too," I said, feeling as if all our differences had just taken a backseat to the vital connection between us in that moment.

We needed no more words than that. I know of no scripture or any spoken prayer that could have been more holy. We'd just fallen together, heart first and eyes wide open, into a profound experience of love.

In Your Own Words

Materials needed: Have on hand a small number of magazines, a book or photo album, or a website that will offer you quick browsing access to a collection of photos showing close-up images of faces. They can be photos of people you know or don't know, or a collection that includes both.

Flip through the photos you have on hand and without asking yourself why you've picked it, choose one that captures your attention and evokes love or some warmth of affection in you. Gaze at the photo for a minute or two. Notice what your own face feels like as you do; imagine what it might look like if the person in the photo could see it. Imagine an exchange that might take place if you were looking at the person face-to-face, participating in something greater than either of you separately or both of you together—perhaps participating in the larger wholeness that holds you both.

Begin writing with the prompt, and follow wherever it leads.

In your face, I see . . .

CHOOSING LOVE

We do not have to love. We choose to love.
—M. SCOTT PECK[9]

The literature of love often refers to love as our natural state, but this is not the same as saying we do not need to cultivate it and choose it. As our hardened hearts have shown us (see the earlier reflection "The Hardened Heart" on page 106), we have many defenses against love and its necessary vulnerability, some of them personally constructed and others a part of our culture.

One common defense raised against love comes as naturally as love itself when we have been hurt by loss and understandingly pull back in sorrow, pain, or disappointment. Well-meaning people may tell us time will heal, but in the moments of deepest grief, it often seems no lifetime could be long enough for us to ever willingly open our hearts again. Fortunately, time often does bring healing or at least it brings us to a place where we can choose to love again, even knowing how it hurts to lose it. As poet Ellen Bass puts it in the poem below, even in our grief, we might just have to tenderly hold our own life in our hands, and say yes to love again.

The Thing Is

to love life, to love it even
when you have no stomach for it
and everything you've held dear
crumbles like burnt paper in your hands,
your throat filled with the silt of it.
When grief sits with you, its tropical heat
thickening the air, heavy as water
more fit for gills than lungs;
when grief weights you like your own flesh
only more of it, an obesity of grief,
you think, How can a body withstand this?
Then you hold life like a face
between your palms, a plain face,
no charming smile, no violet eyes,
and you say, yes, I will take you
I will love you, again.[10]

It is not only healing that takes time. Love itself requires time. It will not be hurried. Which is why, in a world racing around at a 24/7 pace, we must *choose* love if we are to have room for its full presence in our lives. The authors of *A General Theory of Love* note that both experience and brain science tell us we cannot take shortcuts in fostering relational love:

[R]*elationships live on time.* They devour it in the way that bees feed on pollen or aerobic cells on oxygen: with an unbending singularity of purpose and no possibility of compromise or substitution. Relatedness is a physiologic process that, like digestion or bone growth, admits no plausible acceleration. And so the skill of becoming and remaining attuned to another's emotional rhythms requires a solid investment of years.[11]

When we choose love, we make our choice real by making time for it and by fostering the patience and flexibility to let love grow. Choosing love, in other words, may be a matter of choosing to slow down.

For many of us, this is extraordinarily challenging. Our typical pace in the United States is faster than any in recent history, with more hours at work and less time for sleep than one hundred years ago. Then we frequently fill the rest of our time to the brim with other commitments and with online multitasking that can make it difficult to give even the smallest attention to the person sitting at our side. Sometimes this busyness is necessary. But it can also be yet one more way of shutting out our feelings and avoiding our face-to-face connection to others.

Remember the parable of the Good Samaritan told by Jesus? A man on his way to Jericho is attacked by a thief and left on the side of the road, beaten, robbed, and half dead. First a priest and then a Levite passes by, each one seeing the wounded man and crossing to the other side of the road without pausing to learn if the man needs help. Then along comes the Samaritan, who would have been an outcast to the people first hearing this story, and he stops his journey to draw near and aid the man in distress, taking the time to dress his wounds, place him on the Samaritan's own donkey, and bring him to an inn to recover.[12]

In ancient times and in our own, the parable certainly stands as a warning not to let our prejudices and rules override our compassion. But it also serves as admonishment against barriers of any kind that keep us from loving our neighbor. It was, after all, the parable that Jesus told when asked what it means to love your neighbor as yourself. When I hear this story now, I have to wonder if a modern-day telling of it might have the first person walk by too busy texting to even notice the man lying in the road, while the second person, rushing to a meeting, crosses to the other side to catch a bus or call a taxi.

It takes time to choose love. Whether it's choosing to love after we've suffered personal loss, or making time for loved ones at home and afar, or taking time for a loving response to those we barely know, love requires that we pause long enough to let our hearts catch up with our hurrying feet.

In Your Own Words

Materials needed: You will need a timer of any kind that can be set for thirty seconds to one minute.

What new form of love might grow in your life if you choose to grant it all the time it needs? (Maybe you currently take plenty of time for one kind of love, but not so much for another.) What might happen if you paused long enough to let your heart catch up and speak?

Before starting this exercise, set your timer for one minute. (If you are a fast writer or a person whose natural pace is swift, you might want to set your timer for thirty to forty seconds instead.) Start the timer, and write from the prompt below as continuously as possible until the time is up. When the timer goes off, stop wherever you are without finishing your sentence. Without much pause, restart the timer and repeat, writing the same prompt over again and either following a new train of thought or writing about something else related to your first writing. Again, stop wherever you are when the timer goes off. Repeat this until you've written from the prompt five times—or whenever you get so frustrated you're ready to stop! (Do this part first before reading on.)

If I had more time for love . . .

After writing five interrupted prompts, turn your timer off. By now, you may have discovered that a one-minute writing prompt is just your thing. If that's the case, I encourage you to make use of that gift often, using any one-minute pause you come across in your days as an opportunity to write. However, if this has been as frustrating an exercise for you as it can be for me when I do it, take a deep breath and reset your inner state of mind. Assuring yourself that now you will take the time to write a longer, deeper reflection, begin with the same prompt again, either continuing from where one of the five one-minute starts left off or starting a fresh line of thought. In either case, let yourself continue writing for as long as you like or are able.

If I had more time for love . . .

ALL LOVE IS IMMIGRANT

All Love Is Immigrant
There is another other
in the other of every

Another
                         —ED BOK LEE[13]

In the 1980s, before leaving on an around-the-world adventure, David and I read everything we could about what to expect when visiting India. We thought we were prepared. But within ten minutes of our landing in New Delhi, with 115-degree heat pressing down on us, a blanket of hot smells wrapping around us, and our horn-beeping rickshaw swerving through a chaos of bicycles, cars, and an occasional ambling cow, we found that nothing we had read could have ever prepared us for something so unfamiliar. We were stunned, our senses overwhelmed, and all previous knowledge centers in our brains shut down for the day. There was nothing to be done but leave our preconceived notions behind and walk into that new land and new day one wide-eyed step at a time.

Years later, we would recall that experience when our first child was born. Like so many new parents, we had read stacks of books, trying to be prepared. But that first night, returning home from the hospital with Charlie less than twenty-four hours after he was born, we still felt like we'd landed in some place wholly foreign. It was dinnertime, Charlie was sleeping, and we'd picked up a carryout pizza. Walking in the door, we set the baby carrier, slumbering newborn and all, in the middle of the dining room table along with the pizza, and as we ate, gazing at our new, beloved child, we were speechless, filled with wonder, and more than a little terrified by the precious, impossible responsibility that now claimed our hearts and our lives. We were embarking on a journey of love that promised to take us through so much unknown terrain we would have to feel our way along one day at a time.

Love can be like going to India for the first time. Or if you're from India, maybe it's like coming to the United States. Either way, when you finally land in the place you have long dreamt of visiting, you discover you have not a clue about what it will require of you and how you will be changed. As Ed Bok Lee's poem says, love makes immigrants of us all.

Because love is a virtue that binds us to others, it is necessarily a connection with the unknown. Which is perhaps why, in Christian scripture, Paul described faithful living with the simple instruction, "Let love be your aim."[14] In the same way that a runner targets the far side of the finish line and not the line itself, with love, we aim our hearts out further than our knowing can ever reach. In the wordplay of Lee's poem, this might be described as opening our hearts to the "other" nested within every person in the simple command to "Love one another."

This is why love thrives where imagination is at play, and similarly, imagination reaches its fullest potential where love is at play. As the twentieth-century theologian and writer Howard Thurman put it, "[L]ove always sees more than is in evidence at any moment of viewing."[15] Love helps us train our eyes and our hearts beyond the separate identities that Eastern religions refer to as "the ten thousand things" and to focus instead on the connectedness as real as bedrock beneath all distinctions.

"Ultimately," wrote Thurman, "there is only one place of refuge on this planet for any [person]—that is another [person]'s heart. To love is to make of one's heart a swinging door."[16]

In Your Own Words

If you made of your heart a swinging door, who might come in? And where might you find yourself headed when you go out? What migrations might love bring about in your life?

Begin writing with these words and see where the door leads you.

Through this swinging door . . .

A LOVE STORY IN AN ENTIRELY NEW GENRE

In the procession of the soul from within outward,
it enlarges its circles ever, like the pebble thrown into the pond,
or the light proceeding from an orb.
—RALPH WALDO EMERSON[17]

As Emerson pointed out, we mostly venture into love largely unaware that it might open us to a new relationship with all of humanity; but this is the power of love. As we come to more deeply trust the ones we love intimately, we learn to open our hearts more compassionately to a host of others. Have you ever, in the first blush of a new romance or a newly sparked friendship, felt your heart warming toward your difficult neighbor, toward a cranky uncle or the stranger who rudely pushes you aside on the bus? When love softens the heart, we begin to see beneath the surface of things wherever we look, and it can be hard to find a person or a place without some shimmer of attraction.

Who would suspect that the pleasant, inner glow felt with love's first romantic glimmer could lead to something as far reaching—and potentially life changing—as this? Culturally, we are more inclined to privatize love. With almost surgical precision, and with dire results, our focus on romance often severs the love exchanged between two people from the larger love in which healthy, intimate relationships are naturally embedded.

But love is not meant to be isolated, and it is the work of religion to restore our connectedness, inspiring and equipping us to choose and practice love. Despite our culture's messages that love is desirable but fleeting, personal but not political, attractive but impractical. Despite the forces that say we can have love in our lives without challenging the lovelessness of oppression in the world.

In 1980, after calling upon Christian soldiers in El Salvador to stop carrying out government-sponsored torture and terror, the Catholic archbishop of El Salvador, Óscar Romero, was assassinated while celebrating mass. Romero's words, though, have survived. "Let us not tire of preaching love," he said; "it is the force that will overcome the world [. . .] love must win out; it is the only thing that can."[18] In the name of love, we are called to imagine and remember the larger wholeness in which we all belong and, in so doing, to recover our wholeness within.

In a letter written from a Nazi concentration camp in 1944, the French poet Robert Desnos told his lover, Youki, "I kiss you as tenderly as honorability permits in a letter which must be passed by the censor."[19]

Desnos had been active in the French resistance. Upon his capture, he was tortured and interrogated before being sent to camps at Compiègne, Buchenwald, and Flöha. In his letter to Youki, he said he had many ideas for poetry and novels, and apologized for not having the time and freedom in his internment to write them down. He promised, however, that within three months of his return, he would complete a manuscript "for a love story in an entirely new genre."[20]

Desnos died of typhus two days after the liberation (as noted in the "Opening Our Story" writing reflection on page 72), leaving behind neither the love story nor the new genre that came to him as he toiled in the camp's trenches. But, reading his letter today, we receive the powerful inclination contained in his promise. Imagine it now—a love story in an entirely new genre, conjured in the loveless conditions of imprisonment, composed in the days of long labor, divined in thin-veiled dreams that arrived in cold nights on hard cots. Can you glimpse the power and the beauty of a love story strong as that? Can it be that we, reading Desnos's letter in the twenty-first century, have been entrusted with writing this love story today, with discovering and describing a love so muscular it could raise its head and capture a poet's attention even in the death camps of the Nazis?

It would be a story about love strong enough to stand up to history, to suffering and separation, a love that holds us accountable to ourselves and to others, a love worthy of being our life's aim and purpose. Love like that calls us out. It helps us discover and uncover a part of ourselves that has not yet risen to the surface. Love ripens new possibilities in our lives and in the world just as nature coaxes new fruit from the bud and the bloom. Each time we choose love, we are participating in writing its story in a whole new genre for a whole new day.

In Your Own Words

What might happen if love ripened in your life? What new possibilities might you discover? What new story might be written—in your personal life or in the wider world? What new genre might be creative enough, strong enough, and true enough to tell that story?

Begin writing with the prompt, and follow wherever it leads.

What if love . . .

10

WRITING ABOUT JUSTICE

SCALES OF JUSTICE

Justice is what love looks like in public.
—CORNEL WEST[1]

Ask anyone, of almost any stripe or leaning, if they believe in justice, and they will probably say they do. Ask them to define it, though, and you'll likely encounter a long, deep silence. The concept of justice, embedded in the human heart as it seems to be and examined thoughtfully by the best minds in history, can paradoxically be harder to catch hold of than a feather riding on the wind.

Instead of words, what comes to mind for many of us when we think of justice is the balance scale, often seen dangling from the left hand of the blindfolded goddess, as if right and wrong could be weighed one against the other, and justice could be measured with gravity and known by its mass. The Egyptian goddess Ma'at, the Roman goddess Justicia, and the Greek goddess Themis were all associated with justice and all were depicted with scales in their hands. Johannes Vermeer's painting *Woman Holding a Balance*, completed by the Dutch artist circa 1664, carries the image into domestic life with its famous portrait of a pregnant woman, as serene as she is expectant, paying no attention to a painting of the Last Judgment on the wall beside her and holding an empty set of scales in the gentle light from a window.

The image of the scales of justice can be misleading, though. For if justice is measured on a scale, then we might rightfully ask who or what serves as the Office of Weights and Measures, verifying the scale's calibration across history, geography, and context. On the other hand, the image also carries some truth. For who among us has not known injustice as that fluttering sensation in the body that tells us something has gone awry? It is as if our inner scale has been unsettled, whether tipping subtly or swinging with wild, erratic imbalance, or in one swift move, bottoming out altogether under the burden of some heavy injustice.

In Your Own Words

Think of an injustice that you once experienced or witnessed, something that caused your internal balances to swing and sway with alarm. Something that stirred a strong reaction in you, whether you acted upon that or not. It might have been recently or long ago. Perhaps it was a wrong committed against you, or it might have been an injustice that you, wittingly or unwittingly, participated in against someone else. It could have been something you witnessed directly or by reading or hearing about it.

Choose one such incident, and recall the details of the event and your own internal reaction to it.

Now, imagine your internal scales set off balance by this incident, whether subtly or suddenly, and use the prompt to begin writing about this injustice and how you experienced it inside.

The scales in me . . .

JUSTICE AS BLESSING

And if he takes one step towards Me, I take ten steps towards him.
And if he comes to Me walking, I go towards him running.
—ISLAMIC HADITH INTERPRETING
THE STORY OF THE PRODIGAL SON [2]

Another early image dating back to medieval Europe is the Hand of Justice. Carried by many European kings, this was a staff topped with a hand bestowing a blessing. Two fingers up, two fingers down, the hand was a gentle gesture stopped in mid-action, as if the blessing would never stop flowing. The staff was carried on the king's left side, as one of three representations of the king's power, together with the scepter and crown.

The connection between justice and blessing invites an understanding that is often lost in the image of the scales and the focus on judgment. The hand of blessing reminds us that justice is based on relationship, perhaps especially our relationship with those whom we do not know. The term "right relationship" is sometimes used to describe this profound and extended web of kinship and connection in which each party is mutually respectful and loving and all are serving the well-being of one another. In what some have called "mythic reciprocity,"[3] justice involves a mutual exchange of gift and sacrifice compelled toward generosity, rather than measured and cut by the calculated weighing of costs and benefits.

The Chilean poet Pablo Neruda described one such exchange in the fenced backyard of his childhood. Looking for adventure as a young boy, one day he put his eye to a hole in the fence and peered upon an unkempt landscape wholly foreign to him. He stepped back, as if something were about to happen, and a tiny hand about the size of his own appeared in the hole, leaving behind a small and worn, white, woolly sheep. Taking the sheep, he looked through the hole again but the child who put it there was gone. Neruda ran into his house and retrieved a prize of his own, a favorite pinecone, and left it there for the boy, whom he never saw again but recalled for the rest of his life. This kind of mysterious exchange of gifts, Neruda suggests, can put us in relationship with all living things, a relationship that, for him, led to a lifetime of sharing the gift of his poetry with others whom he would never personally know:

> I have been a lucky man. To feel the intimacy of brothers is a marvelous thing in life. To feel the love of people whom we love is a fire that feeds our life. But to feel the affection that comes from those whom we do not know, from those unknown to us, who are watching over our sleep and solitude, over our dangers and our weaknesses—that is something still greater and more beautiful because it widens out the boundaries of our being, and unites all living things.[4]

In Your Own Words

When have you received a gift from another that prompted you to pass your own gifts along as well? Perhaps it was a two-way exchange like Neruda's, or maybe it was something offered just to you—a random object or a kind word, directions when you needed them, or bus fare when you came up short—that inspired you to pass on to another something else of yours. How might these gifts you've received from others give you an experience of "right relationship" or draw you into the "mythic reciprocity" of justice?

Describe one such exchange you've known, what was given, how it made you feel, and what generosity it might have set in motion in your life. How might it represent the Hand of Justice raised in blessing?

Begin writing with the prompt below, following wherever it leads.

It was a gift . . .

JOURNEYING TOWARD JUSTICE

The arc of the moral universe is long,
but it bends toward justice.
—Martin Luther King Jr., paraphrasing abolitionist
Theodore Parker[5]

In Australia, the aboriginal tradition of the walkabout beckons people to drop what they are doing and go on a pilgrimage, following the footsteps of their ancestors. Navigating land they have not crossed before, walkabout pilgrims depend on something called songlines left behind by their earliest ancestors, said to have traveled in mythic time. As the story goes, these ancestors scattered a trail of music and words with their footprints, naming creation as they went and bringing it into being as they spoke, sang, and walked.[6]

When we are engaged in the work of justice, we too have songlines we can follow that will guide and enliven our way.

In late August of 1967, over a hundred civil rights activists calling for open housing in Milwaukee marched three miles across the city's wide industrial river valley on an extended viaduct known at the time as the "longest bridge in the world." Said to stretch all the way from Africa to Poland, the bridge connected Milwaukee's predominately black north side and the city's nearly all-white and predominately Polish American south side. Reaching the south end of the bridge with their hand-lettered signs that read "We Need

Fair Housing," the marchers were met by a crowd of eight thousand counterdemonstrators who were loudly insulting, heckling, and cursing them. The fair housing marchers said a brief prayer, turned, and walked back across the bridge without incident.

The next night, the marchers returned and were met by a crowd that had grown to nearly thirteen thousand, this time hurling rocks and bottles along with angry and violent words. The marchers again walked back to the north side and later that night their headquarters were burned to the ground.

Far from being deterred, the marchers resolved to continue. For the next 198 nights, the fair housing marches continued in Milwaukee, often led by James Groppi, a priest who was arrested nine times for his protests, each time returning to the streets to march again as soon as he was freed.[7]

The marchers did not know when or even if change would come. There was no guarantee they would succeed. Most evidence suggested otherwise. Only now, many decades later, can we see the songlines they made—the true distance they traveled, the much-needed path they opened, and the justice they walked and sang into being. Congress passed the Civil Rights Act in April 1968; Milwaukee passed its own stronger fair housing law just weeks later. And the Milwaukee viaduct once called "the longest bridge in the world" has been officially renamed the "James Groppi Unity Bridge."

Every place in every time has its stories of justice seekers who went before. If we listen, we might hear their songlines ringing out even now—the notes of freedom in the making, the rhythms of feet marking a new way, the sound of voices joined in common aspiration and in creating justice anew.

In Your Own Words

Are there justice songlines beckoning you today? Where have you found footprints, words, and music left behind by others that might guide your way? Whose story do you know that might serve as a songline in your own march for justice?

Begin writing with one of the prompts below, and follow wherever it leads.

This song I hear . . .

Or

If I follow these footsteps . . .

JUSTICE WITHIN

To be just toward oneself means to actualize as many potentialities as possible without losing oneself in disruption and chaos.
—PAUL TILLICH[8]

In pursuing the long work for justice, we might take a page from the book of customer satisfaction and several recent studies about the nature of waiting and what makes it tolerable. It turns out that the worst kind of waiting is not necessarily the longest but rather the most idle. So if we find ourselves waiting for the doors of justice to open, we might employ a useful discovery made long ago by the interior designers of high-rises. When waiting for an elevator, it turns out, we will bide the time more patiently if we wait in front of a mirror. Studies of this phenomenon suggest that mirrors allow us to pass the time more happily by fixing our hair or adjusting our clothes. Perhaps we might also find it more difficult to be impatient when we see what impatience looks like on our faces.

So too, in the enduring wait for justice, we have good reason to begin with a long look at ourselves. Such is the message of an old Jewish tale retold by writer Howard Schwartz, a collector and translator of Jewish folklore:

A man long ago set out to find justice. He traveled year after year, searching place after place, until he had crossed the entire known world, and came at last upon one final forest. Journeying deep into the woods, this last place on earth, he arrived at a small clay cottage and saw through its windows thousands of flickering flames. Intrigued, he knocked on the door, and, receiving no answer, he admitted himself. Inside he found an expansive space filled with hundreds of shelves, each holding dozens of oil candles of different kinds. Some of the candles burned brightly with a full supply of oil; others flickered, their oil about to run out.

To his surprise, an old, bearded man in a white robe appeared in the room. "Shalom aleikhem," the old man said.

"Aleikhem shalom," the pilgrim replied. And he told the old man of his search for justice, and asked him the meaning of the candles.

The old man explained that each candle was the candle of a person's soul. As long as the candle burned, the person was alive. When the candle burned out, the person's soul left the world behind.

"Can you show me my candle?" asked the pilgrim. The old man led him deep into the endless rooms until they came to a simple clay candle burning on a low shelf. Seeing the small flickering flame and the nearly expired supply of oil in his candle, the pilgrim, who had been fearless at every other juncture of his journey, began to tremble. Then he noticed the candle next to his, full of oil, its wick still long and its flame still strong. "Whose candle is that?" he asked.

The old man told him he could only reveal each candle to its own person, and then he left, just as a candle on a higher shelf began to sputter and then went out.

The pilgrim shuddered with fear. Somewhere a person had just died, and he, with only a few drops of oil remaining in his candle, would soon follow.

He turned and looked around every corner, unable to find the old man anywhere. Then he picked up the candle next to his own and tilted it to pour. The old man, reappearing in that moment from nowhere, stopped him, asking, "Is this the justice you seek?"

The man closed his eyes. When he opened them again, the man was gone, the cottage and the candles too. Alone in the forest, he could not know if his candle had gone out and if his journey and his life were both over.[9]

Sometimes the most difficult view we can face is the one we find in the mirror. Lao Tzu reminded us, though, that this is exactly where the work of justice and reconciliation must begin. "Compassionate toward yourself," he wrote, "you reconcile all beings in the world."[10]

Justice depends on compassion as surely as it begins by looking honestly at ourselves. In treating ourselves justly, we discover that compassion gives justice a reach and durability well beyond that of judgment. Only compassion can give justice the supple resilience that it needs to be true.

In Your Own Words

Materials needed: You will need a mirror for this prompt.

Close your eyes and recall a time when you were deeply at peace with yourself and with others. Remember what it felt like to truly be yourself in a way that also made you fully and deeply connected to the world. Recalling this feeling, let it rise to the surface as you take in a deep breath. Breathing out, relax your body, your shoulders, your jaw, your face. Breathe in and out slowly, several times, letting this feeling of peace and order wash over you.

Whenever you are ready, open your eyes and look into your mirror. Gaze softly at your own reflection, noticing what the feeling you've been experiencing on the inside looks like on the outside. If, while you are gazing, you see a flicker of judgment come across your face, close your eyes and start again, breathing deeply, awakening self-compassion, and then opening your eyes again.

Begin writing with the prompt below, following wherever it leads.

Looking for justice, what I see is . . .

COSMIC ORDER

She who is centered in the Tao
. . . perceives the universal harmony,
even amid great pain,
because she has found peace in her heart.

—LAO TZU[11]

Little is known about the specifics of ancient Egyptian law, but what has survived across the millennia is the spirit of justice, or *Ma'at*, on which Egyptian law and society were based. For the ancient Egyptians, the term Ma'at meant essentially the way things are in the natural world, the right and reliable order of the cosmos that keeps the sun rising every day and the seasons turning every year. Egyptian rulers were said to have "done Ma'at" when they ruled justly, aligning with this larger order. Ma'at was also a name for the goddess of justice, truth, and order who judged the dead in the Egyptian underworld by weighing the heart of each arrival on a swinging balance against a feather. Only those with hearts sufficiently lightened by "doing Ma'at"—hearts, unburdened by wrongdoing, that could balance the weight of a feather—were permitted into the afterlife.

This emphasis on the underlying order of the universe was prominent in ancient matriarchal and agricultural societies, and is found in many indigenous religions around the world. Overriding the dualities of good and evil, the concept of justice in these cosmologies was holistic, embedded in the natural world with its cycles encompassing both birth and death while leaning in the larger sense toward life.

In varying degrees, Taoism, Hinduism, Buddhism, and even the Abrahamic religions carry similar ideas of justice as the underlying order of the universe. It is free will that has opened the hatch through which we keep slipping out of this larger relationship and order. Perhaps, then, before justice was ever carved into stone or in human decrees of law, first and foremost, it was tucked more indelibly into the essence of all life, written into the fiber of being itself, woven into all right relations. No wonder we keep missing it; it's been hidden inside the very fabric of relationship and love, and in the ecological web of life that holds us all.

Today, insulated as many of us are from wilderness or even from small natural landscapes, and accustomed as most of us are to unsustainable levels of consumption, we are often blind to the justice found in nature's underlying order. Instead, we regard justice as something that must be imposed on humans as a correction to our inclination toward violence and self-interest. But sociologists and ancient sages alike say it isn't so. Many recent studies have explored the ancient roots of cooperation as a necessity for human survival and flourishing. And as far back as the fourth century BCE, the Chinese philosopher Chuang Tzu noted that we might lack awareness of foregone societies built on justice, because they were so well aligned with the natural order that no one thought to record them:

> In the age when life on earth was full, no one paid any special attention to worthy men [. . .] they were honest and righteous without realizing that they were "doing their duty." They loved each other and did not know that this was "love of neighbor." They deceived no one yet they did not know that they were "men to be trusted." They were reliable and did not know that this was "good faith." They lived freely together giving and taking, and did not know that they were generous. For this reason their deeds have not been narrated. They made no history.[12]

Even in the twenty-first century, when the news and our history books are shot through with violent conflict, there exists an understory (often untold) of more gentle and mutual relations. Just one example of many is a small circle of bereaved mothers that for many years has gathered in a home in the West Bank village of Beit Ummar, while the blood conflict between Israelis and Palestinians drags on. They are Palestinian mothers and Israeli mothers, and they come together to share photographs and stories of the children they have lost in the violence. The grieving mothers share their pain with one another, and as they do, they are together beginning a new story, a story of relationship with the possibility of reconciliation seeded within it. Like the low growth in the shadows of the forest that often goes unnoticed, in every age, the story of quiet and resilient coexistence, cooperation, and collaboration—which is to say, of just and right relations—continues to unfold, though often unrecorded in history or in headlines. It is that common. It is that sure.

In Your Own Words

Materials needed: For this exercise you'll want to have one or more items from the natural world on hand, especially things with some visible design or pattern. These could be seashells, seedpods, pinecones, flowers—dried or still living—a plant, fruit, or vegetable (especially cut open to view the seeds).

Choose one of the objects from nature assembled ahead of time and observe it closely. Pick it up. Notice how it feels in your hand—its surface, size, and heft. Turn it over and look at all sides. Observe the patterns of its design and construction. If it's a fruit, vegetable, or seedpod, you might want to cut it open to see the patterns inside. Is there wisdom to be found in these patterns and their purpose?

What might it mean to align your life with the deeper order embedded in the cosmos, to "do Ma'at" by aligning yourself with this order?

Describe the item you have chosen, exploring its characteristics and its structure, and considering what might be learned from it regarding justice as a return to nature's order. If you prefer to write from a prompt, you might begin with the words below, completing the sentence, making reference to the item in your hand.

If I live according to this order . . .

WHEN JUSTICE LISTENS, WHEN JUSTICE SEES

In order to know what is just in a person-to-person encounter,
love listens. . . . Listening love is the first step to justice
in person-to-person encounters.
—PAUL TILLICH[13]

More than one philosopher has noted that the more laws we have, the more injustice seems to flourish. In one way of thinking, this might seem counterintuitive if we subscribe to the notion that laws are meant to uphold justice. But it's almost as if the laws themselves miss the larger point that injustice rises first from a lack of compassion, and without tending to these origins, the laws simply train injustice to jump higher or run faster to get to where it's going.

If justice is indeed a matter of right relationship, of joining in on the give-and-take of mutual respect, concern, and care, the path we make and take to reach it will become a determining factor in whether we ever get there. Zen master Charlotte Joko Beck said, "In spiritual maturity, the opposite of injustice is not justice but compassion. Not me against you, not me straightening out the present ill, fighting to gain a just result for myself and others, but compassion, a life that goes against nothing and fulfills everything."[14]

How does this compassionate approach to justice relate to the blindfolds so often tied around the eyes of our Western understanding? It is interesting that many of the oldest surviving personifications of justice are not blindfolded. The Greek goddess Themis, for instance, was neither blindfolded nor equipped with a sword. Rather, it was her ability to see and foretell the future that qualified her as the goddess of divine justice, and the justice she represented was one of consent, not coercion.

This is especially important when considering systemic injustice, or the way in which oppression itself is often codified into laws and systems that make it largely invisible. So it is no surprise that work for justice often must begin by resisting the notion that justice is blind. Blindness in an oppressive system only serves to aid the invisible privilege that those in power have and exercise over those without it. Injustice thrives on what is not seen and not named.

Improving Justice's vision might also be accompanied by checking her hearing too. Almost a thousand years ago, in the northeastern forests of what is now North America, a spiritual and political leader who came to be known as the Great Peacemaker began a forty-year quest to peaceably unify five warring nations in the region. But the Peacemaker began his campaign with neither oration nor war. He began by listening.

At that time, Mohawk leader Hiawatha had withdrawn into bitter seclusion as he grieved the deaths of his daughters. When the Peacemaker heard Hiawatha's great grief, he performed a traditional ceremony of condolence—a ritual of compassion that involved wiping Hiawatha's tears so that he might see again, clearing his ears to allow him to hear again, and unstopping his throat that he might speak again. As Hiawatha's grief was released, it was transformed into strength. In gratitude for the renewal of his spirit, Hiawatha then listened to the Peacemaker's vision for unity and joined him, performing the condolence ceremony for the five nations that would unite in the Iroquois Confederacy. For the People of the Longhouse, as the united nation was known, justice was understood as the result of healing relationships, when every part of creation flourished and ripened.[15]

How might our own experience of justice be transformed if we began our work toward it with acts of listening, condolence, and conversation? How might we be changed if we removed the blind-folds from our eyes and regarded one another with clearer vision?

In Your Own Words

Imagine a statue of Justice in a park, a blindfolded woman with the scales in one hand and a sword in the other. It might be a statue you've seen or one you create in your mind. Imagine walking past her on a sunny afternoon, and as you walk by her, she moves. You stop to look, and she removes her blindfold. She looks at you from her pedestal and then steps down to stand at your side. She asks you what you're concerned about as you think about justice, and listens while you tell her all that is weighing on your heart. Together, you walk through the park, talking with one another.

Write about your exchange. If you like, begin with the prompt.

And Justice listened when I said . . .

11

WRITING ABOUT HOPE

HOPE SURPRISES

Hope in the face of difficulty, hope in the face of uncertainty, the audacity of hope: in the end, that is God's greatest gift to us . . . a belief in things not seen, a belief that there are better days ahead.
—BARACK OBAMA[1]

Hope, I am grateful to note, has a habit of showing up at my door when I least expect it. Sometimes (not always), on those days when I am overwhelmed by everything not yet done and all that has gone wrong, when the odds against me are stacked as high as the unwashed dishes in the kitchen sink, when my hair is disheveled and I haven't a prayer of turning things around, it is then that hope has a way of knocking on the door and walking right in. If I'm lucky, it is then, when I need it, that hope comes unbidden, with an energy and determination beyond anything I could imagine. Of course, there are also times when hope fails to show up, and I need to send out a search party just when I am least equipped to organize one. But for now, we might begin our reflections on hope by considering how surprisingly commonplace it can be when we open our eyes to its many forms, as this excerpt from Lisel Mueller's poem helps us to do:

Hope
It hovers in dark corners
before the lights are turned on,
* it shakes sleep from its eyes*
* and drops from mushroom gills,*
*   it explodes in the starry heads*
*   of dandelions turned sages,*
*   it sticks to the wings of green angels*
*   that sail from the tops of maples.*

It sprouts in each occluded eye
of the many-eyed potato,
* it lives in each earthworm segment*
* surviving cruelty,*
*   it is the motion that runs*
*   from the eyes to the tail of a dog,*
*   it is the mouth that inflates the lungs*
*   of the child that has just been born.*[2]

We're so accustomed to Emily Dickinson's observation that "hope is a thing with feathers" that sometimes we forget hope's remarkable shape-shifting and many activities. Consider the furry and industrious description from Julie Neraas's book *Apprenticed to*

Hope: "[A] fierceness resides in me that exhibits all the busyness and fury of a small, persistent animal. It digs and digs, bites and claws at any corral that threatens to fence it in."[3]

It's a description that helps me think of hope as something common, industrious, and tenacious, like the squirrels running across my backyard, burying their nuts for a winter's day. Have you ever received hope from a simple glance exchanged with a stranger? In glimpsing a bud on the end of a branch? In hearing a single refrain of music or catching the scent of a tree in bloom as you walk beneath its branches at night? Noticing hope's many faces and forms of animation can awaken us to the presence of hope in the most unexpected times and places.

In Your Own Words

Materials needed: For this prompt, you'll need a magazine or two with interesting photos of varied events and scenes. (Or if you have internet access, you could visit a media site's collection of photos of the day.)

Where do you see hope? What does it look like, and what is it doing? From a magazine, choose a photograph of a scene or event that piques your interest. It might work best with a picture that presents some interaction or dynamic element, conflict, or story, rather than a still-life composition or a close-up. But don't overanalyze what you select or why. Just pick a photo and look for one thing in it that might represent hope. It can be the main subject of the photo or a very small part of it—anything that, for whatever reason, reminds you of hope and what hope does as you look at that picture.

What is hope, and what does it do? Write about the image of hope you've found in the photograph, describing what hope is and what it does using the following prompts. Use them however you like, writing at length on each, or alternating between them:

Hope is the thing with . . .
Hope is the thing that . . .

TO HOPE AND TO WAIT

Hope is believing in spite of the evidence,
then watching the evidence change.
—JIM WALLIS[4]

The verb *hope* means "to want something to happen," while the noun *hope* refers to "a feeling of expectation and desire" and, in its oldest sense, trust. The word is traced back to the old English *hopian*, which was well vested with desire, meaning to wish or to look forward to something. Some even suggest a connection with the Low German word *hop* and its accompanying image of "leaping in expectation."[5] When we really expect that something we've hoped for will come to pass, it's enough to lighten both our hearts and our steps. Sometimes, when our son was young and his walk would suddenly turn to skipping for no apparent reason, David and I regarded it as a bit of embodied hope. "We've got skip," we would say to each other, an expression for a moment of delighted hope that we still use today.

This forward-looking, forward-leaping character of hope is the essence of the word's theological meaning too. For whether ours is a faith that draws from theism, naturalism, or humanism, when we link our lives to a religious community that believes in and works toward liberation, we are hitching our hearts to hope—not an otherworldly hope tightly focused on some other time or place or life, but a forward-leaning hope planted in the present and well rooted in history and in patient practice. It is a hope that grows in the here and the now.

In Spanish, the expectant nature of hope is linguistically built in. The same word, *espero*, is used to say both "I hope" and "I wait." One cannot talk about waiting for something without also expressing hope that it will come to pass, and one cannot express hope for something without being reminded that it will involve waiting. It is a double meaning that grammatically engages us in the future. As theologian Eleazar Fernandez notes, "[T]hose who wait in hope are already being grasped by its power as they wait."[6]

In the mid-1700s, a farmer named Thomas Potter living in the coastal town of Good Luck, New Jersey, knew something about the junction between waiting and hope.[7] Potter believed in universal salvation—the idea that God is too loving to cause any being to suffer in eternity for wrongs committed in this life—and it was a belief radically out of step with the dominant Calvinist teachings of the day. Calvinist proclamations of predestination then prevalent said that our fate is predestined at birth and only a precious few of us are predestined to salvation.

Eager to bring the good news of universalism to his town, in 1760, Potter built a chapel on his own land and then waited, hoping for a preacher who would deliver the message of universalism from its pulpit. For ten years he waited, and the chapel stood empty. Then one September day in 1770, a large ship became stranded on a sandbar, and a passenger named John Murray made his way into the bay in a smaller vessel.

Murray had been a Methodist minister in England and had lost his standing in the church because he'd been preaching universalist salvation. After his wife and only child died of illness, he sailed to America with the hope of starting over, vowing never to preach again. But when Potter met Murray on the shore and learned of Murray's history and theology, he insisted that Murray stay to preach in his chapel that Sunday. Murray refused, saying he was no longer a preacher and that he needed to leave as soon as the wind would take his ship back out of the bay. To which Potter famously replied that the winds would never change until Murray agreed to deliver his message in the chapel that awaited his arrival.

When Sunday came, the ship was still stuck in the bay, and Murray preached in the chapel, delivering a long-anticipated universalist message to Potter's family and neighbors. As the story goes, as soon as the sermon was over, the winds changed and Murray's ship was free to sail. Murray left but soon returned to the area, preaching a message of universal salvation for years to come, and eventually founding America's first universalist congregation in Gloucester, Massachusetts.

Hope is the kind of faithful waiting we do despite all evidence that would persuade us not to. Hope is how we prepare ourselves for a new possibility we have longed for but never seen. It is a kind of waiting that builds new spaces for the yet unspoken messages we most need to hear.

In Your Own Words

What are the messages you've been longing to hear? It might be something meant for all of us, a message of saving grace that many yearn to hear. "I am with you always," said Jesus in one such message.[8] "Whoever is planted in the Tao / will not be rooted up," wrote Lao Tzu in another.[9] "Do not fear," said God to the Israelites, "for I am with you."[10] Or it could be more personal encouragement—such as healing words of forgiveness, support, courage, or companionship (e.g., don't give up; we're in this together; I've got your back; or you're loved just the way you are).

Imagine your empty page as an invitation for these messages to be spoken. Make a list of them. As you wait to hear them, is there hope in your waiting? Begin writing with the prompt below and keep writing:

While I wait . . .

PANDORA'S JAR

Despair and hope are inseparable. One can never understand what hope is really about unless one wrestles with despair.

—CORNEL WEST[11]

Some of the most hope-filled people I have known have been those for whom favorable outcomes might be described as a long shot at best. This tendency of hope's to show up in the bottom of our suffering is said by some to be the meaning of the Greek myth of Pandora's jar, also known as Pandora's box. It is a story with as many versions as it has interpretations, many of them quite critical,[12] but the earliest literary references trace it back to Hesiod in the eighth or seventh century BCE. And a basic common component of the story's many tellings is that when all the chaos and suffering had escaped Pandora's mythic jar, only one thing remained at the bottom, and it was hope.

Some say this is a tale of woe in which hope is locked up by Pandora, kept out of reach while suffering roams with free rein. But I am more inclined to see this as a tale of origins, one that points us toward the source of hope, which is mixed in with all our suffering, there at the bottom of the jar, where we might least expect to find it.

Hope is often found in the last place you would expect it to be, which may actually be bad news for those of us whose lives are relatively comfortable or privileged. In my own experience, I have found that when the world is tilted in my favor, for whatever reason, I have less awareness of hope's presence and persistence. It is when things go wrong, or when I find myself in a system stacked against me, that I start exercising hope with greater need and rigor.

Perhaps this is what W. E. B. Du Bois meant in *The Souls of Black Folk*, published in 1903, when he described the heartbreak he experienced in looking at his newborn son. "How beautiful he was," Du Bois writes, "with his olive-tinted flesh and dark gold ringlets, his eyes of mingled blue and brown, his perfect little limbs, and the soft voluptuous roll which the blood of Africa had moulded into his features!" Then quickly followed Du Bois's realization, equally fatherly, that already in his young son's head was "a hope not hopeless but unhopeful," acknowledging that as an African American child born into a world still governed by systemic racism, his son would soon enough see "a land whose freedom is to us a mockery and whose liberty is a lie."[13]

A hope not hopeless but unhopeful is one born into the harsh realities of racism, sexism, poverty, and oppression. Sadly Du Bois's son did not survive but died of diphtheria at the age of two, leaving his parents with unredressable sorrow. However, Du Bois maintained enough "hope not hopeless but unhopeful" to record his candid and painful observations about race and racism, giving hope to generations to come by naming the often-unnamed veil separating black from white in a country that claims to value equality.

When working for any long-term change unlikely to be achieved in our lifetime, we are advised by many wise teachers to let go of the hope of fruition, to aspire toward a new world while letting go of our need for results. As the Catholic priest Thomas Merton counseled a young activist:

> Do not depend on the hope of results. When you are doing the sort of work you have taken on, [. . .] you may have to face the fact that your work will be apparently worthless and even achieve no result at all [. . .]. As you get used to this idea you start more and more to concentrate not on the results but on the value, the rightness, the truth of the work itself.[14]

In Your Own Words

Think of a time when your hope waned but then showed up at the bottom of Pandora's jar after all the suffering and chaos had escaped. Perhaps you felt a "hope not hopeless but unhopeful," as Du Bois put it. Perhaps you found hope in the value and "the truth of the work itself," as Merton said—or the truth of your life's experience regardless of the results.

Begin with one of the prompts below:

Who would have thought I'd find hope there . . .

Just when I thought hope had left me . . .

BORROWING HOPE

[T]hat's what hope is, no shining thing but a kind of sustenance,
plain as bread, the ordinary thing that feeds us.
—MARK DOTY[15]

Unfortunately, hope doesn't always show up when you need it. Sometimes it fades or disappears without so much as a coattail in sight. Hope sometimes vanishes when we are facing insurmountable personal difficulties, or it might go running when we try to absorb the daily news of so many tragedies and injustices. We can simply run out of hope.

When this happens, we might need to borrow hope in the same way that we might ask a neighbor for a cup of sugar. Borrow, of course, is a loose term for these exchanges—for neither the sugar nor the hope is typically returned in the same form, but often makes its way back transformed, whether in the form of cookies freshly baked and shared or in the open-hearted presence of one whose hope has been restored.

Each of us has a storehouse of symbols from which we borrow hope when we need it. We might turn to nature, in the garden outside our door or in the endless forests of a wilderness area. Or we might turn to religious symbols—the rainbow or the dove, the lotus rising out of mud, the Bodhi tree, the Taoist bowl of fruit, the Mesopotamian tree of life, or the Christian cross. We look to these and other symbols as reminders of what is possible but not visible in the present moment. They provide us with a promise on which to fix our eyes, what the poet and former Czech president Václav Havel described as a wider horizon that reorients the heart. "[Hope] is an orientation of the spirit, an orientation of the heart; it transcends the world that is immediately experienced, and is anchored somewhere beyond its horizons."[16]

Havel knew something about borrowing hope in dire circumstances. As a dissident during his country's occupation, he was imprisoned numerous times, once for almost five years. From his prison cell, he wrote repeatedly about that wider horizon, what his translater Paul Wilson calls "the outer rim of the discernible, intelligible, or imaginable world," as his source of hope.[17]

For others, despair works like a heavy weight on the eyes, preventing us from looking up or out toward anything that distant. In his memoir, *Heaven's Coast*, Mark Doty wrote about looking for hope as his partner, Wally, was dying of AIDS. Doty observed that sometimes hope is just the "ordinary thing that feeds us," the leavened sustenance of our days. It's not optimism, he points out, because in dire circumstances it carries no expectation that things will get better. But, like bread or the countless ordinary things that feed our will to live one day at a time, it does keep us going.[18]

Michèle Najlis, a writer I met in Nicaragua almost thirty years after the Sandinista revolution, shared her own story of borrowed hope. She was a former Sandinista who had been heavily involved in the struggle that overthrew Nicaragua's longtime brutal dictator in the late 1970s, and she described the victory of the revolution that occurred in her youthful years as seeming like a fairy tale. By the 1990s, though, when the revolution's short-lived victory had already given way to the combined forces of a major hurricane, corruption, and international interference, Najlis lost all hope and fell into a severe two-year depression.

She described how a friend helped her by suggesting that she focus on living just one day at a time. She started in even smaller increments, living just two hours at a time. Then three. Then four. Eventually one day at a time. For two years, she struggled to live this way, hour by hour, day by day, with the care of gentle friends and family, until finally what saved her was a basic act of resistance she learned from a story told by Viktor Frankl. In *Man's Search for Meaning*, Frankl described how a dying woman he knew in the concentration camps took hope—and joy—from a single branch of a chestnut tree with just two blossoms visible through her window.[19] Recalling this, Najlis looked around her room and mustered what little strength she had to get rid of the symbols of death that she found there. Instead, she began to focus on a plant—the one thing alive in the room—as the only act of resistance she had left in her. The plant's green promise, resisting despair and insisting on life, was eventually enough to call her back from her long depression.

The power of symbols is strong, both in the moment and on the page as we pass them on to others. Just as Frankl's story about the branch of the chestnut tree helped Najlis to find hope, perhaps her story about the plant in her room extends that hope to others as well.

In Your Own Words

Materials needed: For this prompt, you'll need some colored markers or pencils or crayons and a plain unlined piece of paper (although you can do this in a journal if you like).

Where do you go to borrow hope? What objects, symbols, scriptures, places, people, rituals, and other practices lend you hope when you need to borrow it? Make a list. It might be a tree or a plant, a loved one, or maybe a religious symbol—a statue of Kwan Yin, a crucifix, or a set of prayer beads. Or it might be something practical like a cane that helps you walk, or a computer that helps you talk. But it should be something that "happifies" you, as the universalist Hosea Ballou would have put it in the 1800s, as it leads you back to hope.

Now, write the names of these sources of hope on your page, recording some in large type and others smaller, in any arrangement or direction and using different kinds of writing, if you want. Choose different colors for each source of hope and spin the page as you work to record the words in different directions, outlining them in bubbles or squares or any shape that comes to mind. Or turn the whole thing into a word picture, if you like.

When you're finished with your cluster of words, notice which words are prominent and which might seem to whisper more softly, and how the words might be related or where they stand alone. Then consider where you might keep this page for easy retrieval when you need it. You might want to paste it in your journal or post it near your desk. Or, if you want to make your own Pandora's jar, take a bowl or any container you like and fold the page to store it in the bottom, where you can reach for it when needed.

If you wish to write more after making your word cluster, you might begin with the following prompt:

It was there when I needed it . . .

A ROAD CALLED HOPE

Hope can be neither affirmed nor denied. Hope is like a path in the countryside: originally there was no path—yet, as people are walking all the time in the same spot, a way appears.

—Lu Xun[20]

"Try to focus your attention on the space above your head and below your feet," I was instructed by Wang Maohua, a Tai Chi master in Beijing. "Extend your awareness to the space beyond your fingers," he said. Gradually, my monkey mind let go of its aimless grip as my teacher led me in a meditative journey through my body, awakening me first to the space within my body and then beyond it. "Now," he said patiently, after I had launched myself through the first few Tai Chi forms, "try not to move by pushing your body. Instead, let your body move by a gentle intention into the space around it, where your awareness is already waiting to meet it."

Hope, it occurs to me, involves this practice of "gentle intention." Hope takes full stock of where we are now, and then casts our awareness and imagination out beyond. It is not satisfied with the way things are but leans toward a new possibility, one not in evidence around us but one already inhabited by our awareness. It lifts our eyes and beckons us to Václav Havel's wider horizon, a place he also called his *domov*, or home, claiming it as a place of true belonging.

Notice hope is not about standing still. In the biblical account of the Israelites' flight from Egypt, they had barely left when they lost their hope. Camped on the shores of the Red Sea, with nowhere to go as the Egyptian army approached from behind, they complained to Moses, asking why he brought them there. Was it to die in the desert because there were no graves for them in Egypt?

Moses was making his best effort to reassure them when God spoke up and said to Moses, "Why do you cry out to me? Tell the Israelites to go forward."[21] Don't stop now. Move on. Keep going. So they did, and of course, as the story goes, the sea parted, making a path from no path, allowing them to cross from shore to shore.

The Hebrew word for intention, *kavannah*, literally means direction, reminding us that to change where we're headed, we don't need to make a sharp turn or travel far down the road. With the smallest shift in intention, we will already be going in a different direction, on our way toward a new destination. Casting our awareness out ahead of our feet, we make a path, step by step, moving forward to meet our awareness, our gentle intention, our prayer. This is what life is all about, said Martin Luther: "[N]ot rest but exercise. We are not now what we shall be, but we are on the way.[. . .] This is not the goal but it is the right road."[22]

In Your Own Words

Materials needed: For this prompt, you'll need scissors, two different colors of pen or pencil, and a piece of paper trimmed to about two thirds the width of your other writing paper. (If you are writing in a journal, use a freestanding piece of paper that you can paste into the journal after completing this prompt, if you like.)

On the two-thirds-width page, write a paragraph briefly describing something you find to be hopeless on some level, whether in your personal life or in the world. Jot it down as if you were casually ranting to a trusted friend about what the situation is and why it feels hopeless to you.

After you have written a paragraph's description, cut the paragraph roughly in half from top to bottom in a line that gently curves to move between the words. Place another sheet of paper (of a different color if you want to accentuate the gap) behind it with the gap opened about two to three inches, or as wide as you can, in the middle of the page, and glue or tape the two pieces of the paragraph down on either side. (If using a journal, you can glue or tape the two pieces in your journal with a gap in the middle.)

Notice the words on either side of the gap on your page. Circle any that interest you. Using some of these words in a new arrangement and possibly with new meanings, and using a different colored pen or pencil, write several sentences or a stream of words unrestrained by grammar that flows through the gap from top to bottom. If you want to start from a prompt, you might use the words:

If I follow the command to move on . . .

WHAT HOPE ASKS OF ME

"Hope" is the thing with feathers—
That perches in the soul—
And sings the tune without the words—
And never stops—at all—

I've heard it in the chillest land—
And on the strangest Sea—
Yet—never—in Extremity,
It asked a crumb—of me.
                    —EMILY DICKINSON[23]

Is it true? Does hope never ask a crumb of me or you?

Whether it asks or compels might be debated, but it can seem that when hope comes to visit us, we can expect consequences. The wind often changes when hope speaks in our lives. And one of the biggest changes is that hope frequently shows up with a traveling companion named love. Have you ever noticed the way hope often arrives with the opening of the heart? When we are moved to love, our vision is widened, allowing us to see well beyond the way things are. Love gives us the reason and ability to aspire toward a greater possibility for ourselves and for others whom we love.

Etty Hillesum's life and words remind us of the connection between love and hope, and hope's insistent call to resistance. A young Jewish woman living in Amsterdam in 1941, Hillesum left one of the twentieth century's most powerful legacies of hope in the diary and letters she wrote during Amsterdam's Nazi occupation and, later, in the death camps, where she died in 1942.

"Why is there a war?" Hillesum asked, writing in her Amsterdam apartment after an unsettling encounter with the Gestapo in the streets. "Perhaps because [. . .] I and my neighbor and everyone else do not have enough love. Yet we could fight war and all its excrescences by releasing, each day, the love that is shackled inside us, and giving it a chance to live."[24] For Hillesum, unshackling the love within meant she was compelled to keep her hopeful stance and to share it as a posture and act of resistance to the horrors of Nazi occupation and death camps. Waiting for her own deportation to the camps, she wrote, "There is no hidden poet in me, just a little piece of God that might grow into poetry. And a camp needs a poet, one who experiences life there, even there, as a bard and is able to sing about it [. . .] and I prayed, 'Let me be the thinking heart of these barracks.'"[25]

What does hope ask of us? More than a crumb, it turns out. Hope brings with it an orientation of the heart that will change your life. If I made a list of the changes I have noticed accompanying that orientation of the heart in myself and others, it might include some significant effects: nonjudgmental acceptance of what is (without assuming it must continue to be so); future orientation, *especially* when the future looks bleak; openness to more possibilities than those most apparent; forgiveness—of others *and* ourselves; and commitment and action, a willingness to allow ourselves "in the obedience of faith, to be used by God's Love," as Thomas Merton put it, in his letter to the young activist.[26]

In Your Own Words

Imagine hope sitting down next to you and picking up something heavy that you've been carrying for a very long time. As hope takes this burden from you, every part of your body feels lightened. Maybe it almost seems like you could get up and skip. But before you can, hope leans close and whispers into your ear. What does hope say? What does hope ask of you?

Begin writing from the prompt below and follow wherever it leads you.

Hope whispers in my ear . . .

12

WRITING ABOUT REDEMPTION

THE REDEMPTION STORE

I believe that the world was created and approved by love,
that it subsists, coheres, and endures by love, and that, insofar
as it is redeemable, it can be redeemed only by love.
—WENDELL BERRY[1]

In 1896, a company named Sperry & Hutchinson began printing large sheets of adhesive stamps in the color of money and with the initials S&H emblazoned in the center of each stamp. The company sold these S&H Green Stamps to retailers, who in turn gave them out to their patrons with each purchase, awarding more stamps the more customers purchased. Customers saved the stamps, licking their adhesive backs and pasting them into little books. When you'd filled enough books, you took them to an S&H redemption store, where the stamps worked like cash and could be exchanged for anything from dishes to a garden hose—often desired items that were just beyond reach of one's disposable income.

In their heyday in the 1960s, S&H Green Stamps were saved and redeemed by over 80 percent of US households before use of the stamps declined dramatically in the 1970s. Today, however, the kind of redemption practiced by S&H has become even more ubiquitous in the form of customer-rewards and frequent-flyer programs, where points substitute for stamps and redemption usually occurs online. What's interesting is the common motivation of these programs. Whether they involve licking stamps or not, they all aim at deepening relationships and increasing customer loyalty.

In Your Own Words

Imagine a rewards program designed to give you stamps or points for every redemptive act or good deed you do. Over time, you accumulate these and have the chance to cash them in at a redemption center for rewards that might otherwise be unattainable to you. What kinds of good deeds will earn points in the program you imagine, and what might be the rewards you receive when cashing them in?

Describe your imagined rewards program, playfully answering some of these questions. If you wish to start from a prompt, you might begin with:

I'm saving up for . . .

or

It's a chance to get . . .

REDEEMING WHAT IS BROKEN

I have woven a parachute out of everything broken.
—WILLIAM STAFFORD, DESCRIBING HIS OWN WRITTEN WORK[2]

Redemption also refers to the restoration of what has been broken, and we need not look far for examples and experiences of brokenness, writ large or small.

Not long after September 11, 2001, writer Terry Tempest Williams explored the nature of mosaics as a redemptive metaphor for how we might understand our brokenness in the new millennium, nationally, globally, and personally. In her book *Finding Beauty in a Broken World*, she wondered what to do with the broken pieces after the September 11 attacks and the shattered peace that resulted when the United States chose war as its response. Answering her longing for wholeness, the word that came to Williams was mosaic. "A mosaic," she writes, "is a conversation between what is broken."[3]

On any day when I am feeling broken, I am grateful for those who remind me that I need not be whole in order to be part of something beautiful. Williams's message counters the castaway assumption that what is broken must be repaired or discarded and left behind. What if instead our brokenness—and the world's—might be seen as a breaking *open*, like the splitting of a seedpod or the cracking of an egg about to hatch? What if that breaking open to new meaning and possibilities brings a beautiful play of light shining on our shattered and sharp surfaces? What if our brokenness might actually be our salvation? "God breaks the heart again and again and again," said Sufi master Hazrat Inayat Khan, "until it stays open."[4]

It may be that the most redemptive work we can do, in our own lives and in our work to repair the world, is to break open the story we have been telling ourselves—the story of certain outcomes, of sure-footed correctness, of entitlement, of privilege—and to humbly ask, what might we make of our brokenness? How might we reassemble the broken parts of our lives and our communities and our earth to weave a parachute like William Stafford's poems, something that will save us as we fall?

In Your Own Words

Materials needed: For this exercise, you will need a broken object of any kind. It can be as common as a pencil with its lead or its eraser broken away, or as treasured as a vase that is chipped or cracked. The brokenness can be visible or not.

Hold the object in your hand if you can. Explore it with your senses and with your understanding of its brokenness. Is it something that could be repaired or mended? Could it be used as it is, for its original purpose or a new one? Can you touch the edge of its brokenness, and if so, what does it feel like? What does it tell you about brokenness you have experienced or might be feeling now?

Begin writing with the prompt below.

Broken like this . . .

NOT EVERYTHING IS LOST

God entrusts and allots to everyone an area to redeem:
this creased and feeble life, "the world in which you live,
just as it is, and not otherwise."
—ANNIE DILLARD QUOTING MARTIN BUBER[5]

Although religious usage of the word redemption may be waning in some circles, the word has been widely adopted by secular cultural critics today, who frequently describe literature, films, and theater productions as having a redemptive message. What do you suppose they mean?

A story from Naomi Shihab Nye suggests one answer. A Palestinian American, Nye was traveling in the United States some time after the September 11 attacks, waiting in the Albuquerque airport after learning her flight had been delayed several hours. Among the airport's prerecorded messages about heightened security alerts and the need for passenger vigilance and suspicion, she heard another announcement asking anyone who understood Arabic to please come to gate A-4, which happened to be her gate.

Arriving at the gate, she found an older woman in Palestinian dress weeping on the floor and an airline service person helplessly standing by, unable to communicate. In faltering Arabic, Nye first explained to the woman that their flight had not been canceled, just delayed. Then the two of them began to pass the time by making phone calls to their family members on Nye's cell phone and introducing each other to the loved ones on the other end. They told their stories to each other, laughing together, with infectious results at the gate. When the woman opened a bag of homemade cookies she was carrying and passed them around, powdered sugar landing on everyone's laps, the airline's staff enlisted two young girls to hand out apple juice. And looking around the waiting area at Gate A-4 that day, Nye noticed that everyone had taken the cookies and no one looked apprehensive anymore about anyone else. "This can still happen, anywhere," Nye asserted. "Not everything is lost."[6]

Redemption, it seems to me, happens in this story because the ending opens into possibilities not easily foreseen in the beginning. And like this story, redemption can occur anywhere and anytime we live through stories of our own that might begin with apprehension of one form or another; with long, unbearable waiting; or with strangers in cold, impersonal settings. And then, often starting with some small act of kindness, the stories open up into a different, wider narrative, where trust and new relationships are again made possible and real.

In Your Own Words

Have you, recently or long ago, lived through a redemptive story of your own? What does the airport scene described by Naomi Shihab Nye stir in your thoughts, your memories, your imagination, and your heart?

Begin writing with the prompt below, following wherever it leads.
Not everything is lost . . .

REPAYING WHAT WE OWE

They used to say we're living on borrowed
time but even when young I wondered
who loaned it to us?

—JIM HARRISON[7]

When considering redemption, it is fitting, if perhaps uncomfortable, to think about debt. As a theological concept, redemption differs from salvation in that it carries with it an added notion of exchange or repayment. It requires something that needs to be redeemed—something lost to be recovered; something broken to be restored; something enslaved to be released; but especially something borrowed to be repaid.

This is difficult, especially in a time so burdened by national and personal debt. I am a pay-as-you-go kind of person, among the first to recoil from linking notions of debt to salvation. I do not like being indebted, financially or otherwise, but current events have reminded me that indebtedness is an inescapable characteristic of life's intricate and global weave—environmentally, socially, economically, and politically. By the middle of 2012, a newborn child drawing her first breath in the United States owed more than $50,000 as her share of the country's growing national debt.[8] Depending on how you balance history's books, this number could be much higher. If we added in the value of labor and land once taken without full payment through slavery or conquest, we would owe a greater sum by far. So even as we work to pay down what we owe, the national debt riddling the United States and many other countries reminds us that every life owes something, much of it untallied and some of it entirely uncountable in numbers. It may seem like a leap, but if you stop and think about it, in its healthiest form, debt is just one of the threads holding us together in the weave of relationship.

When you look at debt this way, in terms of relationship, doesn't love itself require its own terms of exchange? When we are loved, it is hard not to be compelled to pass it back or pass it on to others. For whether we pay it back or pay it forward, in matters of love, there really is no way to bank it or to hoard it. Just as when we breathe, every inhalation carries a debt of exhalation that must be paid, so too every gift of love we receive incurs its own debt to be paid back out again, if not directly and immediately, eventually and to some-one, somewhere, at some time.

Redemption, then, is a matter of honoring our debts. The word's origins in old French refer to "buying back" or re-buying what had been previously owned. In early Roman and Egyptian times, the sacrifices made before harvest were a repayment to the gods and goddesses for the season's growth and abundance. In the traditions and mythology of the Dakota nation, the performance of the buffalo dance and song was considered to be repayment for the fruits of a successful buffalo hunt and a payment forward for the next hunt. In Buddhism, redemption is found in the sacrificing or giving up, you might say "payment," of attachment on the path to enlightenment; and in Sufism or Islamic mysticism, redemption occurs when the prayers, devotion, and other practices of mystics and faithful others "pay down" the debts incurred by the world's profligate sinfulness.

Christian theology perhaps develops the notion of repayment furthest, describing redemption as God buying back what belonged to God before, namely humanity before sin ran off with our original state of goodness and belonging. In this understanding, each of us is born into the world with such great debt we could not begin to repay it. So God steps in and pays it for us. In traditional Christianity, the price paid to "repurchase" the human soul is exorbitant—nothing less than Jesus's own suffering and torturous death. Of course, many Christians, Unitarians, and Universalists in recent centuries understand it differently, noting the redemptive exchange that occurred in Jesus's life and is still occurring daily in our own. In other words, what makes Jesus a redeemer in this theology is not how he died but how he lived—and how we live, following his example.

Redemption, in this sense, has a lot in common with the simple give-and-take of breathing. It is a humble and grateful admission of all that we have received and a confession of the debt we owe and give back—to the earth, to the holy, to one another, and to ourselves—in repayment.

In Your Own Words

Make a list of IOUs that you might leave for others noting you will pay them back for something you've received or taken from them. Then make a second list of IOUs that you might receive from others, reminding you of things they owe you. Look at both lists; choose one IOU and write about it, considering whether it should be repaid in part or in full, with identical reimbursement or some other replacement or alternative reciprocation. Be creative in considering how the exchange might be made. Begin writing with the words:

The note says, IOU . . .

REDEMPTION AS DELIVERANCE—
IMPRISONED AND FREED

*In every generation, all people are to see themselves as if
they personally departed from Mitzrayim.*
—**FROM THE LITURGY OF THE PASSOVER SEDER**

Another meaning of redemption is deliverance, or liberation, and one of the best-known stories of deliverance ever recorded is that of the ancient Israelites and their liberation from slavery in Egypt. Beginning with their flight in the middle of the night and their passage through the parted waters of the Red Sea, led by Moses and guided by a holy pillar of fire, the Israelites' exodus story has strengthened and inspired numerous struggles for liberation around the world and is recounted by the Jewish Passover Seder every spring.

This may be a story from long ago and one more mythical than historical, but it is a story that will shake your world even today if you let it—and if you consider its metaphorical meaning. The Hebrew word for Egypt, *Mitzrayim*, derives from another Hebrew word meaning "narrow places" or "constricted places." So the exodus story is a mythological reminder of enslavements of all kinds—not only physical enslavement but also any confinement or restriction within our hearts and minds, or within the relationships and circumstances of our lives. Who has not, at some time, experienced an emotional, spiritual, or psychological constriction or bondage sufficient to stop us from freely claiming the sacred expression and ground of our true being?

This is the profound meaning of the phrase recited during the Jewish Seder "In every generation, all people are to see themselves as if they personally departed from Mitzrayim." Which is another way of raising the question: although we like to affirm our condition as a free people or as human beings with free will, who among us can truly say we are and always have been living free?

Fatima Mernissi, in her memoir *Dreams of Trespass*, describes growing up in her family's Moroccan harem. Mernissi explains to Western readers that *harem* is the word for a Moroccan household, usually a set of buildings constructed around an inner courtyard, creating a compound of sorts in which the household patriarch made the rules and the family's women and children were confined as much by rules and tradition as by the walls and the man posted at the gate. As a young girl trying to understand this confinement behind the tall walls of their household, Mernissi was guided by a wise aunt who told her, "A harem was about private space and the rules regulating it. [. . .] It did not need walls. Once you knew what was forbidden, you carried the harem within. You had it in your head, 'inscribed under your forehead and under your skin.'"[9]

Each of us has rules inscribed somewhere under our skin, sometimes confining us without our awareness, often unarticulated but significantly restricting what we do and who we are allowed to be.

Learning to see these rules and the "harem within" that confines us is the first step toward liberation and redemption. "First," said priest and spiritual writer Anthony de Mello, "realize that you are surrounded by prison walls, that your mind has gone to sleep. It does not even occur to most people to see this, so they live and die as prison inmates."[10]

In Your Own Words

What enslaves you now or has enslaved you in the past? What keeps or has kept you from being free? What rules have created a "harem within" that you might want or need to leave? When have you been in an Egypt of your own? Think of one form of Mitzrayim, or inner tyranny or enslavement. Write about it for five to ten minutes, describing the walls of this prison and the rules that keep you from claiming your freedom. You might start with the following words:

This narrow place I have been in . . .

After describing your own Mitzrayim, pause and ask yourself how you have escaped those walls or rules, or how you might escape them in the future. What is or might be your redemption? Write about this, beginning with the prompt below, following wherever it leads.

When I see myself as if I have just left Mitzrayim . . .

REDEMPTIVE LIVING

*A man cannot find redemption until he sees the flaws in his soul,
and tries to efface them. . . . We can be redeemed only
to the extent to which we see ourselves.*
—Martin Buber[11]

It may be tempting to think of redemption as something that happens like a miracle or epiphany breaking through the hardened ground of our days dramatically like a geyser of liberation or salvation. But in these lines from his poem "Ordinary Time," Tim Dlugos suggests that redemption is both more common and requires more effort than that.

> *Which are the magic*
> *moments in ordinary*
> *time? All of them,*
> *for those who can see.*
> *That is what redemption*
> *means, I decide*
> *at the meeting.*
> . . . .
> *Mine consists of understanding*
> *that the magic isn't something*
> *that I make, but something*
> *that shines through the things*
> *I make and do and say*
> . . . .
> *when I am fearless and thorough*
> *enough to give it room*[12]

Just how does one make room for redemption? Dlugos's full poem pays tribute to the recovery community that supported his twenty-three years of sobriety and the redemption found in recovery from any addiction—be it chemical or behavioral, or other addictions of the body, soul, or mind. The redemption experienced in recovery, he points out, doesn't occur overnight nor does it happen once and for all time. It takes place one ordinary and difficult day at a time, and is marked by paying attention to the way each day is lived and to the choices we make along the way. It also often involves acknowledging our indebtedness. The Twelve Step program, for instance, requires an honest accounting of the wrongs that we have done to others and ourselves, a willingness to seek and give forgiveness for those wrongs, and a lifelong commitment to service as the debt of engagement that makes recovery successful.

In Christian theology, this daily commitment is at the root of Jesus's words "Those who try to make their life secure will lose it, but those who lose their life will keep it."[13] In Islamic theology, it is a debt paid down regularly with repentance and righteous living— including the practices of prayer, fasting, pilgrimage, and giving to the poor required of every Muslim.[14] In other world religions, the ethic of the Golden Rule serves a similar purpose.

Whether in recovery, in religion, or in any personal effort to change, redemption is about how we live our lives one ordinary day at a time—by our willingness to make room for new possibilities and by making a commitment to see, believe, and work toward something better, for ourselves and for others. It recognizes that all our time is borrowed time and that we pay it back by choosing how we will spend it, day by day, hour by hour. Theologian Forrest Church wrote:

> Love's power comes in part from the courage required to give ourselves to that which is not ours to keep: our spouses, children, parents, dear and cherished friends, even life itself. It also comes from the faith required to sustain that courage,

the faith that life, howsoever limited and mysterious, contains within its margins, often at their very edges, a meaning that is redemptive.[15]

When we live lives "worth dying for," as Church put it,[16] we redeem what was given to us, debts and all, on the day we were born.

In Your Own Words

Draw a large box on your page, just inside the edges of the paper. Imagine this box is your life. "Howsoever limited and mysterious," Forrest Church said, it "contains within its margins, often at their very edges, a meaning that is redemptive." What aspects of your life so far have redeemed it, given it meaning, or made it a life "worth dying for"? These can be single events or experiences, or a wide arc of devotion over many years. Remembering that redemption is available to all and occurs day by day, what intention comes to mind that might give your life meaning today?

Inside the box you have drawn, write about redemption that has occurred or is occurring now within the margins of your life. Record your words right up to the outline of the box, remembering Church's observation that often the meaning of our life will be found there at its edges. Begin with the words below and continue writing until a good portion of the box on your page is filled *but not all of it.* Leave one small space open without any writing in it.

On this day, my life is being redeemed . . .

In the remaining white space inside your box, now write just one word or brief phrase, chosen after you pause to consider: what is the one redemptive thing you wish to save room for in your life on this day and the days to come?

13

WRITING ABOUT GRACE

THANKS BE

Grace is the ability to redefine the boundaries of possibility.
—MANNING MARABLE[1]

Few words have stirred as much theological debate and division over the centuries while still arriving in the current millennium as untarnished, as frequently and comfortably spoken, and as difficult to define as *grace*.

Depending on whom you ask and when, grace might be equated with salvation or with sacraments, with the presence of God or with beauty or movement or life itself. Grace is resilience. Grace is forgiveness. It is sin's opposite. It is healing. It is revelation, the oneness of all being. It is enlightenment. It is light. It comes before faith. It comes after faith. Some say it is faith.

But in its Latin root, *grātia*—which gave us not only the word *grace* in English but also *gracias* in Spanish and *grazie* in Italian—we find one theological meaning of the word that is perhaps the least questioned and most frequently used. For the ancient Romans, in addition to meaning a pleasing quality and favor or goodwill, *grātia* meant simply gratitude or thanks. In English, we have these meanings (and more), but when we talking about "saying grace," we are referring to this root meaning of gratitude.

In a poem by Rafael Jesús González titled "Grace" in English and "Gracias" in Spanish, we are invited into a state of grace through the naming of our gratitude and blessings:

Gracias

Gracias y benditos sean
el Sol y la Tierra
por este pan y este vino,
    esta fruta, esta carne, esta sal,
      este alimento;
gracias y bendiciones
a quienes lo preparan, lo sirven;
gracias y bendiciones
a quienes lo comparten
(y también a los ausentes y a los difuntos.)
Gracias y bendiciones a quienes lo traen
   (que no les falte),
a quienes lo siembran y cultivan,
lo cosechan y lo recogen
   (que no les falte);
gracias y bendiciones a los que trabajan
   y bendiciones a los que no puedan;
que no les falte—su hambre
   hace agrio el vino
      y le roba el gusto a la sal.
Gracias por el sustento y la fuerza
para nuestro bailar y nuestra labor
   por la justicia y la paz.

Grace

Thanks & blessing be
to the Sun & the Earth
for this bread & this wine,
    this fruit, this meat, this salt,
      this food;
thanks be & blessing to them
who prepare it, who serve it;
thanks & blessing to them
who share it
   (& also the absent & the dead.)
Thanks & blessing to them who bring it
   (may they not want),
to them who plant & tend it,
harvest & gather it
   (may they not want);
thanks & blessing to them who work
   & blessing to them who cannot;
may they not want—for their hunger
   sours the wine
      & robs the salt of its taste.
Thanks be for the sustenance & strength
for our dance & the work of justice, of peace.[2]

The poem brings us into a basic posture of thanksgiving. It is a good place to begin on any day; but especially when pondering the vast presence and reach of grace in our lives, it can position us to recognize and receive grace ourselves.

In Your Own Words

What are you thankful for on this day, in this time of your life? Begin with the concrete and the near at hand. Give thanks for your paper, your pen, your hand that holds it; for the rain or the sun, the trees or the grass or the snow; for the chair beneath you, the clothes on your back, the meal you last ate . . . you get the idea. Work outward from what is tangible and near and see where it takes you, repeating one of the phrases below and completing it differently each time.

Thanks be (to or for) . . .
Or
Thanks and blessing to . . .

GRACE AS RECEIVING

Grace fills empty spaces but it can only enter where there is a void to receive it, and it is grace itself which makes this void.
—SIMONE WEIL[3]

One of my favorite confessions of Augustine's is about grace and its unknowable nature. "What is grace?" he asked, right away admitting in a nearly palindromic puzzle, "I know until you ask me; when you ask me, I do not know."[4]

I concur. When I woke up this morning, I knew exactly what to write about grace. It was when I got out of bed and put my fingers to the keyboard that things got a little difficult.

Perhaps this is as it should be. Grace, after all, begins with beyond. Grace shows up in the portal of not knowing, in moments of confusion or doubt, and often in experiences of loss and grief, in fear or loneliness—times when we have been emptied in one sense or another, whether certitude, confidence, or ego. In a sermon, Paul Tillich once said:

Grace strikes us when we are in great pain and restless-
ness. It strikes us when we walk through the dark valley of
a meaningless and empty life. It strikes us when we feel our
separation is deeper than usual because we have violated
another life, a life which we loved, or from which we are
estranged [. . .] Sometimes at that moment a wave of light
breaks into our darkness, and it is as though a voice were saying: "You are accepted."[5]

Playwright Eugene O'Neill more succinctly said that all humans
are broken and each one of us "lives by mending. The grace of God
is glue."[6] Is it possible to receive grace if we are not broken? Given
the universal state of human frailty and limitation, perhaps the more
useful question is whether it is possible to receive grace if we do not
know we are broken.

When the heart is clenched like a tight fist, whether in anger or
certitude, in fear or in grief, it is grace that coaxes the fist open, looks
into the palm, and reads there a lifeline of a larger possibility. Grace
is an open hand—extended to the stranger, to the loved one, to the
wounded one within us all. It is the open hand of relationship, kindness, and blessing.

When a room is closed and stuffy, it is grace that opens the window and grace that then blows in. Grace *is* an opening. Just when we
think we know exactly what's going on, who we are, who everyone
else is, and what can and cannot happen next, grace draws back the
bolt of our knowing and flings wide a new view.

In a well-known story, a Zen master is visited by a learned man,
asking to be taught about Zen, and the Zen master begins without
speaking, pouring his visitor a cup of tea and continuing to pour
until the cup overflows. When the visitor cries out for him to stop
pouring, the Zen master says, "Your mind is like this cup. How can I
teach you about Zen unless you first empty your cup?"

Grace cannot be compelled to arrive at our bidding. But it can be repelled by a heart so full it holds no space open to receive grace when it comes.

In Your Own Words

What is it that fills your heart and your mind on this day? What knowledge or sorrow, what resentment or certitude, what story, opinion, bias, or fear fills and clenches your heart in this moment? What might you put down, clear out, or set aside, making a void that grace could then fill?

Make a fist with one hand. Squeeze it tight. (Modify these embodied gestures and those that follow, as needed for your own situation.) Pound the air with it, if you can, as if making a point or a charge. (Notice what happens to your face as you do.) Pound it once or twice into the flattened palm of your other hand. Notice how hard it is, how compact and full of tension it is.

Now, take in a deep breath and as you breathe out, release your fist. Open it, palm up. As you breathe in again and release that breath through your mouth, feel the touch of air on your open palm. Turn your other hand over too, opening it. Hold both hands, palms up, relaxed, fingers curved toward you, breathing deeply as you regard them, empty and open. Breathing in again, now open your arms wide to either side, shoulders down, head back, shoulder blades pulled together, down and back, behind you. Feel your chest relaxing and stretching and your heart opening as you do, breathing out.

Gently draw your open hands back together, still curved and relaxed with palms toward you, in front of your face. Look at the empty cup they make. Notice their wrinkles and lines carved by movement and time—and perhaps their calluses too, made by work and by touch. Regarding your hands as instruments of love and connection, pull them up to touch either side of your face, fingertips on or above your cheekbones, wrists together under your chin, cheeks gently cupped in your palms. Notice how well they fit there, the curve of the palm matching the curve of the cheek. Pause for a moment, closing your eyes, if you wish, and letting your hands feel the shape of your own face and all that it holds—your beauty and your faults, your gifts and your failures. Imagine, if hands could speak, how they might now say, "You are accepted. Just as you are, you are accepted."

Begin writing with the prompt below, and follow wherever it leads.

Hearing that I am accepted, just as I am . . .

FALLING INTO GRACE

You are so weak. Give up to grace.
The ocean takes care of each wave
till it gets to shore.
—JALAL AL-DIN RUMI[7]

Perhaps one of the reasons it can be hard to describe or define grace is that it does not stay put. Grace moves. Grace dips and bends. Grace dances. It spins and it turns. Grace heals. Grace stirs within. Grace is the movement just beginning when a work of art ends, the sigh we release on the song's last note or when the end of a poem becomes clear.

Grace can knock us off our feet when we stand on the shore looking out. Then it's grace that catches us before we are washed out to sea.

In Christian theology, grace is often said to be what saves us after the fall. But grace can be a kind of falling too, a loss of self-determined footing, a tumbling *into* something sacred and whole, into forgiveness, into love.

Philip Simmons was an English professor in his fruitful midlife years when he was diagnosed with ALS, the illness my mother had, commonly known as Lou Gehrig's disease. Like my mother, as Simmons's illness progressed and weakened his muscles, he experienced many falls. He wrote a book of reflections on his experiences with ALS aptly titled *Learning to Fall*. In the title essay, Simmons notes there is more than one way to think about falling and says our attitude toward it has everything to do with what we might be falling into:

> We fall on our faces, we fall for a joke, we fall for someone, we fall in love. In each of these falls, what do we fall away from? We fall from ego, we fall from our carefully constructed identities, our reputations, our precious selves. [...] And what do we fall into? [...] We fall into humility, into compassion, into emptiness, into oneness with forces larger than ourselves, into oneness with others whom we realize are likewise falling. We fall, at last, into the presence of the sacred, into godliness, into mystery, into our better, diviner natures.[8]

In Your Own Words

Imagine yourself falling into grace. Perhaps it's that sensation when you are just falling asleep and your body believes it, too, is falling, dropping through open air until you suddenly jolt awake again, or the feeling of giving yourself over to a good dance partner, the kind of graceful falling involved in every good twirl. Perhaps it's the way the ground opens up beneath you when you are falling in love, or the feeling of finally letting go of certainty when you acknowledge you really don't know—and might not control—what happens next, and you begin an extraordinary free fall into the possibility of something new, something beautiful you had been wholly unable to apprehend before.

Imagine yourself falling in any of these ways—letting go of your own center of gravity and your own sense of control, and then being caught— the way the ocean catches every wave and carries it to shore, or the way a good dance partner catches your hand, pulling you back before you touch the floor. What do you feel as you begin to fall? What do you feel as you move farther into the fall? What do you feel when you are swept up, turned, and twirled in a dance or a new direction?

Begin writing with the prompt below.

Here I am, falling . . .

THE SAME AND NOT THE SAME

*Grace is not a strange, magic substance which is subtly
filtered into our souls to act as a kind of spiritual penicillin.
Grace is unity, oneness within ourselves, oneness with God.*
—THOMAS MERTON[9]

Where does grace come from? From outside or within? From an
experience of the extraordinary, the exalted, the magnificent? From
spiritual practice, meditation, prayer? From paying attention to the
ordinary, the everyday, the ground beneath our feet? The answer to
these questions is, perhaps, simply, yes. For like truth, grace springs
from multiple sources, and our task in the spiritual practice of writing—as in any spiritual practice—is to notice it when it does and to
ready ourselves to receive it.

A story is told about the artist Henri Matisse who agreed, late
in life, to design a set of stained-glass windows for a chapel. Picasso,
learning of this project, reportedly challenged Matisse with some
anger, asking his friend how he could lend his artistic talents to the
church, which he pointed out represented a vision so different from
the modern ideas of liberation that he and Matisse had both empha-
sized in their long careers. Matisse replied with the observation that
they had both, as artists, devoted their lives to recovering a state of
grace they had known in their early, churched years, what he called
the inner "atmosphere" of their First Communion.[10]

The inner atmosphere of grace, whether it has arrived from above
or below or within, is one known by artists, writers, and mystics alike.
It is also known by worshipers, wilderness journeyers, and seekers of
all kinds, all with their own ways of pausing to look and listen for the

presence of grace. Experiencing it can be a life-changing epiphany or it might just be a moment of wonder on any given day, the discovery of connection, beauty, compassion, or wholeness.

Frederick Buechner, writer and contemporary Christian theologian, wrote about a day when he expected grace to arrive as a miracle, as a moment of hearing the holy speak on a bright sunny day, only to have the miracle escape him, and then have grace arrive anyway:

> [T]he time was ripe for miracle, my life was ripe for miracle, and the very strength of the feeling itself seemed a kind of vanguard of miracle. Something was going to happen—something extraordinary that I could perhaps even see and hear [. . .]. But [. . .] nothing like what I expected happened at all.
>
> This might easily have been the end of something for me—my faith [. . .]—but it was not the end. Because something other than what I expected did happen. Those apple branches knocked against each other, went clack-clack. No more. No less. "The dry clack-clack of the world's tongue at the approach of the approach of splendor." [. . .] the clack-clack of my life. The occasional, obscure glimmering through of grace. The muffled presence of the holy.[11]

In Your Own Words

When have you heard a "clack-clack" in the middle of an ordinary day, awakening you to "the occasional, obscure glimmering through of grace"? "The muffled presence of the holy" nearby, right there next to you? It might have been brought on by a gesture from someone else—a stranger or a loved one, a word or the touch of someone's hand. It could have been an image, a work of art, a note of music, a moment in nature. It might have been in worship, in prayer or meditation. Or maybe it was a sound or a sudden silence, a dream, a smell, your own movement or body. If a memory doesn't come readily to mind, let your imagination run free, creating a scene where the "clack-clack" of grace might have been heard. Where were you in that moment? What happened around you and inside you? How did you feel in the presence of grace?

Begin writing with these words and follow wherever they lead:

It was grace, glimmering through . . .

THE MURMUR OF GRACE

I want . . . to live "in grace" as much of the time as possible. . . .
By "grace" I mean an inner harmony, essentially spiritual,
which can be translated into outward harmony.
—ANNE MORROW LINDBERGH[12]

The three Graces in Greek mythology are sisters bearing names meaning splendor, mirth, and abundance. Frequently presiding over festive gatherings of all kinds, they were sometimes associated with the Muses, capable of inspiring poets and artists alike. The details of their lineage and lives, and even their number and names, vary from one mythological source to another; but the impressions they have made on artists across the centuries have been strikingly clear as one of harmonic movement, or what the poet Martha Heyneman calls "unity in diversity; diversity in unity." A triad embodying beauty, creativity, and festivity, they are seldom depicted individually but often appear woven in an animated circle, bearing gifts and dancing with visible joy, fidelity, and love. It is their flowing image of grace that Heyneman describes in her essay "Morning Wind in the Leaves":

> They are so close to the Source they can scarcely bear to part
> from it or from each other. One steps out, another draws back,
> and the third holds the other two together. They are the uni-

versal form of a single vibration; the hum that underlies all sound: Om, sound of the world turning; [. . .] Creation and evolution in a nutshell, the form of every melody, every journey, there and back again.[13]

The experience of grace depicted here is an expansion of consciousness, blurring the borders we often fiercely patrol in guarding our individuality. It awakens an awareness of what Merton described as the "unity within," or what French writer and mystic Romain Rolland called the boundless "oceanic feeling" of religious awakening, a sensation that has as much to do with the tidal rhythms of unity and diversity as it does with infinity's wide horizon.

If this begins to sound too abstract or far-fetched, perhaps we do well to rein it back in to the tangible realm of kinship, for sometimes the most powerful way we know grace is in a relationship that becomes more than the sum of its parts. It might be experienced between two people—soul mates, lovers, siblings, parent and child, mentor and learner—or in a community, *sangha*, congregation, or any gathering of two or more coming together in love and joined by another presence: welcome, if difficult to name. Some say that presence is God. Others simply regard it as love itself. Theologian Sharon Welch calls this a "surplus connoted by grace—the deep joy of loving and being loved."[14]

However we name it, we can experience it in our kinship with other creatures as well as other people. One October morning, while on retreat in the middle of the Minnesota prairie, I rose at dawn and walked alone in a light rain, following a path mowed through the tall grass outside the retreat center. At the end of the path, I stopped to take in the expansive rolling landscape around me and heard the sound of a stream rushing over rocks, even though I was surrounded by dry land as far as the eye could see. It drummed like distant applause growing in volume.

As I stood there, straining to hear and name the approaching sound, a flock of starlings, called a murmuration, appeared on the northern horizon. Massive in size, claiming almost the full width of my vision, it rolled across the sky like a beautiful black blanket loosely woven of thousands of small, chirping birds, all flapping their wings. The blanket unfurled, obliterating the clouded sky, and then folded over in a turn of direction and narrowed into a long, undulating ribbon that rippled away from me, curling this way and that, all the while still filling the air with a symphony of wings and chatter.

My jaw dropped wide open. I laughed out loud as the birds kept coming, my laughter easily absorbed in the sound of their wings' endless applause. I lost all awareness of the ground beneath my feet, as if gravity had momentarily let go and some part of me had been swept up in the murmuration, twirling through the air with grace and glee, still laughing in astonishment and joy.

Finally, the last fringe of the flock came into view, then passed overhead, and the murmuration disappeared over the horizon. The fields fell under the spell of a new silence—perhaps the same one that had been there before, but now I heard it with new ears. I was remarkably alone and yet more a part of everything than I had ever felt before.

In Your Own Words

When has a murmuration of grace, of any kind, swept you up in a moment of weightlessness? Where have you seen and heard grace moving in the world recently? Perhaps it didn't cover the sky but appeared instead as the smallest or most ordinary speck, barely discernible, before your eyes or right there at your feet, reminding you with sharp clarity that you are a part of life's great unity. When have you felt the "surplus connoted by grace," perhaps in the deep joy of loving and being loved, or maybe in the harmony of music, in the eyes of a child, or in the jeweled dew on a spider web at dawn? Consider such a scene from your memory or your imagination and notice where you feel it in your body. What emotions does it stir? Where do you feel its lift, if you do?

Begin writing with the prompt below and follow wherever it leads:

I heard grace murmuring . . .

MIDDLE VOICE—PARTICIPATING IN GRACE

Grace is free, but when once you take it you are bound forever to the Giver, and bound to catch the spirit of the Giver. Like produces like. Grace makes you gracious, the Giver makes you give.
—E. STANLEY JONES[15]

If grace brings movement into our lives, it is the movement of reciprocity and surplus, in which gifts and gratitude are passed back and forth in a kind of call-and-response, not in a closed loop but always expanding. When we experience grace, we respond with gratitude, and as we experience gratitude, we become more receptive to grace. This exchange lies at the heart of the biblical covenant between the Israelites and God; it amplifies the muezzin's call to prayer from minarets around the world; it is the rule, spoken and unspoken, in many indigenous cultures that the gift must always keep moving— and the teaching that everything we cherish comes to us as a gift.

It is difficult to wrap our minds around this kind of radical reciprocity, where gratitude and grace and givers and receivers tumble over one another in a participatory tangle that defies not only our culture of possession but also our contemporary syntax itself. Long ago, a verb tense wholly lost to us today made it easier to grasp. The "middle voice," used in Sanskrit, Greek, and Indo-Persian, was neither active nor passive but described events as happening of themselves while in collaboration with those affected by them. Writer and editor Christopher Bamford says the closest we might come to this in today's English would be to say "It thinks in me" or "It acts in me." He notes that the meaning of this verb tense was lost as the individual will and ego emerged in ancient Greece and as agency became prized over receptivity.[16]

Though we have lost the grammar to express the participatory nature of grace, we can still experience it. The "middle voice" of grace that moves us while moving *in* us and *through* us is both active *and* passive. When we receive grace, we also become its instruments, unfurling it further into the world.

Theologian Catherine Keller suggests this is the meaning of the one-sentence parable Jesus told about yeast. "The kingdom of heaven," Jesus said, "is like yeast that a woman took and mixed in with three measures of flour until all of it was leavened."[17] Grace works like the yeast, a small organism with the enormous ability to make dough rise but *only* with the participation and added effort of a bread maker willingly doing the work of kneading. Keller says, "grace is simply not a unilateral force."[18]

In Your Own Words

When have you participated in bringing grace into the world? How might you be moving grace into the world? Or how is grace moving in or through you? What is the "surplus" of grace in your life spilling over as you go about your daily activities?

Begin with the prompts, alternating between them, and following wherever they lead:

By grace, I was given (or moved) . . .

By grace, I am giving (or moving) . . .

14

WRITING ABOUT HOSPITALITY

SUCH AS WE'VE GOT

[Hospitality] is the first step toward dismantling the barriers of the world. Hospitality is the way we turn a prejudiced world around one heart at a time.

—JOAN CHITTISTER[1]

The German word for hospitality says it literally and simply: *gast-freundschaft*, or "friendship for the guest." It is a definition that reminds me of a 1920s framed plaque that used to hang in David's family cottage, inviting guests to share the modest physical accommodations of the cottage along with the extraordinary emotional space to "be at ease" without pretense or expectation. In the middle of the plaque, it declared plainly, "We're happy to share with you / Such as we've got"[2] and then went on to name the modest offerings of a leaky roof and a potful of soup. "Such as we've got" can be humble but when offered and received in a spirit of hospitality, it invites us into generous exchange.

While it is true that hospitality is about not holding back in sharing the best of what we have and who we are with others, it is also about not holding back for fear of having—or being—too little. It's about sharing our lives just as they are. On the receiving end, as guests, it's about accepting the generosity of others, "such as they've got," as well. After all, "such as they've got" might be just what one needs. I remember sleeping on a friend's couch during one of my last visits with my mom, near the end of her life. When I woke in the middle of the night, my heart aching with grief, I discovered my friend's cat had curled up in the crook of my arm and with the softest feline paw was gently stroking my cheek, practically wiping my tears as she did.[3]

Advertisements from the hospitality industry can give the impression that true hospitality has the shine of brass and crystal and is populated by white-gloved attendants. But the same industry provides a wide range of "red carpet" treatment. A few years ago, two friends of mine arrived at an inexpensive motel where they'd made reservations on a road trip. Walking into the lobby they were surprised to find a sign saying "Welcome Ed and Kristin, Our Special Guests of the Week." When they identified themselves to the front desk clerk as Ed and Kristin, they received hearty congratulations along with a small brown lunch bag, stapled shut on the top. Once settled in their room, they opened the bag to find one raspberry pop tart, a mini bag of M&Ms, some gum, and a few other candies. They laughed heartily at the collection of treats, about as random as something salvaged from a parent's handbag for a hungry child, but they did admit to feeling special and welcomed.

Hospitality doesn't need a fancy wrapper. Sometimes, in fact, all it takes is to make sure the door is open and that a chair is available inside. I once led a retreat for a men's group that had been meeting weekly for almost twenty-five years while still welcoming new members. They told me that when they first formed the group in their church, the door to the room where they met was permanently locked, so they propped it open with a brick to make sure latecomers could join in. Over the years, they came to call their group the "Order of the Brick," each of them being a fellow "Brick," a subtle, perhaps even unconscious, reminder of their commitment to keep the door open to newcomers and latecomers alike.

In Your Own Words

When have you felt fully welcomed as a guest? Maybe it was something your hosts prepared for you before you arrived, or it might have been something they said—or something they didn't say—in greeting you. Perhaps it was a hand on your shoulder or a kiss on the cheek, a brick in the door, an open chair, a stepping stool, a wheelchair ramp, a gender-neutral bathroom, a room with child care, or a pet that sat by your side.

As you recall a time when you received a gesture of warm hospitality, begin writing with the prompt below:

I knew I was welcome when . . .

THE DOOR OF YOUR HOME

[Abraham] looked up and saw three men standing near him.
When he saw them, he ran from the tent entrance to meet them,
and bowed down to the ground.
—GENESIS 18:2

It was Abraham who long ago set the bar for hospitality so high. His storied welcome of three total strangers, told in the book of Genesis, gives us a picture of extraordinary hospitality. Sitting in the entrance of his tent one afternoon, Abraham spotted the unannounced visitors approaching, but he did not wait for them to arrive at his tent. He ran out in the heat of the day to greet them. Although he did not know them, he did not ask for names, country of origin, mutual acquaintances or references, or even the length and purpose of their visit. Instead, he bowed down and requested the privilege and favor of washing their feet. Then, offering them "a little bread," he did not serve whatever he had on hand. He ordered fresh cakes made from choice flour and a tender calf from his own herd slaughtered and prepared especially for the three strangers whose names he did not know. Only later did he learn that they were angels, delivering the word that Abraham and Sarah would at last bear the child they had longed to conceive.[4]

Hospitality, it turns out, is not just friendliness to the guests we know but especially to those we don't, and it flows in more than one direction in a profoundly mutual exchange. The word's roots trace back to the Latin word *ghosti*, a lineage shared by the words "host," "hospital," and "hospice," as well as "guest" and "stranger" in an etymology beautifully intertwined as a reminder that hospitality is born of a rich reciprocity in which guest and host are merely roles exchanged over time. Both Greek and Arabic share this understanding, each offering one word meaning both guest and host.[5]

In ancient Greece, this relationship was initiated by none other than Zeus himself as the protector of strangers. Were I living in ancient Greece, a stranger on my doorstep could appeal to the rule of *xenios Zeus* (meaning Zeus of the strangers), which would entitle the stranger to the rites of hospitality, not only garnering my care and attention while under my roof but also my concern for the stranger's safe return home. If I refused these rites of hospitality to the stranger, I would pay no small price, thereafter being regarded as a "monster" and "unfit for human fellowship" and denied relationship with the gods.[6] Similarly, the Israelites, having received God's hospitality during their escape from Egypt and long and homeless wandering in the desert, were then expected to share hospitality with other wanderers as a way of passing it on.

By contrast, in contemporary society, we have few requirements or expectations that we will welcome the stranger. It sometimes seems to me that as we become more quick to share our lives and musings with strangers online, we seem to be increasingly wary of face-to-face encounters with strangers in our streets and on our doorsteps.

On a national level, the hundreds of immigrants who die in Arizona's desert each year trying to enter the Untied States without visas offer tragic testimony of our response to the stranger. Individually, the many ways we have of locking our doors, screening our calls, and insulating our lives from those we do not know offer a more quotidian picture of our capacity to turn strangers away before we've even seen them. What would it mean to lift our eyes to the horizon instead, individually or nationally, like Abraham running out to greet the strangers, asking them the favor of allowing him to care for their needs?

In Your Own Words

Imagine yourself in your home, comfortably seated and facing the door but without expectation.[7] The door is wide open. All is well. As you sit there peacefully, someone approaches and knocks, saying nothing. Lit from behind, the person presents only a silhouette; no features are visible, but the person's posture is expectant, forward leaning without being imposing or threatening. You see this stranger standing on your threshold, already halfway through the doorway and pausing there. You cannot imagine who the person is or where they've come from. Their palms are held open to you, as if offering a blessing—or perhaps asking for something they need, you think. It is impossible to tell, and it occurs to you, the two might be the same. Your heart, you notice, is beating more rapidly. What are you feeling? What do you hope? What do you do?

Begin with the prompt below and follow wherever it leads:

Standing in the doorway . . .

MAKING SPACE FOR DIFFERENCE

It is the not-me in thee that makes thee precious to me.
—QUAKER PROVERB

I sometimes think of hospitality as the things my mother taught me to do and to offer, which is largely in terms of what is there—a bowl of fruit or a glass of water, a flower at the bedside, a set of towels by the sink. And yet, at a more basic level, it often comes down to what is not there, to the space we willingly make for another—at our tables, in our homes, in our lives, and in our hearts—space with enough room for others to enter *as they are* without contortions of identity, belief, or spirit. Creating this opening in our inner space, in our thoughts, feelings, and assumptions can be hospitality's most challenging aspect.

Theologian Henri Nouwen called this "free space." He said:

> The paradox of hospitality is that it wants to create emptiness, not a fearful emptiness, but a friendly emptiness where strangers can enter and discover themselves as created free; free to sing their own songs, speak their own languages, dance their own dances; free also to leave and follow their own vocations. Hospitality is not a subtle invitation to adopt the lifestyle of the host, but the gift of a chance for the guest to find his own.[8]

I could read Nouwen's explanation of free space every day and still learn something new from it, because every time I read it, it reminds me that the first rule of hospitality, the requirement that precedes all requirements, is to lay my ego—and my expectations—down. To make space, not only at the table but more essentially in my mind, in my own preconceptions. To let go of my assumptions about others and my need to pin them down to one identity or another, to one story or another, to labels that I can use to pigeon-hole them without ever really knowing them.

One of the uncomfortable truths accompanying the hospitality teachings of many world religions is that we are already in relationship with strangers regardless of how we receive one another. We cannot choose *not* to be in relationship; we can only choose *how*. In the short term, we might find it useful to pretend the relationship does not exist and that we are not accountable to people we do not know, but religious lessons are rarely about the short term. In the long view, these teachings remind us that we are all related, we are all in relationship, and whether we know one another or not, we owe one another acknowledgment at the very least and an openness to encounter without assumptions. In these daily acts of simple hospitality, we repeatedly have the chance to break down the walls that divide us.

The relationship between strangers can be traced back to count-less creation stories in which the world comes into existence as a matter of separation and sorting: sky from land, land from water, and one creature from another, all particular beings emerging from their original unity. The phrase "ten thousand things" is a reference to this multiplication act of creation, carrying within it the unspoken reminder of the oneness from which they spring. Not surprisingly, this relationship between separation and oneness is equally present in the Big Bang theory and in the long evolutionary trails leading to our present-day existence. These stories, scientific and mythologi-cal alike, tell us that if we all originate from the same stardust and oceans, the same lotus flower or turtle back, or the same earthen mud and breath of God, when we meet a stranger today, we are already in relationship with them, encountering some unknown part of our oldest unity, of our larger self and being. Hospitality and its welcoming of the stranger is one small, daily way in which we honor and restore the unity from which we have emerged.

The practice of hospitality teaches us to welcome strangers as strangers, honoring their apparent differences as well as what is unknown to us in their stories. We are asked to make room for them without requiring that they be or become like us, or even that they be or become our friends. Although the encounter itself should be friendly and as such, it might seed a new friendship in time, its deepest hospitality rises from letting go of *expected* friendship and trusting the sanctity of relatedness between one stranger and another. When we do this, we take a small step in repairing the brokenness of human experience, and we prepare ourselves to learn from the other what is outside of our own experience and ken.

In my own tradition of Unitarian Universalism, the first of seven principles that our congregations share as values succinctly affirms "the inherent worth and dignity of every person." Older biblical teachings note that we are all made in the image of God and a spark of divinity resides in each one of us. The poet Samuel Taylor Coleridge once connected this teaching to what he described as an old Jewish custom of never stepping on a scrap of paper left on the ground lest the name of God might be written on it. "Though there was a little superstition in this," he said, "yet truly there is nothing but good religion in it, if we apply it to [humanity]. Trample not on any; there may be some work of grace there that thou knowest not of. The name of God may be written upon that soul thou treadest on; [. . .] therefore, despise it not."[9]

When we extend hospitality to strangers, making room for their strangeness or unknowns to enter our lives too, we are acknowledging the sacred connection that includes all of us while we are also opening our hearts to the widest possibilities of mystery without the need to tame or claim what remains unknown.

In Your Own Words

In the corner of your page, sketch the lines of a simple web, spaced apart at least the width of a fingertip. Wherever the lines meet, make a small dot, imagining it to be a person or a being, each connected to the others through the web's fine filaments of lines. The web can be any size, but try to draw it so that it has a dozen or more dots. Choose one of the dots anywhere in the web to represent you, and circle it or make it a little bigger. Using your finger, begin on your dot and trace the lines that connect your dot to every other one on the web.

If the dots represent people to whom you are linked in the web of life, what do you notice about the lines or paths that join you, one to another? What does it feel like to consider the threads that connect you to every being, in every place, in every time? Whenever you're ready, begin writing with the prompt below, repeating it each time you start a new sentence or a new paragraph.

These threads between us . . .

ENTERTAINING ANGELS UNAWARES

Every [human being] is a divinity in disguise.
—RALPH WALDO EMERSON[10]

As an act of reciprocity, hospitality does not trace its origins to any human being. Rather, in most religious teachings, it is regarded as a human response to the hospitality we each receive in our relationship to God or in response to the holy blessing of life itself. However, because the hospitality we each receive at birth is so basic to our existence, we are often wholly unaware of it. Or we may, in everyday acts of hubris and self-reliance, simply fail to acknowledge it. Often it is only when taken by surprise that we are awakened to both the gifts and the demands that hospitality places at our feet.

In folklore from around the world, the divine shows up disguised and usually uninvited—as beggar, foreigner, undesirable neighbor, or even pesky creature. In these stories, it is the one who opens the door and welcomes the uninvited, unannounced stranger to the table who is then said to have "entertained angels unawares."[11] In the stories, this kind of hospitality often earns the individual divine favor. Not coincidentally, as we pass the stories on and are shaped by them ourselves, their example of hospitality also creates a harmonic social order in which food and shelter can be shared, basic needs met, and the possibility of cooperation and friendship invited. Hospitality is then both an ethical and a practical virtue, developed across the millennia by a species often living in most inhospitable conditions.

In one ancient story of hospitality, the Greek myth of Baucis and Philemon recorded in Ovid's *Metamorphoses* over two thousand years ago, the gods Jupiter and Mercury were roaming the earth disguised as mortals searching for rest. Turned away from a thousand homes, the two gods arrived finally on the doorstep of a simple thatched cottage, the home of Baucis and Philemon, an old and impoverished couple whom we are told "faced their poverty with cheerful spirit." Long wedded, the two were woven into a relationship of equality in which Ovid explains "*both* gave and followed orders," a partnership steeped in love and reciprocity that spilled over in their welcome of the unknown guests at their door. The strangers were invited in, and Philemon pulled up a rustic bench for them to sit on while Baucis tucked up her skirts to set the table.

With neither the assistance of servants nor with extravagant fare, the old man and woman then set about generously preparing and serving "such as they've got," laying it before the two visitors with no idea of their divine identity. Only when the couple decided to kill their valued goose in order to complete the meal—and the goose went running to Jupiter and Mercury for protection—did the gods reveal their identity, sparing the goose and blessing Baucis and Philemon. Jupiter and Mercury then took the couple to the top of a nearby mountain from which they saw that all the houses of their neighbors who had turned the strangers away were now flooded while the couple's home was being transformed into a temple. Jupiter asked them what wish they had for themselves and, after consulting with each other, the two replied that they would like to become the priests and caretakers of the temple and, when the end of their lives came, they wanted to die in the same hour. Their wish granted, Baucis and Philemon lived out their days in the temple; and in time, one day, standing side by side, each began to sprout leaves, one as an oak, the other a linden. After saying their human good-byes to each other, they remained silently as trees growing side by side for years to come, each unique but with roots and branches intertwined.[12]

In this and many other hospitality tales, we can see the long trail of gifts and gratitude that precedes each act of welcome and also follows it, as if playing out any role of host and guest merely marks our brief participation in a story old as time and continuing still. Baucis and Philemon's gratitude for one another and for the blessing of their modest home is what allows them, perhaps even compels them, to share what they have and who they are with the two strangers at their door. And long after they have died, the two intertwined trees live on, blessed by the gods in their continuing companionship.

The hidden identity of the gods in hospitality tales is required in order to create a culture of generosity that embraces the stranger, but the gods' disguise is also what gives them access to human lives often carefully constructed to avoid surprises and to maintain a sense of privacy and individual control. Theologically, many religious teachings point out that the truth of our sacred origins and connectedness can *only* arrive as the uninvited stranger. In a culture that makes little room for the unknown and the unfamiliar, the sacred *must* break in without invitation. This is why, in a beautiful expression of welcoming the sacred unknown, the monks in many medieval monasteries would greet any stranger at the door, saying "O Jesus Christ. Is it you, again?"

Like this, with each single act of hospitality to the stranger and the uninvited guest, we begin to repair our relationship with the holy; we become more aware of our own role as guests and of the greater hospitality on which each of our lives depends. It is not easy. True hospitality to the stranger can be profoundly demanding and life changing. It requires, as theologian Eleazar Fernandez points out, not only that we create welcoming spaces and communities but that we also challenge the inhospitable systems that turn strangers away before they can reach our doorstep.[13] The practice of hospitality begins when we overcome our fears long enough to open our whole selves; and when we do, it makes us available to something larger moving through our lives, as D. H. Lawrence suggests in the final lines of his poem "Song of a Man Who Has Come Through":

> *What is the knocking?*
> *What is the knocking at the door in the night?*
> *It is somebody wants to do us harm.*
>
> *No, no, it is the three strange angels.*
> *Admit them, admit them.*[14]

In Your Own Words

Think of several strangers you have recently encountered. Make a little list. Maybe it includes a salesclerk, a bus driver or rider, or the tollbooth operator who took your coins. Maybe you list a neighbor or coworker not well known to you, or the homeless person standing on the corner. It could include someone calling on the phone, or the one who bused your dishes in the restaurant, or another who cleaned the restroom just before you arrived. Or, if you were the one cleaning, it might be the stranger who arrived as you finished. What would it mean to admit these strangers to your awareness? How might you admit them—remembering that hospitality requires friendly acknowledgment, generosity, and reciprocity, but not necessarily friendship with all that it entails?

Choose one of the strangers on your list whom you have encountered in the past week, and imagine looking beneath the surface of that person's human "disguise" to see a faint but sacred glimmer within, as if the person might be standing in for some holy presence that's come to visit you. Then imagine an exchange you might have with that person, having seen that sacred glimmer. Write about that exchange, beginning with the prompt below and following wherever it leads:

If I greeted you like the sacred one that you are . . .

DESERT TIME

[Y]ou neglect and belittle the desert.
The desert is not remote in southern tropics,
The desert is not only around the corner,
The desert is squeezed in the tube-train next to you,
The desert is in the heart of your brother.

—T. S. ELIOT[15]

The Arabic word for hospitality, *djiwar*, means "neighborliness" or "granting refuge to wayfaring strangers not a member of your own tribe."[16] In the desert, where turning travelers away could threaten their survival, old Arabic customs called for providing strangers three days' food and shelter, after which they were expected to be strong enough to move on.

In contemporary Western culture, where many of us feel harried by overscheduling and multitasking, we might ask if our own landscape isn't a bit of a desert too, parched by an extended drought of time. The busyness that claims and fills our lives leaves few shady oases where we can linger with others; it also makes it difficult for us to encounter the quiet and less-known parts of ourselves, the stranger we each carry within, still waiting to be welcomed. Years ago, while training our first puppy, David and I chose our own words for the standard command to "Go lie down." Instead, we taught our dog to lie down and wait when he heard the phrase "I'm busy." Now it occurs to me that many of us have trained each other (and ourselves) with this phrase as well, using it as a not-so-subtle way of buying time or space to separate us from others or from those parts of ourselves we may unwittingly keep at arm's length.

When I am on deadline, I often make use of my phone's caller ID to avoid unnecessary interruptions. One week, while diligently focused on a big project, I noticed the same caller kept showing up in repeated rings, identified only as coming from a long-term care facility in a neighboring community. When I listened to the messages, they were from someone named Mavis, a woman I'd never met, who thought she was reaching the voice mail of another person named Paul. For a few days, I avoided the calls. But when they continued, I thought perhaps if I answered the phone and spoke to Mavis, we might clear things up.

It turned out not to be so easy. In the early stages of dementia, Mavis was confused enough by me answering the phone that at first she just hung up on me. When we finally connected, though, I learned she was trying to reach her brother who lived in the same town as me. We tried several approaches, beginning with me simply telling her she'd reached a wrong number, but by the time she hung up and tried again, it was my number she called once more. So it went on, until finally, I asked for her brother's last name. I looked him up in the phone book and called him myself. Thereafter, what seemed to work best for all of us, when Mavis called me, was for me to answer, assuring her that I would leave a message for her brother and then he would call her back.

Eventually, she came to remember me, in a general, short-term way. When I would pick up the phone and tell her she'd reached me again instead of Paul, we'd laugh. She'd thank me. After a while, she'd often say she hoped we'd meet one day. We'd wish each other well, and then I'd hang up and call her brother's number.

When a friend of mine asked if I wasn't starting to get annoyed with the calls, I realized that far from being a nuisance, the whole exchange had become a gift. As a naturally forgetful person, I often criticize myself for not remembering one thing or another—the cup of tea in the microwave; the soup cooking on the stove; the clothes in the washing machine, spun but not dried. But the more exchanges I had with Mavis, brief as they were, the more accepting—and forgiving—I became of my own forgetfulness.

The last time Mavis called was the day before Thanksgiving. Again, we laughed. We wished each other a happy Thanksgiving. And again she said, "I hope I get to meet you someday. It almost feels like we know each other." To which I answered, "You know, Mavis, I think maybe we actually do."

In Your Own Words

Materials needed: If you have access to a small bowl of sand, have it on hand and start this writing exploration by taking a fistful of sand in one hand and letting it run through your fingers. If no sand is available, use sugar or rice and imagine it as the whitest sand.

What part of yourself might be out in a desert today, longing for your time and attention? What is the parched voice within you that is waiting to be heard? What part of your life might be running through your fingers like sand because you lack the time to welcome this unknown or unwelcomed part of yourself?

Imagine a conversation you might have with a wayfaring part of yourself. How do you greet this "stranger" approaching from the distance?

What do you offer this part of yourself normally kept at a distance? What does this wayfarer say and what does he or she bring you in exchange for rest beneath your oak tree? Begin writing with the prompt below and write about the encounter that might follow it:

If I offer you shade and a drink of water . . .

THE GIVE-AND-TAKE OF HOSPITALITY

What do I mean "open to God"? I mean . . . a courageous and confident hospitality expressed in all directions. . . . I mean an openness which is in the deepest sense a creative and dynamic receptivity— the ability to receive, to accept, to become.
—SAMUEL H. MILLER[17]

Inevitably, when considering an ethic of hospitality, we run into the question of boundaries and how, or even whether, they apply to hospitality's wide-open door. Few among us have not had the experience of hosting people who hold us "hostage," whether by overstaying their welcome, by disregarding our real limits (in time, space, or resources), or by simply failing to take turns and thus dominating the conversation. It is, after all, no accident that the word *hostage* derives from the same root as *hospitality* and *host*.

Even those who have taken vows of hospitality in their calling to religious orders will face the difficult question of how to honor their personal needs while generously welcoming guests, invited and uninvited alike. For if we continually ignore our own needs to tend to the needs of others, we will soon dry up, with nothing to offer for their needs or our own. As Sufi poet Hafiz put it,

> *There are different wells within your heart.*
> *Some fill with each good rain,*
> *Others are far too deep for that.*[18]

True hospitality requires a radical reciprocity between guest and host, an exchange so fundamental it is occurring every moment in our encounter with each other. Writer Paul Jordan-Smith notes that these roles are especially fluid in our spoken exchanges.[19] If you visit my home, for instance, where I am host and you my guest, and you begin to tell me a story, in that moment, as a storyteller, you become the host, and I, the listener, am your guest. If your story goes on and on and on, without end, according to Jordan-Smith, I might become your hostage.

Because true equality can be hard to find or to create, hospitality can be abused or "deformed," as theologian Letty Russell liked to put it,[20] and it needs to be held accountable to a healthy and humble give-and-take between guest and host. Both must be willing to admit each other, in some way, into their heart and their awareness, and would do well to consider the ways in which we sometimes simultaneously play the roles of both guest and host as well as the ways in which we pass these roles back and forth. Denis Heurre, OSB, was a Benedictine monk from France, elected as abbot president of an international congregation of Benedictines in 1980. In a collection of letters to the monastic members of that congregation, he wrote about the Benedictine rule of hospitality, saying, "Unless we treat a guest with all the respect due to a human being and in the faith that God is manifest in this encounter, our hospitality will not be monastic. [. . .] But the monk, too, has an equilibrium and rhythm in his way of life, and unless he can present himself in his own character as a monk, he can be of no value to the guest."[21]

It is in the equality and the give-and-take of this relationship that it becomes holy, attended by a larger sacred connection and context. Elsewhere, Huerre writes, "If the guest and the monk remain superficial, there will be no *humanitas*" (i.e., human kindness and benevolence) "circulating between them, none of the respect that ought to encircle the mystery of each man. If, in the place of an encounter between monk, guest, and God, the third term is forgotten, there is only chatter."[22]

The question of boundaries, then, is a matter of drawing a larger boundary that can hold both guest and host in a circle wide enough to retain and respect the identity of each; to make room for exchanging their roles freely and frequently; and to honor and invite a relationship larger than the sum of guest and host alone. Making room for all three of these possibilities requires a circumference larger than many of us often draw.

In Your Own Words

Think back to anytime you remember exchanging the roles of guest and host with another. It might be recently or long ago. It could be with someone you know well or someone you just encountered briefly. While thinking about this memory, consider how the exchange happened. What did it feel like? Did it make room for something more between the two of you? If so, you don't need to name what (or who) it was that joined you in the exchange. Often there are no words to describe that "something more." But do consider how you experienced it. What was exchanged? What was shared? Begin writing about the person in this exchange with these prompts below. You can keep repeating them, completing them in new ways each time, if you like, or after completing them the first time, just keep writing, following wherever it leads.

At first you were . . . and I was . . .

And then . . .

For an interesting extension or variation of this, do your writing in well-spaced lines, five inches wide or narrower, and when you're finished writing, cut the lines apart and reassemble them in any order, using all or only a few. Play with the order a bit, letting it reveal the many ways in which the roles of hospitality were exchanged. If you find a sequence you like, feel free to adjust a few words to make it say what you want it to say.

15

WRITING ABOUT REVERENCE

LIFE'S GRAND ECOLOGY OF BEING

If all the heavens were parchment, if all the trees were pens,
if all the seas were ink, and if every creature were a scribe,
they would not suffice to expound the greatness of God.
—RABBI MEIR BEN YITZHAK NEHORAI[1]

In a Northern California park, the cross section of an old redwood trunk about ten feet in diameter has been balanced on its side so you can step up and view its many rings.

When the tree fell over seventy-five years ago, it was about 350 feet tall and 1,392 years old. It's a lifespan difficult to fathom, so park interpreters have provided cues to help. In the center of the trunk's cross section, a small note says the tree sprouted in the year 544 CE, when, on the other side of the globe, the emperor Justinian ruled the

Byzantine Empire. Nearby, another note marks a ring of the tree that was growing when Mohammed was born, and a third points to the ring that grew when the Mayan civilization began in 680 CE. Across the width of the trunk, you can touch your finger to the ring that grew during the Sung Dynasty in China or the Aztec civilization, or the year Columbus arrived in the Caribbean, at which time the tree was 948 years old—and still growing.

I am accustomed to feeling awestruck in the company of great old trees that dwarf my stature, but standing next to that redwood's cross section also made me feel small—and fleeting—in time.

Reverence, it has been said, begins with an acknowledgment of human limitations in the presence of something greater, something more than we can ever be. Praised in ancient Greece as the "guardian of civilization," reverence has been lifted up around the world as the virtue that sensitizes the conscience.[2] It reminds us we are neither immortal divine beings nor immoral monsters but somewhere in between. Reverence is as much about us remembering our common humanity—with our wonder and our weaknesses alike—as it is about taking our shoes off to honor the holy ground on which we stand.

"But one must first become small," May Sarton wrote in her poem about reverent listening. "Nothing but a presence / Attentive as a nesting bird."[3]

The opposite of reverence is hubris. In our supersized culture, in our superpower fantasies, do we even know how to "become small" and "attentive as a nesting bird"?

Listening is a good place to start. And watching. Go outside on a clear, dark night in a place where you can see the moon and stars. Listen to the wind rustling through the leaves. Or wrap your finger inside the soft, curled fist of a newborn child. Or step into a worship sanctuary with its soaring ceiling and light-filled spaces. Look up. Look around you. Listen to the choir.

Notice that the feeling of reverence is not really about *becoming* small. It is about finding ourselves in a web of life and deep kinship so trustworthy we can safely admit we have always been small. In life's grand ecology of being, reverence is actually a matter of profound belonging.

Reverence is about seeing and naming holiness. Many of us are happy to sing along with songwriter Peter Mayer praising the sacred shimmer of the world and declaring, "Everything is holy now."[4] But to experience reverence in a world brimming with holiness, it helps to focus on just one thing. Listen to it. Let it remind you of your place alongside it, your place in the world and in time, small and mortal and passing—and beautifully tucked into a vast cosmos shining with grand miracles and mystery from one eternity to another.

In Your Own Words

Think of a time when you have felt reverently small in relationship to another—perhaps when experiencing nature's grandeur, history's vast expanse, the fellowship of others in a community, or in witnessing the infinite reach of the cosmos. Maybe it was an experience of human creative expression—an extraordinary cathedral, a sweeping symphony, a delicate poem or a piece of art—that filled you with awe and a sense of understanding and of being understood, which is to say a sense of belonging, a trustworthy kinship felt at the core of your being.

Begin writing with the prompt below:

Small as I am, it is here I belong . . .

ALL IN A NAME

I am the one whose love
overcomes you, already with you
when you think to call my name . . . .
—JANE KENYON[5]

Reverence does not require a belief in God. While it is an important element of many religions, throughout human history, reverence has surfaced as a virtue independent of beliefs in specific deities and doctrines. Contemporary philosopher Paul Woodruff has written an eloquent exploration of what he calls the "forgotten virtue" of reverence, a virtue he finds at play in every human relationship, personal and societal. For those who tug possessively at reverence as belonging more exclusively to the domain of creedal religion, Woodruff points out that agnosticism itself is a posture of extreme reverence, acknowledging humbly as it does that the existence of God is beyond all human capacity for knowing. "True reverence," Woodruff writes, "does not kill heretics or unbelievers. Reverence knows the limits of human knowledge and never presumes to represent literally the mind of God."[6]

What *is* required by reverence, if not belief, is this: it insists on relationship and a posture of humility. We cannot experience or express reverence without holding ourselves in relationship to something or someone outside the circumference of our own control. Reverence is, at its most basic, an acceptance that we do not exist in isolation, and that we are not God, which is a reminder to check our hubris. While each of us carries a spark of the divine, none of us is immortal, all-knowing, or all-powerful, no matter how we stack up in the world's measurements of privilege through class, race, gender, education, strength, and talents.

The dictionary tells us *reverence* can be defined as "deep respect," which seems desirable enough. But if you look more closely at the Latin root of the word, which means "to stand in awe of" or "to fear," that's when it gets a little tricky. In the twenty-first century, fear is a word that makes many of us uncomfortable, especially when it's hitched to religious words, ideas, or practices. Ironically, in fearful response, we often either run from reverence or raise our defenses against it.

Reverence invites a different understanding, though, a way of placing ourselves in relationship with our fears. (The Hebrew word *yir'ah* means both fear and awe or reverence.) In the Hebrew Bible, for instance, "the fear of the Lord" means more than temerity when we hold it in context. Theologian W. M. Rankin points out this phrase is embedded in the profound relationship and covenant between God and God's people, suggesting a reverence based "not on servility but on a foundation of fellowship and trust."[7]

Names can be an invitation into both relationship and reverence. The first step in any relationship is often to learn and speak another's name, and as a relationship becomes more intimate and trusting, we might give one another special names—nicknames or names of affection—whether particular or common. *Sweetie, love, pal, buddy, dear*, even *dude*, all endearments for another, can also become a way of naming our relationship with that person.

I once met a man in Nicaragua, José Carlos, who knew the names of over two hundred birds he could identify by their songs. He learned this while working for seven years in Chocoyero Park, a nature preserve outside of Managua. Working and living side by side with the birds day after day and listening to them one by one, José learned how each was unique and what each one had to say. He was clearly in reverent relationship with them.

Islamic teachings say there are ninety-nine names for God—names often written in careful calligraphy and framed on the walls of mosques—but in fact, the Qur'an and Sunnah contain more than ninety-nine names; and one hadith, or historical Islamic teaching, says that some of God's names remain hidden to us, which means there are still more than any list we find in print. The names that are recorded, though, comprise a generous litany of abundance, beauty, and grace: the Greatest Name, the All Compassionate, the Source of Peace and Safety, the Exceedingly Merciful, the Guardian, the Irresistible, the Repeatedly Forgiving, the Bestower, the Savior, the Exceedingly

Beneficent, the Exceedingly Gracious, the Inspirer of Faith, the Shaper of Beauty . . .

The Bible poetically offers many names for God, but the emphasis in rabbinic and kabbalistic teachings is on the unknowable, unpronounceable nature of God's true name, YHWH, uttered by God to Moses, as Moses stood before the burning bush. In Howard Schwartz's anthology of Jewish mythology, he notes the belief in one tradition that after God's name was revealed to Moses, only one true sage of every generation knew its proper pronunciation, a pronunciation now considered to be lost.[8] In its place, the Hebrew word *Adonai*, or "My Lord," is often substituted in prayer, and *Hashem*, or "the Name," is used in other references.

In my own tradition of Unitarian Universalism, where many names for the holy are honored and none is privileged over others, our hymnal includes over ninety names including:[9]

Wholeness	God
Eternal One	Lover of All
Grander View	Stream of Life
Fount of Justice	Living Waters
Circle of Peace	Deepest Mystery
O Liberating Love	Help of the Helpless
Spirit of Truth, of Life, of Power	Music of the Spheres
Streams of Mercy Never Ceasing	Goddess
Highest That Dwells Within Us	Author of Creation
Mother Spirit, Father Spirit	Blessed Radiance
Power of Love	Beauty of the Earth
Web of Life	Deep Yearning
Grandeur of Creation	Source of All
Boundless Heart	Being in All
Care That Cares for All	Mother Earth
Stillness	Creative Light and Dark

Power of Hope Within   Peace Profound
Wonder of Wonders   Mother of the Generations
Eternal Home   Truth That Makes Us Free
Spirit of Love   Hope Undaunted
Truth Within   Source of Body and Soul
Wise Silence   Fruits of Peace and Love
Ever Spinning Universe   Creative Love
The One   Giver of All

Finding, learning, and claiming our own names for the holy is a way of awakening reverence in our lives and opening our senses to sacred movement. It is also a first step in understanding and being able to translate the languages of reverence and names for God used by others. The Buddhists' warning not to confuse the finger pointing at the moon for the moon itself is an important reminder that the deepest truths and mysteries always lie just beyond all words we might use to point toward them. Our ability to see past or through the names others use for the holy will give us many more sightings of the holy, many more views of the sacred, and many more experiences of wonder and reverence. As we become more fluent in our own language of reverence, we will gain new understanding of the languages others use as well.

In Your Own Words

What are the names you use for the holy, the sacred ground of your being, the source of life and of love? Look at the names above and note any that describe your experience of the holy on this day. Write these names in a list on your own page, adding others that come to mind as words, phrases, or whole sentences naming your own experience of reverence.

Take a moment to read your list of names out loud, varying your pace and volume and tone, however it feels right. Notice the sound of the words, their vibration inside you as you speak them and the images they conjure. Read your list through more than once, if you like. Then, return to the page and begin writing with the words below:

When I say your name(s) . . .

Variation: Let your own list of sacred names be your opening prompt and continue writing, whether in list form or in full sentences.

PAYING ATTENTION

> *Earth's crammed with heaven,*
> *And every common bush afire with God:*
> *But only he who sees, takes off his shoes,*
> *The rest sit round it and pluck blackberries*
> —**ELIZABETH BARRETT BROWNING**[10]

For many of us, experiences of nature offer one of the primary ways in which we know the feeling of reverence. Whether writ large across the vast stretch of a night sky generously salted with stars, or writ small in the delicate design of a dragonfly's wings or in a bud just loosening its buttons outside our front door, nature can coax us to let down our guard, to set aside our schedules, and to sit for a moment—or more—in rapt and reverent attention.

Art offers other on-ramps to reverence in poetry, painting, music, dance, stage, and story—and science too, with its lenses both telescopic and microscopic, focusing with reverence and with reason on life's mysteries large and small. As Elizabeth Barrett Browning poetically reminded us, nothing is too small, too distant, or too unknown for our reverent attention.

> *And truly, I reiterate, . . nothing's small!*
> *No lily-muffled hum of a summer-bee,*
> *But finds some coupling with the spinning stars;*
> *No pebble at your foot, but proves a sphere;*

No chaffinch, but implies the cherubim:
And,—glancing on my own thin, veined wrist,—
In such a little tremour of the blood
The whole strong clamour of a vehement soul
Doth utter itself distinct.[11]

On a good day, many of us would agree that the world is chock-full of wonders within and all around us; the challenge is that noticing them takes time. It requires time to look and listen, time to pay attention in a world where we often hurry from here to there and where our full schedules and our distracted preoccupation shield us from the here and now. How do we stop and pay attention in a world like that?

Albert Schweitzer, the German-born physician and philosopher known for the ethic he named "Reverence for Life" almost a hundred years ago, showed what it can mean to open oneself reverently to the here and now, and to the future all at once. With Reverence for Life, Schweitzer called upon his fellow humans to honor a kinship with *all* of life, crossing the categories of race, nationality, and species that deeply defined the early-twentieth-century Western thinking of his times.

It's interesting to note, in the accounts of how this philosophy came to him, that it didn't first appear to him in his library surrounded by books; nor did it come in any soaring architectural space nor in music, which Schweitzer played and composed with great talent; it didn't even come under the night sky in central Africa, where he moved in 1913, living and working as a physician and doggedly pondering what the key to a moral society might be. Rather, this wisdom came to Schweitzer in a flash, he claimed, its phrasing and comprehension instantly complete, while he was traveling for days up the Ogowe River in Africa as a passenger on a barge. It was the dry season, he reported, and they had to creep slowly upstream, carefully navigating between sandbanks. In the first three days of their trip, he'd sat on the deck of the barge covering whole pages of paper with incomplete sentences, trying to articulate the key to ethical living. And then, late on the third day of his trip, as the sun was setting and the barge was slowly making its way through a small herd of hippopotamuses, the words "Reverence for Life" flashed upon his mind, "unforeseen and unsought," he later said, describing it as an iron door in his thoughts that gave way.[12]

Of course, when the phrase came to him, it was in German. *Ehrfurcht vor dem Leben*, a phrase that carries a deeper connotation in German than its English translation can convey. Says one scholar, "'Ehrfurcht' is more awesome than 'Reverence,' and 'vor dem Leben' is more direct and intimate than 'of life.' We stand in awe not of life *out there* but of life *right here in us, in front of us, and all around.*"[13] It was an intimate reverence that flashed into Schweitzer's thoughts on that day—a deep awe not for life far flung or abstract, but the kind of life breathing right beside him through wide hippopotamus nostrils, wallowing right there with him, sharing what was left of the shallow stream he was trying to navigate in an oversized barge.

When have you felt an intimate awe for the life within you, right there in front of you, or all around you? As contemporary writer Barbara Brown Taylor put it, "Earth is so thick with divine possibility that it is a wonder we can walk anywhere without cracking our shins on altars."[14] Have you ever cracked your shin on one of these altars, been stopped midstep with the world demanding your reverent attention?

In Your Own Words

When have you been surprised by a close-up encounter with divine possibility? Can you recall a time when something interrupted you, insisting on your reverent attention, whether listening to the hum of a bumblebee or picking up a pebble at your feet? Writing about one of these memories, or making up an imaginary situation that might invite a reverent gaze, begin writing from the prompt below.

There it was, right next to me, demanding . . .

THE TEA HOUSE DOOR

Zen teaches that we should feel reverence for all beings no matter how insignificant they might seem . . . from the most basic and small to the most complex and vast. Each has the whole reflected within. The tea ceremony represents this relationship. The tearoom, the utensils, the tea, and every action is treated with reverence for its being.
—C. ALEXANDER SIMPKINS AND ANNELLEN M. SIMPKINS[15]

In Japan, one of the ancient practices that cultivates and preserves reverence is the Japanese tea ceremony. Developed over many centuries, the tea ceremony is an elaborate combination of ancient systems of aesthetics, etiquette, and order, all designed to note one's proper place among others, beginning with the ritual arrival of guests in order of their age, experience, and relationship to the host. Lasting several hours, the ceremony takes place in the teahouse, a simple structure separate from one's living quarters, where the doorway is often so small that you practically have to crawl in on your knees, as one writer explains, leaving all worldly things behind as you enter. For the samurai, or noble warriors of years gone by, this meant actually removing their swords and hanging them on a hook outside because the swords would not fit through the intentionally small teahouse doors.[16]

What does your doorway into the practice of reverence look like? What does it require that you leave behind as you enter? For some of us, it might be the swords of our opinions or the shield of knowledge held protectively over our hearts, an armor of certainty that we know all that we need to know. Perhaps it's the privilege of race, gender, age, or class that, visibly or invisibly, with or without our awareness, can keep us from our proper place among others; or for some, it might simply be the height of confidence or the fluency of language. It could be something we have worked very hard to attain, which might prevent us from passing through the doorway into reverence if we cling to it too fiercely, unwilling to set it down even for the shortest time.

Consider, for a moment, what might happen if the doors into our present-day exchanges—our electoral debates, editorial pages, or conversations online—were metaphorically as small as teahouse doors. Imagine, if you can, how our exchanges might unfold if we each had to enter on our knees, with the swords of our sharp words left hanging on a hook outside. If we realized that reverence begins with a willingness to kneel and then to look up—to another, to beauty, to mystery, to life itself—we might begin to apprehend a kinship with others that includes all people, across differences in class, race, gender, and age, and even differences in religion and political leaning. What might we have to leave behind to cross the thresholds of differences like these and enter a reverent exchange with others?

My friend Dottie Mathews tells a story about two of her children when they were young. She was playing dress-up with her two-year-old, Angie, spinning an air of glamor and make-believe with costumery and curls and a few well-placed rhinestones. When Angie finally walked into the other room, her older brother, Philip, almost four, was struck speechless by the transformation. He stuttered and stammered, at a loss for an adequate word. "Anch," he said, wide-eyed and breathless before his little sister, "you look . . . you look . . . you look ENORMOUS!"

Are we willing, are we able, to open our eyes and hearts to the enormity of reverence, of seeing the beauty and blessedness in others, especially those who are different from us?

In Your Own Words

When has something inspired such awe that it made you feel reverently small? What behaviors, attitudes, or habits sometimes guard you against feeling small like this? What might you need to leave behind at the door in order to experience the enormity of an exchange with another person, especially a person with whom you have difficulty and difference?

Draw a small square door on your page with space around it. Make a short list on either side of it, brainstorming things you might leave at the door as you bow to enter. Then draw from your list as you begin writing with the prompt below, describing what it's like to pass through the small door, leaving some things outside.

The door is small. As I stoop to enter . . .

BUILDING A HABIT, PRACTICING REVERENCE

Reverence the highest, have patience with the lowest.
Let this day's performance of the meanest duty be thy religion.
Are the stars too distant, pick up the pebble that lies at thy feet,
and from it learn the all.
*—*MARGARET FULLER[17]

I have heard it said that reverence is disappearing from our culture largely because so many institutions, traditions, practices, and even beliefs themselves have been proven unworthy. But reverence is perhaps not unlike beauty, cultivated as much, or more, within the beholder as in what we behold. Woodruff claims the seeds of reverence exist in every one of us, but they may need to be cultivated in our irreverent age. You learn reverence, he says, "by finding the virtuous things you do and doing more of them, so that they become a habit."[18]

What is it you do that inspires or teaches reverence? Are there ways in which rituals—of your own making or learned from tradition or from others—might help make reverence a daily habit?

Woodruff takes us to ancient China to explore the use of rituals in fostering reverence. Acknowledging the hollow ring to many rituals that have been handed down over time, he says it's not the ritual itself but the attitude we bring to a ritual that coaxes our reticent reverence to the surface. The *Analects of Confucius* describe the concept of *Li*, which Woodruff tells us has often been translated as ritual but is more accurately understood as the attitude of reverence we bring to our rituals. "[W]ithout *Li*," the *Analects* say, "courtesy is tiresome; without *Li*, prudence is timid; without *Li*, bravery is quarrelsome; without *Li*, frankness is hurtful."[19]

What regular habits do you have that beckon an attitude of reverence? Maybe it's your morning cup of coffee or tea, the way you make it as well as the way you drink it. Perhaps it's a prayer or meditation you use at the end of each day, or the way you greet the dawn. It might be the way you tuck your child into bed at night or sign off in a phone call with a loved one. Or it could be a matter of simple manners, how you shake someone's hand, when you look them in the eye and when you don't, when you stand to meet them or remove your hat or your shoes.

If we take a moment to study our own manners, we might identify a host of things we do, small practices and habits, of times, places, and experiences in which we feel or foster an attitude of reverence. In what common rituals and ceremonies—formal or informal, civic or religious, personal or collective—do you participate with a feeling of reverence, awe, or respect? Is it Election Day, standing in line until the person at the table finds your name on the page in her book? Is it practicing a musical instrument or another art form? Or maybe it's taking a daily walk or run, doing yoga or Tai Chi, or any number of religious rituals, such as lighting a candle, saying a prayer, repeating a mantra. What are your habits of reverence?

In Your Own Words

Make your own list of practices and habits, daily or less frequent, in which you encourage or welcome an attitude of reverence. What common rituals, ceremonies, or experiences, personal or collective, inspire your own feelings of reverence, awe, or respect? What practices of good manners cultivate reverence when you do them? Be specific. Be creative. List whatever comes to mind. Then pick one from your list. Consider what it involves. What do you do? How do you feel when you do it? What does it awaken and stir in you? What do you notice, in yourself, in others, and in your surroundings, when you do it? What kind of awe or respect rises in you and how does it feel?

Whenever you're ready, begin writing with one of the following two prompts, and follow wherever it leads.

It's a little like bowing my head . . .
or
It's a habit of mine . . .

HITCHED TO EVERYTHING ELSE

> *I know to love is to respect.*
> *And reverence*
> *is the nature of my love.*
> **—THICH NHAT HANH**[20]

In the middle of the twentieth century, a young girl set out to collect firewood for her family in Kenya. "Do not take the wood of the fig tree, though," her mother warned. "That is the tree of God," was her mother's explanation. "We don't cut it. We don't burn it. We don't use it. They live for as long as they can, and they fall on their own when they are too old."[21]

The young girl was Wangari Maathai, the first African woman to receive the Nobel Peace Prize and founder of the Green Belt Movement, which, at the time of her death in 2011, had planted over thirty million trees in Africa to fight erosion while providing jobs for women and firewood for fuel. In adulthood, Maathai recalled her childhood lesson in reverence as one that taught her to honor nature itself as sacred. Looking back, as the fig trees in the Kenyan high-lands were cut down and the fertile soil on the hillsides eroded away, she realized that the trees had provided important protection—not in a mystical or religious sense, but in a very physical way. By hold-ing the soil in place there on the steep inclines of the highlands so prone to erosion, the old trees honored as trees of God served a critical purpose, growing deep roots that broke up the underground rock, and bringing the subterranean water system up nearer to the surface, where it formed life-supporting streams.

We come to recognize what is sacred, Maathai said, by notic-ing and honoring that which is life sustaining. Carrying this lesson forward in a remarkable life's work that made profound connections between environmentalism, economics, civil rights, and peace, Maathai exemplified John Muir's phrase written nearly a century earlier: "When we try to pick out anything by itself, we find it hitched to everything else in the Universe."[22]

Reverence, it turns out, is most apparent—and most important—in our relationship with power and how we wield it. It connects us, up and down, with the chain of being and requires that we reverently regard that which falls beneath the blows of our axes, the imprint of our feet, and the theft of our consumption. As Woodruff puts it, "[R]everence comes most into play when the strong have the weak at their mercy."[23]

In the ancient Greek story recorded by Herodotus, in the sixth century BCE, the last Lydian king, named Croesus, once considered himself to be the happiest, most blessed of any human who had ever lived. When he asked a visiting wise man named Solon to confirm this, however, Solon would only say, "Call no man happy until his life is over."

Not long after, Croesus started a war with Persia, and his fortune turned as he was captured and defeated. Bound for execution by fire, as the flames began burning the wood beneath his feet, he remembered Solon's words and let out a loud moan, shouting Solon's name. Cyrus, the Persian king, heard this and instructed his interpreters to find out the meaning of Croesus' cry. When the interpreters learned the story from Croesus and relayed it to Cyrus, the Persian king immediately recognized his own story in that of Croesus. Struck by their common humanity, he feared that his execution of Croesus would bring great punishment to him as well. He ordered the fire extinguished, and seeing that it was already burning far out of control, he also prayed. A heavy rain began to fall, Apollo's answer to his prayers, the story says, and the fire was extinguished, saving both Croesus and Cyrus as their common humanity was restored.[24]

The Jewish theologian Martin Buber famously called for this kind of reverent reciprocity in his work *I and Thou*, with its suggestion that morality requires that we stop objectifying others as "It" and instead address them as "Thou," or as we might say today, "You," with a touch of both warmth and respect. We are called to establish I-Thou relationships with other people, other beings and life forms of all kinds, and with the earth itself. As we do, we find a connection between that which is holy in the other and in ourselves, and our relationship to God, to the sacred, to Life itself is repaired, restored, and rejuvenated.

Writers have long practiced the basic tenets of I-Thou relationships, addressing their words of praise and gratitude to a revered but unnamed "you." Walt Whitman gave us many fine examples:

> *You air that serves me with breath to speak!*
> *You objects that call from diffusion my meaning and give*
>   *them shape!*

You light that wraps me and all things in delicate equable
        showers!
You paths worn in the irregular hollows by the roadsides!
I believe you are latent with unseen existences, you are so
        dear to me.[25]

Honoring our reverence for and connectedness with Life, with God, and with others, we can write our own *you* statements. The twentieth-century minister and peace and justice activist Harry Scholefield made a spiritual practice of writing these statements. In a collection of "You Books" he kept between 1984 and his death in 2003, Scholefield recorded some fourteen thousand *you* statements as a record of his encounters with the sacred in everyday life. During that time, he also served as a mentor to his colleague Laurel Hallman, who in turn shared his practice of writing *you* statements in *Living by Heart*, a guidebook she later published on Scholefield's devotional practices.[26]

Here's a sample of *you* statements from his first book:

#368   You are the poem trying to reach me, and me trying to reach the poem.

#471   You are the routine.

#334   You are what I cannot avoid.[27]

And sometimes he began these statements with the words "I find you [. . .]" as in this entry that reflects Scholefield's ability to find the sacred in his own humility and brokenness too:

#333   I find you in my faults and failures.
        I find you in my growing openness.[28]

Writing these encounters down, Scholefield said, developed what he called his sense of kinship with others. It helped him relate reverently to everything in his daily life as a *You* or *Thou*.[29]

In Your Own Words

To write your own you statements, based on Scholefield's practice, recall an encounter with the sacred that you've had in the past day or week. (If nothing recent comes to mind, think of any encounter and use the writing prompt to explore where the holy might have been hidden in that experience or exchange.) Perhaps it was a person, a pet, an animal, a tree, or another being in nature. Maybe it was an experience of many beings and things—the blowing wind, the singing river, the rising sun. As you recall this encounter, begin writing about it by addressing what was holy in it.

Begin simply with the word "**You . . .**" or, as in the second example above, begin with the words "**I find (or hear, know, see, taste) you . . .**" and complete the phrase with a single sentence or with a short string of sentences.

Then compose a response from the one you are addressing. Let this response lead you into a dialogue between the two of you, an "I-Thou" exchange honoring the sacred within each, and following wherever it leads.

LAST WORDS

How to finish
a book of incomplete sentences,
of questions unanswered and
narratives
still being written . . . .

If there is one thing I have learned, as a writer and as a minister, it is that there are no last words, despite our best efforts to hear them or to have them. Certainly writers have tried, offering memorable closing lines in poems and books and stories. And who hasn't heard or delivered impressive closing arguments that pose as last words, pounded in like nails with percussive insistence and finality? Or, especially and more tenderly, we remember the last words spoken to us as deathbed whispers, sometimes healing, possibly astonishing, and, periodically, entirely indecipherable. We might think of any of these as last words, but as long as we remember them and carry them forward, we are still answering them, still living in conversation with them, still adding to them. Both religion and living in relationship with others remind us that no story is finished while we still have voice and words to continue telling it, often in surprising new ways.

No, there are no last words, only words awaiting our reply—mine, yours, ours, in a conversation started long before we arrived, that will continue long after we are gone.

If there are no last words, though, perhaps it is also true that there are no new words. *Faith, prayer, sin, love, justice, hope, redemption, grace, hospitality*, and *reverence*—all are old and weathered. Yet, when taken up again like just-plucked herbs and rubbed between thumb and forefinger, between heart and mind, and pen and page, they can release scents as fresh as mint.

To be alive is to join a conversation old as time and still being spoken. As long as we have breath, we cannot opt out; we are part of this exchange. Even silence speaks. So this book, its sentences and stories all unfinished, is just beginning, and I eagerly wait to discover how the conversation might continue with reverence and compassion, with curiosity and generative imagination, through a thousand and one nights and many, many more.

Ours is an old, old story still unfolding. Begin writing whenever you are ready and follow wherever it leads.

ACKNOWLEDGMENTS

If it takes a village to raise a child, it seems to me that developing this spiritual practice of writing—and completing this book about it—has taken a whole metropolis and then some. So I thank all those named below while also expressing my deep gratitude to every one of you who, knowingly or not, inspired, informed, and encouraged me, or helped to shape this work. For your support as participants, colleagues, mentors, teachers, funders, friends, and advocates near and far—and for your wisdom, good faith, and generosity—I sincerely thank you.

I am grateful to all of you whose teachings and publications on writing and the writing process have seeded and nurtured my own, but especially those whose writing exercises and prompts have modeled healthy and creative ways to guide others' writing. Many of the writing prompts in this book were inspired by exercises I first learned from teachers, writer friends, and colleagues over several decades of writing in groups and in classes. More recently, the books of Pat Schneider and Natalie Goldberg were particularly important to me in the first months of developing my theological guided writing sessions and the practice of contemplative correspondence that grew from them. Except for specific references, I refrained from rereading their books, listed in the appendices, while writing this one to preserve my own perspective and practices, but I gratefully honor the depth of their work and their impact on mine. I hope they will find my application of their practices in creating this particular form of theological writing to be the tribute that I intend it to be.

I am especially thankful to Unity Church-Unitarian in Saint Paul, Minnesota, for providing a congregational home and incubator for my fledgling literary ministry and the writing sessions and practice that grew from it. The church's co-ministers Janne Eller-Isaacs and Rob Eller-Isaacs were extraordinary in their support, and my work was inspired and sustained by the congregation's entire staff and wider membership. Especially important were my ministry's many advisors—Mary Farrell Bednarowski, Shelley Butler, Kathy Coskran, Sara Ford, Ruth Stryker Gordon, Rick Heydinger, Carol LeBourveau, Jonathan Morgan, Martha Postlethwaite, Linda Myers Shelton, Bob Steller, and Kate Tucker—whose wisdom and good questions for three years running guided me in developing this practice, understanding its significance, and securing the many different kinds of support it needed.

This was a ministry created on a shoestring budget, initially supported by the Fund for Unitarian Universalism and individual donors as well as Unity Church-Unitarian. To every one of you who made a financial gift of any size, I hope you know that without your generosity and your faith in my ministry, this practice would not have been developed and this book would not exist. Thank you for making it possible.

In addition to Unity Church, countless other institutions supported and shaped this ministry by providing a venue where I led writing sessions over these first several years. Of special importance was Wisdom Ways Center for Spirituality in Saint Paul, a public ministry of the Sisters of St. Joseph of Carondelet, where I led writing sessions and served as writer in residence and was blessed by Barbara Lund's generous encouragement. The Loft Literary Center in Minneapolis and United Theological Seminary of the Twin Cities were also valued hosts and sponsors of writing sessions. And for outstanding hospitality of time and space wholly devoted to the writing of this book, I thank Bart and Greta Hammond, the Collegeville Institute for Ecumenical & Cultural Research, in Collegeville, Minnesota, and the Anderson Center, in Red Wing, Minnesota.

Another long list of people has helped me bring *Writing to Wake the Soul* to the computer screen and page. For the many ways you may have encouraged the writing of this book or helped to make it better, I wish to thank Elizabeth Jarrett Andrew, Amy Eilberg, Eleazar Fernandez, Sari Fordham, Beth Gaede, Dottie Mathews, Kristin Maier, Julie Neraas, Kathleen Norris, Donald Ottenhoff, Adil Ozdemir, and Bart Schneider, as well as my treasured colleagues at the Collegeville Institute. Special thanks go to my editors at Beyond Words, Anna Noak, Gretchen Stelter, Lindsay Brown, and Linda Meyer; Sheri Gilbert, who, with great spirit and expertise, tracked down my permissions; and my agent Scott Edelstein, who not only found a publishing home for the book but also ably talked me through more than a few difficult days.

Finally, there are a few whose support has been ongoing and beyond all measure. For being there when I needed you, in so very many ways and for such a long time running, I thank Mary Farrell Bednarowski, Naomi Cohn, and Kate Tucker; each one of you has been a much-depended-on guide and cherished companion on this road. For accompanying my every day of writing and every break taken to walk through the nearby woods, and for not leaving this world until the week I wrote the last pages of this book, I thank my beloved dog, Eliza. And most of all, I thank David and Cat Hammond, you two who are dearest to my heart and have been witnesses to pretty much every point, high and low, along the way, and my larger family. Without the whole bunch of you, I cannot imagine what I would wish to write about or why I would think that it mattered.

Thanks and blessings be to all of you, and more.

Appendix A:

Tips for Leading Groups in Contemplative Correspondence

The practical guide to contemplative correspondence in chapter 5 is a good starting point for trying this spiritual practice, whether you do it alone or with others. But when leading groups in contemplative correspondence, you might wish to consider a few other suggestions as you plan and lead your writing sessions. I offer the following thoughts based on the groups I have led and what I've found to be important in creating a safe and encouraging space for corresponding with the sacred inner voice.

ALL IN A NAME

To start with, consider how you will name and describe your writing sessions as you announce them and invite participants to attend. Although there are times when my hosting organization or conference has labeled a session as a *workshop*, I explicitly avoid that word in my own naming and description to be clear that these are not about craft nor do they include any workshopping or critique of participants' writing. I call them "Open Page writing sessions," and I include the specific theme in their promotional titles. (It is often the theme that attracts people, regardless of their experience with or even fears of writing.) I also include, in my promotional copy, some brief reference to the fact that the sessions are for writers and non-writers alike. No experience required, I often add.

GROUP COVENANT

In many kinds of groups, covenants can help establish trust by making the group's commitments and expectations clear at the outset. Contemplative correspondence is especially dependent upon making and holding safe space, so I start every writing session by articulating a four-part covenant and asking for a nod of heads to confirm it. In one-time groups or the first session of any series, it is especially important both to welcome those who have never attended a session before and to remind those who have previously attended of the agreements we are making to one another as participants. Simply put, it's a way of starting everyone on the same page. (Sometimes, when I have a lot of returning participants in the room, I note that this repetition of the covenant is a form of basic hospitality, making the process and our agreement with one another as clear to the newcomer as it is to the old-timer.) If the same group gathers for multiple sessions, I still review it, albeit briefly, each time we begin as a reminder to all, including me, of our agreement with one another—and as a way of sending off any inner critics that have snuck into the room, as they have a way of doing even when we didn't intend to bring them along.

    You might develop your own covenant as a writing session facilitator or your own way of expressing this one. I use the following four points, some of them inspired by Pat Schneider's wise and useful book *Writing Alone and with Others*[1] but tailored specifically for writing groups that are not workshopping but rather creating a worshipful space for a correspondence with the soul. Most repeat or echo the guidelines discussed in chapter 5 of this book, but I offer them here in the language and explanations I use when leading a writing session as an example of how to translate the ideas in chapter 5 into a group covenant.

GROUP WRITING SESSION COVENANT

1. Everyone is a writer.

The only thing required for contemplative correspondence is to have something to write with, something to write on, and something to write about. When I lead writing sessions, I always have extra paper, pens, and pencils on hand. These are available as people arrive, but when we run through the covenant, I remind people to help themselves to supplies as they need to during the session. This means no one will be without something to write with and something to write on; and because we are drawing from our own experience, I note, no one will be without something to write about. For the duration of the writing session, then, we will regard one another as being equal as writers—no matter how much or how little writing we have done, what kind, or with what goal or result. We are all equally writers.

2. Critics be gone!

With this part of the covenant, I explain that this is not a workshop on the craft of writing or a time for critiquing one another's work or, especially, our own. I acknowledge the value of writing workshops and critiques but say as clearly as I can that this is not what we are doing here. In the practice of contemplative correspondence, there are few things that silence the "still, small voice within" or send the soul into hiding as quickly as a vocal and incisive inner critic. So if you have a particularly active or harsh inner critic—even one that might offer valued guidance in grammar or spelling, punctuation or style—be grateful for these tips when you need them, but for the duration of this writing session, I tell participants, give your inner critic a break. Send it down the hall or outside until the session's done. Let your words fall on the page however they come, as if you were just penning a letter to yourself (which you are!).

3. All writing is fiction until proven otherwise.

Now that your inner critic has moved on, in the space that it left open, invite your imagination to sit down and join in while you write. Sometimes the facts don't seem to convey the full truth of our experiences. It's what novelist Tim O'Brien meant in saying there's "happening truth" and then there's "story truth."[2] If the fish you caught felt like it was two feet long even though it only measured six inches, try telling the story with a two-foot fish and see what you learn from writing it that way. While you wouldn't want to use the inflated numbers in a fishing contest, when you're corresponding with your soul about how that particular fishing experience felt and affected you, the "two-foot-long" description might say more about the muscle or courage it took for you to reel that fish into the boat than the six-inch version could ever express.

Regarding our writing as fiction until proven otherwise also has to do with how we receive any writing shared in the session, and this comes directly from Pat Schneider's guidelines for healthy writing workshops.[3] We agree, in the group covenant, to assume that any writing others share with us is fictional unless they specify that it is autobiographical. This is important for allowing participants to share their writing without feeling like they're revealing their life story if they do not wish to. Also, it reminds all of us, when hearing what someone else has written, that we're not there to analyze, fix, or even discuss at length one another's lives. While personal sharing can and does happen regularly and sometimes very deeply in these writing sessions, they are not therapy or personal encounter groups, and this statement of the covenant helps clarify that boundary.

4. Sharing is optional; confidentiality is required.
Each session includes at least one opportunity for participants to share something they've written or something they've discovered in the session. (Including both types of sharing offers an option for those who want to connect with others but don't wish to read what they wrote.) I say clearly that this is always optional, but I strongly encourage people to share something, noting that it tends to enhance the fruits of this writing both for the one who shares and for others. We need each other's stories. I also underscore that while the sharing is optional, attentive and gracious listening and confidentiality are required. Remember, I like to say, if someone reads something just written in the session, these are newborn words. Receive them as you would a newborn child laid in your arms—with gentle support and gratitude for the gift and the blessing that they are.

As to confidentiality, I remind people we're assuming everything is fiction until proven otherwise. Even if someone identifies a story as autobiographical, I ask participants to let it remain the writer's story to share when and how and with whom *the writer* chooses. If you wish to share the story with others outside the sessions (stories are, after all, meant to be shared), find some way to share it as "story truth" without revealing the writer's identity in any way unless he or she gives permission to do otherwise.

THE PROCESS

Another matter of hospitality in leading a writing practice that will be new to some is to explain the process up front so that people know what to expect. I describe the basic structure of the session in an explanation that goes something like this:

> I'll share different ways of looking at the theme, with definitions, stories, poems, images, objects, teachings from world religions, or information from science, history, or other fields. Then, I'll offer a prompt for participants to use as a starting point for their own writing in silence. The prompts are meant to help get participants' writing started and they can be used any way participants like. If you draw a blank when pondering the prompt as provided, change it. Turn it upside down, backward or inside out, to any form that works. For instance, if I say begin with the words, "What I know is . . ." and nothing comes to mind, begin writing "What I do not know is . . ." If you feel resistance to a particular prompt, though, *and* if you are comfortable doing so today, you might not want to abandon it too quickly. Sometimes our deepest truths are shielded behind our resistance, whether consciously or unconsciously. So if you wish to find your inner truth, you might try peering behind your resistance to see what may be hiding there. (Lower your standards, as Stafford would say.) Try the prompt as is, and see what comes. The most important thing, in any case, is that you use the time and prompts however they work best for you.

I offer the prompts, as well as the stories, poetry, and information leading up to them, as spoken material, usually without a written copy for participants (unless something about the exercise itself requires it). I do, however, write the prompts out on a flip chart or project them via PowerPoint after I've read them through once or twice, to provide the option of a visual reference as people begin their own writing. I also often post the titles and authors of the readings (but not the full content) on a flip chart or via PowerPoint as we go. I tell people they can contact me afterward for readings or other references. If I've prepared a bibliographic list of readings, I wait until the end of the session to distribute it to avoid having people read ahead and anticipate what's next, instead of discovering the prompts one step at a time. During the writing session, I encourage people to settle into the moment as much as they can. This is an invitation to the associative mind to take what it hears and run with it. As we find in the practice of *lectio divina* where a passage of scripture or poetry is read out loud, receiving something by the ear instead of the eye can create different and deeper resonance. Sometimes when we hear a reading, we can be quicker to participate in it rather than holding it at arm's length with the analytical eye we often bring to material read from the page.

People often want to take the readings home with them. This might be the understandable desire to spend more time with a piece of writing either because it rang true or was puzzling upon first encounter. Personally, I have a growing library of books collected on that basis alone, and if that need is strong, I encourage people to track down the published work, whether through a library, by purchasing the book, or online. But sometimes—at least this is the case with me—the desire to have a reading in hand and to take it home can be part of my unwillingness to let the moment in which I heard it stand as having its own value. Have you ever first encountered a poem and felt how perfectly it named your own experience or emotions, only to discover on second reading just days later that although it might be a really good poem, it no longer speaks to you with nearly the same import or impact? I tell participants to trust what they have heard in the moment and how it made them feel because that, after all, is the point of contemplative correspondence—listening to our own inner voice as it responds to what we've heard and seen and experienced. Some participants have later told me they made beautiful discoveries when writing from a prompt they heard differently from whatever I said out loud. In other cases, I've had participants writing from a physical object they chose at the session, and they found the object so evocative they wanted to take it home with them. Sometimes these same participants have later noted, though, that their own writing inspired by that object was perhaps a more profound way of taking it home. As Lu Chi put it several millennia ago, "Work with what is given; / that which passes / cannot be detained."[4]

When explaining the process to participants, I also ask them to hold the silence for one another during each writing prompt and tell them, if you finish writing before the time is up, you might try to keep your hand moving, even writing "I don't know what else to write . . ." Sometimes this produces surprising results. Or, if you prefer to stop, simply enjoy the silence until the writing time is up. It isn't sterile silence but a quietude beautifully embellished by the soft scratching of pencils and pens on paper, the occasional crisp turn of a page, or the groan of a chair as someone shifts position and weight. Someone once remarked at the end of a session that the sounds of everyone writing together gave him the feeling that he was part of a literary chamber group making a kind of sacred music on the page.

At the end of the time for each prompt's writing, I tell the group, I will ring the singing bowl three times to give notice. If you're not quite finished with a thought, you might jot a few notes about where your writing is headed to help you return to it later. When the singing bowl is silent, that's when we'll move on. If people are still writing when I strike the singing bowl the third time, I will run the mallet around the bowl's edge to keep the note going longer until all or most have put their pens down. It doesn't have to be a singing bowl; you can use other methods, including your own voice. But whatever you use, introduce it with care, as you would mark the end of any group time of silent meditation.

PASTORAL CONCERN

I always end my introductory remarks with one more comment acknowledging that writing our inner truths can surface both joy and sorrow, and I remind participants that while writing is a solitary act, we need not carry our sorrows or fears alone. I suggest that if their writing opens up difficult emotions, during the session or at any time, they might want to share their feelings with another—a trusted loved one, a teacher or mentor, a minister, rabbi, imam, or other religious leader, a therapist or counselor or spiritual director. We each have access to people who can companion us through our difficult times. We don't have to walk the hard roads alone.

I maintain a small list of spiritual directors and therapists in my home community—people I either know personally or who have been recommended by trusted colleagues—and when leading sessions locally, I tell my groups they can contact me for referrals. I regularly receive these requests, usually with an interest in finding a spiritual director. Because the writing sessions function as a group form of spiritual direction, I can well imagine spiritual directors might wish to lead them as an outreach tool or to serve their directees in groups. I have also had ministers or managers request a session on a particular topic that their congregation or staff has been wrestling with. In these cases, the writing session itself provides a form of pastoral care for the group.

PRACTICAL MATTERS

If you plan to offer group writing sessions, the following practical considerations might be a good place to start.

Frequency, number, and length of sessions, themes, and size of group

Frequency and number: Writing sessions can be offered individually or as a series. Sometimes it's easier to recruit participants in a new setting by offering a single two- or three-hour session, but often participants in a stand-alone session or even a two-part series will say at the end they would have liked more sessions. When stringing several sessions together in a series, it can work on a weekly or monthly basis. Weekly timing requires a greater commitment from your participants, but it also allows more carryover from one session to the next, both in content and in building community among participants.

Length of session: These sessions work best if they're at least two hours long, with a typical two-hour session allowing time for three or four prompts as provided in Part 2 of this book. The sessions can easily be extended as full-day or multiple-day retreats, allowing time for participants to do their own deep reflection while also sharing with one another, but I've also led them in as little as one and a half hours, or as a kind of introductory session in an hour, by limiting the number of prompts and the sharing among participants. In the shorter sessions, however, it is difficult to create a contemplative atmosphere with enough spaciousness for both personal writing and sharing with one another.

Size of group: Contemplative correspondence can work in a variety of group sizes, but you'll want to make different accommodations for larger groups. I've led sessions with just a handful of participants and as many as seventy-five. With the right room and setup, you could probably handle more. The key thing is to remember that the practice involves an intimate exchange with one's own inner truth and inner voice, so participants' experience will be enhanced however you can appropriately create a safe and comfortable environment that encourages and protects that intimacy.

Smaller groups will be more intimate by definition, but in larger gatherings you can do a few things to create geniality as well. Seating people around tables of four to six can help with a larger group, as does sharing in dyads or triads. I've had some participants in a series attended by about thirty people become so attached to other new acquaintances at their table that after the first session or two, they made an agreement with each other to sit together for the remaining sessions in the series. Other options for building community in larger groups have to do with how you solicit responses from the group in the opening and closing, discussed below under "Session structure."

Physical space, setup, and supplies

Seating: I almost always have tables for people to write at, although in some retreat settings, it can be nice to sit in a circle of couches and chairs as long as people have something hard to write on. If I know we won't have tables, I sometimes bring clipboards or even a supply of thin hardcover picture books people can use as lap writing surfaces.

With small groups, it's wonderful to have everyone seated around the same table or tables arranged in a single group, in which case, I usually sit down too, still able to maintain eye contact with every writer. Of course, people need enough room to comfortably write—and even more space if you're using writing prompts that involve cutting and pasting or other activities—and you'll want to have a "traveler's chair," both to accommodate a drop-in participant and as a reminder of the many stories not present in the room (see page 39).

Equipment: I try to have a flip chart, whiteboard, or chalkboard on hand, even if I use a PowerPoint, so that I can write people's contributions where everyone can see them if we're doing group brainstorming. And of course, for some prompts, I need other equipment for playing recordings or short video clips or projecting images. I often prepare a PowerPoint presentation for my sessions because it allows me to include photographs and other visual images in the setup for different prompts. This can be useful in encouraging associative writing, and a wide variety of noncopyrighted images are readily available from the internet. But PowerPoint can also disturb the intimacy of a smaller group, especially in informal retreat settings, so I don't automatically assume more technology is better. Consider your group and your setting and your purposes when deciding whether to go low- or high-tech.

Making the space worshipful: Chapter 5 discusses the importance of creating a space set apart for your individual writing and gives a few suggestions for how to do that simply. This applies to leading groups as well. Regardless of how you describe your writing session in advance, some people will come expecting a class or a workshop. Anything you can do in the physical arrangements to suggest that it will be more akin to worship or meditation will help your participants enter into a contemplative spirit as soon as they walk into the room. If you have a small group seated around a single table, you might arrange the middle of the table aesthetically with a textile, a candle, a plant, or flower and a few objects related to your theme. If the session is in a larger room with participants at multiple tables, I often use a small table at the front of the room to create an altar similarly appointed. Sometimes, depending on the topic, group, and setting, I might have a single votive for each participant, and I invite all to light their own candles during the opening words of the session. (However, I have learned the hard way that caution is warranted when bringing these small burning candles into close proximity with lots of loose paper on the table!)

Drawing from my own religious tradition, I usually have a chalice with a candle in it that I light with the opening words and extinguish in the closing. It sits next to the singing bowl, which I use after the opening silent meditation and at the end of each writing prompt. The possible variations on this are beautiful and many. The point is to provide a visual cue to participants that they are entering liminal time and space for the duration of the session—something set aside from the bustle of their lives for listening and reflecting, alone and together.

Supplies: As mentioned earlier, I always have extra paper and pens or pencils on hand, as well as any other supplies for the particular prompts. I like to have participants use name tags or names on table tents too, to help all of us (including me) use each other's names in our exchanges. Writing is, after all, an act of naming.

Objects for writing prompts: For the writing prompts that make use of physical objects, bring a variety and quantity that will allow all participants to choose from several options. When selecting objects, consider how they might appeal to different people—if I'm collecting domestic objects, for instance, I try to draw from the workbench as well as the kitchen, and the toy box as well as my sewing supplies and computer accessories. When setting up before participants arrive, keep your objects out of sight until you invite everyone to choose one. Again, this keeps people in the moment and also introduces a modest element of surprise, which can encourage both creativity and the "still, small voice within." Sometimes I arrange the objects on a table at the front of the room and cover them with a cloth. Other times, I divide them among several trays, also covered until the moment I need them, and then pass them around the table or the room. It's often helpful to tell people not to worry about what they pick or why, rather to choose whatever catches their eye or their interest.

Visual images: If you are using a prompt that draws from visual images, follow the same principles as described above for using objects, having enough on hand for people to make their own choice and not passing them out until the prompt begins. You can use old magazines with plenty of photographs, giving each writer one to browse through, choosing a single image to work with. I keep a ready supply of periodicals just for this purpose, mixing very old issues of *National Geographic* (often available free at used book sales of the Friends of the Public Library) with more recent issues of a variety of magazines like *The Sun* with its evocative black and white images. Remind participants to choose quickly and not to get absorbed in reading the articles! Or a different way to go is to gather pictures ahead of time and organize them into packets, from which each participant will choose one. This takes more prep time but will allow participants to choose more quickly, and depending on the prompt, you can decide whether to include a caption to contextualize the photo or not. In addition to clipping from any magazines you have on hand, this option also allows you to draw from the wealth of images available online. I find a good internet source of photos to be the news media, such as *The Christian Science Monitor* or the BBC, that regularly publish evocative news and human interest photos posted in collections called "Photos of the Day." Again, when handing out the packets, remind participants it doesn't matter what they choose or why, just to pick something that captures their interest as they flip through the packets.

Feedback forms: I always prepare a form to request feedback on the writing session in general and list each prompt within it, so participants can quickly comment on which ones worked and which ones didn't. Because so much of the writing is personal and not shared in the group, it's important to me to ask about which of the prompts worked for them and which didn't. I'm usually surprised and grateful that people take as much time as they do to complete the forms before leaving. I've received very helpful comments from people that have influenced the development of this practice, the shape and content of the sessions I lead, and the material in this book.

Typically, the feedback on any given prompt can be varied. What works really well for one person might cause the next writer to draw a blank. Unless someone hasn't had luck with any of the prompts or one of the prompts hasn't worked for most of the participants, I don't worry about one prompt not working for one person. What I do watch for in the responses are those prompts that spurred lots of good writing for most participants (in which case I try to use more prompts like that one) or where a prompt fell flat for many or caused widespread confusion (sometimes causing me to adjust it or give it up entirely). In addition, many people give me specific insights into how the prompts worked for them, and that helps me understand how best to set them up for others the next time I use them.

Session structure

In planning my sessions, I structure them with the intention of inviting people into the topic at an accessible and welcoming place and then working into deeper reflections before coming to an end and closing with words that offer a blessing for the road. The basic template for a two- to three-hour session with four prompts looks like this, with a short break added anywhere in the middle:

- Opening words and pause for silent meditation
- Introductions: name and one word related to the theme
- Explanation of the covenant and the process
- First prompt (brief setup with an easy prompt to get things going)
- Background (often etymology or definition or both)
- Setup with stories, poem, imagery, etc., and second prompt

- Optional pause for sharing
- Setup with stories, poem, imagery, etc., and third prompt
- Setup with stories, poem, imagery, etc., and fourth prompt
- Sharing
- Closing words or poem and blessing for the road
- Feedback forms

The session begins with an opening reading and brief silent meditation, followed by introductions with a simple theme-related question that can be answered in a single word or phrase. For instance, in a session about brokenness, I might ask participants to share their names and one thing in their lives that has broken recently. This invites everyone's voice into the room while demonstrating the variety of answers every question can elicit. (Start with your own name and answer as a way of modeling how to do this quickly.) If the group is too large, of course, you'll have to forego this because it will take too much time, but in that case, I often ask for answers to the question from the group as a whole and write the responses on the flip chart until the page is full.

I don't include sharing after every prompt. I like to let people gain their own momentum from one prompt to the next as the session progresses. In a three-hour session, I might have participants share before a midway break, but often we wait until the last prompt is over before sharing. Then, if the group is large and the sharing happens in dyads or smaller subgroups, you can bring the group back together as a whole and open the floor for any observations or things to be shared with everyone before the session ends. This makes room for any particularly salient discoveries or short written pieces that are begging to be offered to the wider group.

Finally, I close the session by reading one last poem and a blessing for the road, while extinguishing the burning chalice. This offers a gentle ritual to mark the end of our time together.

THEME AND CONTENT
FOR WRITING SESSIONS

As noted earlier, naming a theme for your writing session can be a good way to attract participants. But on a more substantive note, the theme provides an important focal tool for connecting the writing to meaning that transcends our individual lives. As facilitator, you'll find the theme gives you a way to search for stories, images, and poems for your writing session. For your participants, it will package their writing from the session in a way that can make it more meaningful in the moment and in the future.

Any of the ten words in Part 2 can be used as a theme, allowing you to use or adapt the prompts provided here. If you want to develop a new session on a different theme, you might begin by asking yourself what word or theological theme stirs your own curiosity and interest. (As a preaching professor of mine liked to say, if you don't know what to preach about on a given week, ask yourself what is the message that you most need to hear right now. Likely somebody else will need to hear it too.) Or if you're leading the writing session as part of a community of faith or another organization, is there a word or theme that is prominent in the life of that community now? I've led writing sessions for values-based organizations exploring a word from their mission statement as a way to reflect on how the mission relates to their day-to-day work. In one case, the organization convened its senior staff for a half-day session on a particular word from their mission that raised different questions for those overseeing direct services and for those involved in the organization's fundraising. Bringing both groups together to reflect on the word gave them time and language to explore their own perspectives on it and then to talk to each other about how it related to all of their work. In a community of faith, you might choose themes related to the liturgical year or religious festivals, or to words or themes that are prominent in your congregational life or history. If you offer sessions regularly, you might keep a file of ideas for themes, saving related readings or images or stories as you run across them.

A few themes I've found particularly rich in writing sessions, individually or in series, in addition to the ten in this book, are: abundance, belonging, blessing, courage, freedom, incarnation, peace, pilgrimage, thresholds, transformation, and vocation. (A longer and ever-growing list of themes I've used in writing sessions and retreats is available on my website at karenhering.com.)

Once you've chosen your theme, you will likely find a wealth of material for building the content of a writing session in your own library and in the religious stories of your own faith tradition, but try to branch out into new material as well. The internet, the news media, periodicals, libraries, and religious encyclopedias can all be great sources. Of course, if your theme is one of the ten covered in this book, you have ready-made material in the reflections and writing prompts on these pages, and the bibliography in appendix B will steer you toward additional reading and sources. In general, I incorporate more poetry in the writing sessions I lead than I have included in these pages. Especially when it is read out loud, poetry opens up our associative thinking and, with its rhythms and rich imagery, primes participants for their own writing.

Different kinds of writing prompts

When leading writing sessions, it's good to include different types of writing prompts. You'll find a wide variety of options, including many more than are represented here, in the books listed as writing resources in appendix B. Two that are especially full of prompt ideas are *Writing Alone and with Others* by Pat Schneider and *Wild Mind: Living the Writer's Life* by Natalie Goldberg.

APPENDIX B:
ADDITIONAL RESOURCES

For an extensive bibliography and list of additional resources for building your own personal or group practice of contemplative correspondence, visit my website, **karenhering.com**. There you'll find an extended version of the list below as well as books on theology and theory, and print and online sources for poetry, stories, and images. Here I include just a few of the books that have been inspiring, instructive, and informative in my own practice of contemplative correspondence and in preparing and leading writing sessions for others.

I know the list that follows is entirely incomplete and I offer it only as a starting point. I encourage you to add to it, drawing from your own library, reading, and resources. The more you practice contemplative correspondence, the more you will be attuned to noticing good material all around you—in nature, in the news, and in your reading. In the practice's ethic of inclusion, try to look especially for voices that reflect experiences different from your own.

GENERAL: BOOKS ABOUT WRITING AND CREATIVE PROCESS

The asterisked titles indicate content sources for writing sessions. For additional print and online sources, visitkarenhering.com.

*Kevin Anderson, *Divinity in Disguise: Nested Meditations to Delight the Mind and Awaken the Soul*, Monclova, OH: Center for Life Balance, 2003.

Elizabeth J. Andrew, *Writing the Sacred Journey: The Art and Practice of Spiritual Memoir*, Boston: Skinner House Books, 2005.

Roseanne Bane, *Around the Writer's Block: Using Brain Science to Solve Writer's Resistance*, New York: Jeremy Tarcher/Putnam, 2012.

Julia Cameron, *The Artist's Way: A Spiritual Path to Higher Creativity*, New York: Jeremy P. Tarcher/Putnam, 1992.

Julia Cameron, *The Right to Write: An Invitation and Initiation into the Writing Life*, New York: Jeremy P. Tarcher/Putnam, 1998.

*Natalie Goldberg, *Wild Mind: Living the Writer's Life*, New York: Bantam, 1990.

*Miriam Greenspan, *Healing Through the Dark Emotions: The Wisdom of Grief, Fear, and Despair*, Boston: Shambhala, 2003.

*Laurel Hallman, *Living by Heart*, Dallas, TX: Living By Heart, 2003. (Available from First Unitarian Church of Dallas, Adult Religious Education Department, 4015 Normandy Ave., Dallas, TX 75205)

Lu Chi, *The Art of Writing: Lu Chi's Wen Fu*, Sam Hamill, trans., Minneapolis: Milkweed Editions, 2000.

Marilyn Chandler McEntyre, *Caring for Words in a Culture of Lies*, Grand Rapids, MI: Eerdmans, 2009.

Toni Morrison, *Playing in the Dark: Whiteness and the Literary Imagination*, Cambridge, MA: Harvard University Press, 1992.

Mary Pipher, *Writing to Change the World: An Inspiring Guide for Transforming the World with Words*, New York: Riverhead Books, Penguin, 2006.

*Kim Rosen, *Saved by a Poem: The Transformative Power of Words*, Carlsbad, CA: Hay House, 2009.

*Pat Schneider, *Writing Alone and with Others*, New York: Oxford University Press, 2003.

Gregory Orr, *Poetry as Survival*, Athens, GA: University of Georgia Press, 2000.

Louise DeSalvo, *Writing as a Way of Healing: How Telling Our Stories Transforms Our Lives*, New York: HarperCollins, 1999.

BOOKS ABOUT METAPHORS AND FRAMING

*James Rowe Adams, *From Literal to Literary: The Essential Reference Book for Biblical Metaphors*, Cleveland, OH: The Pilgrim Press, second edition, 2008.

Joe R. Feagin, *The White Racial Frame: Centuries of Racial Framing and Counter-Framing*, New York: Routledge, 2010.

James Geary, *I Is an Other: The Secret Life of Metaphor and How It Shapes the Way We See the World*, New York: HarperCollins, 2011.

George Lakoff and Mark Johnson, *Metaphors We Live By*, Chicago: University of Chicago Press, 2003.

ADDITIONAL RESOURCES FOR CREATING THEOLOGICAL WRITING SESSIONS

Books (also see the asterisked books listed above)

J. Ruth Gendler, *The Book of Qualities*, New York: Perennial, Harper & Row, 1988, originally published by Turquoise Mountain Publications, 1984.

Margaret Parkin, *Tales for Change: Using Storytelling to Develop People and Organizations*, London and Sterling, VA: Kogan Page, 2004.

Howard Schwartz, *Adam's Soul: The Collected Tales of Howard Schwartz*, Northvale, NJ: Jason Aronson, 1992.

Howard Schwartz, *Tree of Souls: The Mythology of Judaism*, New York: Oxford University Press, 2004.

Nina Wise, *A Big New Free Happy Unusual Life: Self-Expression and Spiritual Practice for Those Who Have Time for Neither*, New York: Broadway Books, 2002.

Philip Zaleski, ed., *The Best Spiritual Writing* series, annual anthology of poetry and essays, New York: Penguin Books, beginning in 1998 with a new volume each year.

Periodicals and websites

Periodicals and websites provide a wellspring of material for developing writing sessions or supporting an individual practice of contemplative correspondence. For suggested online resources and periodicals, visit my web site, karenhering.com.

NOTES

Unless otherwise noted, passages of Hebrew and Christian scripture are from the New Revised Standard Version Bible (copyright © 1989 the Division of Christian Education of the National Council of the Churches of Christ in the United States of America). Dictionary references, unless otherwise noted, have been taken from the *New Oxford American Dictionary*, third edition (New York: Oxford University Press, 2010).

Epigraph on page viii: Hafiz, *The Gift: Poems by Hafiz, the Great Sufi Master*, trans. Daniel Ladinsky (New York: Penguin Putnam, 1999), 19.

Introduction
1. W. S. Merwin, "Utterance," *The Rain in the Trees* (New York: Alfred A. Knopf, 1988), 44.

2. Jeremy Taylor, *Where People Fly and Water Runs Uphill: Using Dreams to Tap the Wisdom of the Unconscious* (New York: Warner Books, 1992), 45.

3. See chapter 3, note 10.

PART I

1. Hafiz, *The Gift: Poems by Hafiz, the Great Sufi Master*, trans. Daniel Ladinsky (New York: Penguin Putnam, 1999), 293.

Chapter 1: Why We Write

1. Wendell Berry, *A Timbered Choir: The Sabbath Poems 1979–1997* (Berkeley, CA: Counterpoint Press, 1998), 182.

2. Ben Okri, *A Way of Being Free* (London: Phoenix House, 1997), 112.

3. From The Afghan Women's Writing Project, http://awwproject.org/discover -awwp/history-mission/.

4. From a historical exhibit in Managua celebrating the twenty-fifth anniversary of the literacy campaign, seen in August 2006.

5. From a meeting with María López Vígil in Managua, August 2006. Vígil made her literary reputation recounting the stories of the poor and victimized in Central America, and her own work underscores her point.

6. Okri, *Being Free*, 114.

7. Gregory Orr, *Poetry as Survival* (Athens, GA: University of Georgia Press, 2000), 8.

8. Neil Mikesell, "old man," *Cairns: The Unity Church Journal of the Arts*, 3 (St. Paul, MN: Unity Church-Unitarian, 2011), 16.

9. Ralph Waldo Emerson, "The Poet," *The Essential Writings of Ralph Waldo Emerson* (New York: Random House Modern Library, 2000), 288.

Chapter 2: Why Metaphors Matter

1. George Eliot, *The Mill on the Floss* (New York: Harper & Brothers, 1860), 125.

2. T. S. Eliot, "Burnt Norton," *Four Quartets* (New York: Harcourt Brace Jovanovich, 1973), 19.

3. Sam Hamill, "Nine Gates," *Measured by Stone* (Willimantic, CT: Curbstone Press, 2007), 44.

4. George Lakoff and Mark Johnson, *Metaphors We Live By* (Chicago: University of Chicago Press, 2003), 235.

5. Virginia Woolf, quoted by Ursula K. Le Guin in "The Fisherwoman's Daughter," *Dancing at the Edge of the World: Thoughts on Words, Women, Places* (New York: Harper & Row, 1990), 227.

6. Heid E. Erdrich, from "Origin of Poem," *Fishing for Myth* (Minneapolis: New Rivers Press, 1997), 14.

7. W. S. Merwin in conversation with James Richardson, *Poets in Person* (Chicago: Modern Poetry Association, 1991), audiotape recording.

8. Lakoff and Johnson, *Metaphors We Live By*, 245–46.

9. Adrienne Rich, *Poetry and Commitment* (New York: W. W. Norton & Co., 2007), 32–33.

10. James Geary, *I Is an Other: The Secret Life of Metaphor and How It Shapes the Way We See the World* (New York: HarperCollins, 2011), 9.

11. *New Shorter Oxford English Dictionary*, 1993 edition vol. 1 (New York: Oxford University Press, 1993), 1070.

12. Geary, *I Is an Other*, 87.

13. Ibid., 82.

14. Ibid., 88. (Geary is referencing the work of Lakoff and Johnson.)

15. Lakoff and Johnson, *Metaphors We Live By*, 7–9.

16. Ibid., 49, 140–41.

17. George Lakoff, *Don't Think of an Elephant! Know Your Values and Frame the Debate: The Essential Guide for Progressives* (White River Junction, VT: Chelsea Green, 2004), 17.

Chapter 3: Writing as a Spiritual Practice

1. From the Hasidic work *Liqqutim Yeqarim*, Arthur Green and Barry W. Holtz, eds. and trans., *Your Word Is Fire* (New York: Paulist Press, 1977), 49.

2. Anthony de Mello, "True Spirituality," *Song of the Bird* (New York: Image Books/Doubleday, 1984), 11.

3. Yannis Ritsos, "The Meaning of Simplicity," *Repetitions, Testimonies, Parentheses*, trans. Edmund Keeley (Princeton University Press, 1991), 125.

4. Claude Lévi-Strauss, *Myth and Meaning* (New York: Schocken Books, 1979), 18.

5. Ibid.

6. John Calvin, *Institutes of the Christian Religion*, ed. John T. McNeill, trans. Ford Lewis Battles (Philadelphia: Westminster Press, 1960), 1:52.

7. William Stafford, "When I Met My Muse," *The Way It Is: New and Selected Poems* (St. Paul, MN: Graywolf Press, 1998), 222.

8. asha bandele, *The Prisoner's Wife* (New York: Scribner, 1999), 21.

9. Julia Cameron, *The Artist's Way* (New York: Jeremy P. Tarcher/Putnam, 1992).

10. 1 Kings 19: The "still, small voice within" is a phrase that originates in the biblical story of Elijah, who had fled to the wilderness, fearing for his life after all the other prophets of the day had been killed by Ahab. As Elijah hid in a cave, God told him to come out while God was passing by. First, a powerful wind passed by, but God was not in the wind. Then an earthquake came, but God was not in the earthquake, and a fire followed the earthquake, but God was not in the fire. Finally, after all this, came what the King James Version called a "still small voice" that Elijah recognized as the voice of God. Other more contemporary translations have named it "a gentle whisper" (New International Version) or "a sound of sheer silence" (New Revised Standard Version).

11. Henry David Thoreau, *Walden and Other Writings* (New York: Modern Library, 1937, 1950), 723–24.

12. Emerson, "The Poet," *Essential Writings*, 292.

13. Coleman Barks, interviewed by Linda Stankard, "A Valentine to the World," *Book Page*, February 2003, http://bookpage.com/interview/a-valentine-to-the-world. "We are a conversation," Coleman Barks said, describing Rumi's perspective, "between the one who takes bodily form and something else that is flowing through that was never born and doesn't die. So that intersection, that conversation is what a human being is."

14. Lu Chi, *The Art of Writing: Lu Chi's Wen Fu*, trans. Sam Hamill (Minneapolis, MN: Milkweed Editions, 2000), 33.

15. Ibid., 30.

Chapter 4: The Invitation of Ellipses . . .

1. Rita Dove, "Dawn Revisited," *On the Bus with Rosa Parks* (New York: W. W. Norton, 2000), 36.

2. Louise Glück, "Disruption, Hesitation, Silence," *Proofs & Theories: Essays on Poetry* (New York: Ecco, 1994), 74–75.

3. Mahmoud Mustafa Ayoub, "The Idea of Redemption in Christianity and Islam," *Mormons and Muslims: Spiritual Foundations and Modern Manifestations*, ed. Spencer J. Palmer (Provo, UT: Religious Studies Center, Brigham Young University, 2002), 157–69, http://rsc.byu.edu/archived/mormons-and-muslims/13-idea-redemption-christianity-and-islam.

4. Research has shown that for all of us—including white people who strive not to be racist as well as people of color—the frames of white racism subconsciously shape our silent response to people and experiences. Our inner silent process-

ing can still foster unwanted responses. See Joe R. Feagin, *The White Racial Frame: Centuries of Racial Framing and Counter Framing* (New York: Routledge, 2010).

5. Chimamanda Ngozi Adichie, "The Danger of a Single Story," TED Talks, posted October 2009. http://www.ted.com/talks/chimamanda_adichie_the_danger_of_a_single_story.html.

6. Howard Schwartz, "How the Tenth Tribe Lost Its Words," *Adam's Soul: The Collected Tales of Howard Schwartz* (Northvale, NJ: Jason Aronson, 1992), xi–xii.

Chapter 5: A Practical Guide to Contemplative Correspondence

1. Jalal al-Din Rumi, *The Essential Rumi*, Coleman Barks, trans. (Edison, NJ: Castle Books, 1997), 41.

2. Story told by Luis Urrea at the 2012 Festival of Faith and Writing, Calvin College, Grand Rapids, Michigan.

3. Robert McAfee Brown quoted by Luci Shaw, "Reversing Entropy," *Shouts and Whispers: Twenty-One Writers Speak about Their Writing and Their Faith* (Grand Rapids, MI: Wm. B. Eerdmanns, 2006), 210.

4. Louise DeSalvo, *Writing as a Way of Healing: How Telling Our Stories Transforms Our Lives* (New York: HarperCollins, 1999).

5. Yung Y. Chen and Richard J. Contrada, "Framing Written Emotional Expression from a Religious Perspective: Effects on Depressive Symptoms," *International Journal of Psychiatry in Medicine*, 39(4) 2009: 427–38.

6. Charles Simic, *The Uncertain Certainty: Interviews, Essays, and Notes on Poetry* (Ann Arbor, MI: University of Michigan Press, 1985), 5–6. Simic says, "Silence, solitude, what is more essential to the human condition? 'Maternal silence' is what I like to call it. Life before the coming of language. That place where we begin to hear the voice of the inanimate. Poetry is an orphan of silence. The words never quite equal the experience behind them."

7. John Berger, *G.: A Novel* (New York: Vintage Books, 1972), 129.

8. Kim Addonizio and Dorianne Laux, *The Poet's Companion: A Guide to the Pleasures of Writing Poetry* (New York: W. W. Norton, 1997), 21.

9. C. S. Lewis, *An Experiment in Criticism* (New York: Cambridge University Press, 1961), 137–38. Lewis said we read literature seeking "an enlargement of our being."

10. It is a phenomenon summarized by James Geary, *I Is an Other*, 63. "When we concentrate on an inner picture and when we are careful not to interrupt the

natural flow of events, our unconscious will produce a series of images which make a complete story."

11. Eugene Peterson quoted by Shaw, "Reversing Entropy," *Shouts and Whispers*, 204.

PART II

1. Zbigniew Herbert, "I Would Like to Describe," quoted in Jane Hirschfield, *Nine Gates: Entering the Mind of Poetry* (New York: HarperCollins, 1997), 115.

Chapter 6: Writing about Faith

1. Sharon Daloz Parks, *Big Questions, Worthy Dreams: Mentoring Young Adults in Their Search for Meaning, Purpose, and Faith* (San Francisco: Jossey-Bass, 2000), 31, referencing the work of William F. Lynch, SJ, *Images of Faith: an Exploration of the Ironic Imagination* (Notre Dame, IN: Notre Dame Press, 1973), 25.

2. Wilfred Cantwell Smith quoted by Kenneth Cracknell, ed., *Wilfred Cantwell Smith: A Reader* (Oxford: Oneworld Publications, 2001), 131.

3. Ibid., 128.

4. Sharon Salzberg, *Faith: Trusting Your Own Deepest Experience* (New York: Riverhead Books, 2002), 47.

5. Norita Dittberner-Jax, "Away from Home," *What They Always Were* (Minneapolis: New Rivers Press, 1995), 38.

6. Salzberg, *Faith*, 17.

7. Wilfred Cantwell Smith, *Faith and Belief* (Princeton, NJ: Princeton University Press, 1979), 12.

8. Hafiz, "No More Leaving," *The Gift*, 258.

9. Adapted from an exercise used by Reuel Howe, an Episcopal priest, in his seminars on spirituality, as reported by John Buchanan in *Christian Century*, February 22, 2011.

10. Joan Chittister, *In a High Spiritual Season* (Ligouri, MO: Triumph Books, 1995), 82.

11. Paul Tillich, *Dynamics of Faith* (New York: Harper, 2001), 4.

12. Thomas R. Smith, *Waking before Dawn* (Red Wing, MN: Red Dragonfly Press, 2007), 9.

13. Kahlil Gibran, *The Collected Works* (New York: Knopf, 2007), 299.

14. Parks, *Big Questions, Worthy Dreams*, 19.

15. Tillich, *Dynamics of Faith*, 87.

16. Luci Shaw, *Breath for the Bones: Art, Imagination and Spirit, A Reflection of Creativity and Faith* (Nashville, TN: Thomas Nelson, 2007), 102.

17. James Baldwin, *Nobody Knows My Name*, quoted in Tram Nguyen, ed., *Language Is a Place of Struggle: Great Quotes by People of Color* (Boston: Beacon Press, 2009), 225.

18. Pema Chödrön, "No True Story," *Comfortable with Uncertainty* (Boston: Shambhala Audio, 2008), audio recording.

19. Salzberg, *Faith*, 14–15.

20. The story was initially told by a Holocaust survivor and recounted by Susan Griffin in her essay "To Love the Marigold," *The Impossible Will Take a While: A Citizen's Guide to Hope in a Time of Fear*, ed. Paul Rogat Loeb (New York: Basic Books, 2004), 136–37.

21. Alan Watts quoted by Salzberg, *Faith*, 67.

22. Zora Neale Hurston, *The Sanctified Church* (Berkeley, CA: Turtle Island, 1981), 97.

23. Douglas Steere, quoted by *Parks, Big Questions*, 139.

24. Recounted by Salzberg, *Faith*, 39.

25. Hebrews 11:1 (NRSV).

Chapter 7: Writing about Prayer

1. Jalal al-Din Rumi, *Essential*, 36.

2. C. S. Lewis, *Readings for Meditation and Reflection*, ed. Walter Hooper (New York: HarperCollins, 1996), 60.

3. Leonard Cohen, *Beautiful Losers: A Novel* (Toronto: McClelland & Stewart, 2003), 58.

4. James Luther Adams, *The Essential James Luther Adams: Selected Essays and Addresses*, ed. George Kimmich Beach (Boston: Skinner Books, 1998), 77.

5. Mary Rose O'Reilley, "Speaking in Tongues," *Half Wild: Poems* (Baton Rouge: Louisiana State University Press, 2006), 53.

6. From numerous sources including Margaret Parkin, *Tales for Change: Using Storytelling to Develop People and Organizations* (London and Sterling, VA: Kogan Page, 2004), 140–41.

7. José Hobday, *Stories of Awe and Abundance* (New York: Continuum, 1999), 53–54.

8. John Wesley, quoted by Umphrey Lee, *John Wesley and Modern Religion* (Nashville: Cokesbury, 1936), 107–8.

9. Mother Teresa quoted by Malcolm Muggeridge, *Something Beautiful for God: The Classic Account of Mother Teresa's Journey into Compassion*, quoted in Marilyn Chandler McEntyre, *Caring for Words in a Culture of Lies* (Grand Rapids, MI: Eerdmans, 2009), 211.

10. Benedicta Ward, *The Sayings of the Desert Fathers: The Alphabetical Collection* (Collegeville, MN: Cistercian Publications, 1984), 67. Abba Zeno as quoted in Krista Tippett, "Krista's Journal: A Richer Texture of Prayer and Contemplation," On Being (blog), December 31, 2009: http://www.onbeing.org/program /approaching-prayer/journal/613.

11. Several different Sanskrit phrases have been translated as "I am that." The phonetic phrase used by Jeremy Taylor is "*tsam tsvas tvat*," described online at http://jeremytaylor.com/pages/whatsnew.html.

12. McEntyre, *Caring for Words*, 210.

13. Tad Wise, *Blessings on the Wind: The Mystery & Meaning of Tibetan Prayer Flags* (San Francisco: Chronicle Books, 2002), 8.

14. Ibid., 24.

15. Ibid., foreword by Robert A. F. Thurman, 5. Thurman also says Tibetans regard their prayer wheels and flags as "small gestures that remind them of their spiritual aspirations for happiness, love, and compassion."

16. Jeanne Lohmann, "Nothing So Wise," *Shaking the Tree: New and Selected Poems* (McKinleyville, CA: Fithian Press, 2010), 29.

Chapter 8: Writing about Sin

1. David Shumate, "Teaching a Child the Art of Confession," *High Water Mark: Prose Poems* (Pittsburgh: University of Pittsburgh Press, 2004) quoted in Garrison Keillor, *Good Poems for Hard Times* (New York: Penguin, 2005), 102.

2. Sven Lindqvist, *"Exterminate All the Brutes": One Man's Odyssey into the Heart of Darkness and the Origins of European Genocide*, trans. Joan Tate (New York: The New Press, 1996), 2.

3. John Steinbeck, *Travels with Charley: In Search of America* (New York: Penguin, 1986), 78–79.

4. Brad Knickerbocker, "Gandhi Grandson Pursues Peace," *The Christian Science Monitor*, February 1, 1995, 14.

5. Judith Silver, Esq., "Movie Day at the Supreme Court: 'I Know It When I See It': A History of the Definition of Obscenity" (informative article, www.coollawyer. com), http://www.internet-law-library.com/pdf/Obscenity%20Article.pdf.

6. Lao Tzu, *Tao Te Ching: An Illustrated Journey*, trans. Stephen Mitchell (New York: HarperCollins, 1990), 52.

7. Paul Tillich, *The Shaking of the Foundations* (New York: Charles Scribner's Sons, 1948), 154–55.

8. Sallie McFague, *Life Abundant: Rethinking Theology and Economy for a Planet in Peril* (Minneapolis: Augsburg Fortress, 2001), 117. Church teachings change too. Just a few years ago, the Catholic Church added new sins to the original seven deadly ones. The new list includes many social sins, such as environmental pollution, genetic manipulation, excessive wealth, poverty, drug trafficking, consumption, morally debatable experiments, and the violation of the fundamental rights of human nature.

9. Tillich, *Shaking of the Foundations*.

10. Lewis Carroll, *Alice's Adventures in Wonderland* (New York: Macmillan, 1920), 15.

11. Sallie McFague, *The Body of God: An Ecological Theology* (Minneapolis: Augsburg Fortress, 1993), 114–15. In *Life Abundant*, McFague describes sin as taking more than our fair share and "turning away from reality, from the radical, intimate relationships that constitute life and its goodness, [. . .] the false belief that we can live from and for ourselves," 183–84.

12. Carroll, *Alice's Adventures in Wonderland*, 60.

13. John O'Donohue, *Beauty: The Invisible Embrace* (New York: HarperCollins, 2004), 16–17.

14. Matthew 13:14–15 (NRSV).

15. John 8:1–11 (NRSV).

16. Pema Chödrön, *Comfortable with Uncertainty* (Boston: Shambhala, 2008), audio recording.

17. Susan Griffin, *The Eros of Everyday Life* (New York: Doubleday Books, 1995), 146.

18. McFague, *Life Abundant*, 6.

Chapter 9: Writing about Love

1. Mother Teresa, *No Greater Love* (Novato, CA: New World Library, 2002), 22. Originally published as *A Life for God: The Mother Teresa Reader*, ed. LaVonne Neff (Servant Publications, Inc., 1995).

2. For a long, playful list of love's metaphors online, visit: http://grammar.about .com/od/rhetoricstyle/a/lovemetaphors.htm.

3. Diane Ackerman, *A Natural History of Love*, quoted by bell hooks, *All About Love: New Visions* (New York: HarperCollins, 2001), 4.

4. Mother Teresa, *No Greater Love*, 22.

5. Nikki Giovanni, *Reader's Digest*, 1985, quoted in Nguyen, *Language*, 116.

6. Patrick O'Donohue, foreword, John O'Donohue, *The Four Elements: Reflections on Nature* (London: Transworld, 2010), xx.

7. Zora Neale Hurston, *Their Eyes Were Watching God* (New York: HarperCollins, 2000), quoted in *Language*, ed. Nguyen, 119.

8. Thomas Lewis, Fari Amini, and Richard Lannon, *A General Theory of Love* (New York: Vintage Books, 2001), 60–65.

9. M. Scott Peck, *The Road Less Traveled: A New Psychology of Love, Traditional Values and Growth* (New York: Simon & Schuster, 2002), 83.

10. Ellen Bass, "The Thing Is," *Mules of Love* (New York: BOA Editions, 2002), 72.

11. Lewis et al., *A General Theory of Love*, 205.

12. Luke 10:25–37 (NRSV).

13. Ed Bok Lee, "All Love Is Immigrant," *Whorled: Poems* (Minneapolis: Coffee House Press, 2011), 1.

14. 1 Corinthians 14:1, *The Living Bible Paraphrased* (Wheaton, IL: Tyndale House Publishers, 1971).

15. Howard Thurman, *For the Inward Journey: The Writings of Howard Thurman* (New York: Harcourt Brace Jovanovich, 1984), 192. Of the imagination Thurman wrote, "But the imagination shows its greatest powers as the *angelos* of God is in the miracle it creates when one man, standing on his own ground, is able while there to put himself in another man's place. To send his imagination forth to establish a point of focus in another man's spirit and [. . .] so to blend with the other's landscape that what he sees and feels is authentic [. . .] We corrupt our imagination when we give it range over only our own affairs," 187.

16. Ibid., 188.

17. Emerson, "Love," *Essential Writings*, 197.

18. Óscar Romero, *The Violence of Love* (Farmington, PA: Plough Publishing House, 2007), 20.

19. Robert Desnos, "Letter to Youki," *Against Forgetting: Twentieth Century Poetry of Witness*, trans. Carolyn Forché (New York: W. W. Norton, 1993), 237–38.

20. Ibid.

Chapter 10: Writing about Justice

1. Spoken and written numerous times by Cornel West, including in his comments to the Occupy Wall Street protestors on October 7, 2011, and posted on his website: http://www.cornelwest.com/occupy_la_100711.html.

2. Quoted by Ross Fuller, "An Accursed Mirage," *Parabola*, 33:4 (2008), 41.

3. The term draws from the writings of Barry Lopez on animal rights. It was applied to Neruda's poem by Madronna Holden in her essay "Wild Justice" in *Parabola* 33:4 (2008), 78–85.

4. Pablo Neruda, "Childhood and Poetry," *Neruda and Vallejo: Selected Poems*, ed. Robert Bly, trans. Robert Bly, John Knoepfle, and James Wright (Boston: Beacon Press, 1993) 12–13.

5. Martin Luther King Jr. made this statement in many of his speeches, including during the march from Selma in 1965. It was a paraphrase of a quote from an 1853 sermon by Unitarian abolitionist minister Theodore Parker, who said: "I do not pretend to understand the moral universe. The arc is a long one. My eye reaches but little ways. I cannot calculate the curve and complete the figure by experience of sight. I can divine it by conscience. And from what I see I am sure it bends toward justice." See: Melissa Block, "Theodore Parker And The 'Moral Universe,'" *All Things Considered*, September 2, 2010, NPR. http://www.npr.org/templates/story/story.php?storyId=129609461.

6. Bruce Chatwin, *The Songlines* (New York: Penguin, 1987), quoted by Phil Cousineau, *The Art of Pilgrimage: The Seeker's Guide to Making Travel Sacred* (San Francisco: Conari Press, 1998), 43.

7. Margaret Rozga, "March on Milwaukee," *Wisconsin Magazine of History*, 90:4, (2007), 28–39.

8. Paul Tillich, *Love, Power, and Justice: Ontological Analyses and Ethical Application* (New York: Oxford University Press, 1960), 70.

9. Based on "The Cottage of Candles," Howard Schwartz, *Tree of Souls: The Mythology of Judaism* (New York: Oxford University Press, 2007), 43–44.

10. *Tao Te Ching*, Mitchell, trans., 67.

11. Ibid., 35.

12. Thomas Merton, "When Life Was Full There Was No History," *The Way of Chuang Tzu* (New York: New Directions, 1965), 76.

13. Tillich, *Love, Power, and Justice*, 84–85.

14. Charlotte Joko Beck, *Nothing Special: Living Zen* (New York: HarperCollins, 1993), 53.

15. Based on a telling of the story by Kimberly McKeehan, "The Big Harmony," *Parabola* 33:4 (2008), 74–77.

Chapter 11: Writing about Hope

1. Barack Obama, 2004 Keynote Speech to the Democratic National Convention, quoted in *Language*, Nguyen, ed., 251.

2. Lisel Mueller, "Hope," *Alive Together: New and Selected Poems* (Baton Rouge: Louisiana State University Press, 1996), 103.

3. Julie Neraas, *Apprenticed to Hope: A Sourcebook for Difficult Times* (Minneapolis: Augsburg Books, 2009), x.

4. Jim Wallis, quoted by Paul Rogat Loeb, "Introduction," *The Impossible Will Take a Little While: A Citizen's Guide to Hope in a Time of Fear* (New York: Basic Books, 2004), 5.

5. The "leaping in expectation" appears in the entry found at: hope. Dictionary. com. Online Etymology Dictionary. Douglas Harper, historian. http://dictionary .reference.com/browse/hope.

6. Eleazar S. Fernandez, *Reimagining the Human: Theological Anthropology in Response to Systemic Evil* (St. Louis, MO: Chalice Press), 218.

7. John C. Morgan, "About Thomas Potter," *Murray Grove: Retreat and Renewal Center*, http://www.murraygrove.org/potter.html.

8. Matthew 28:20 (NSRV).

9. *Tao Te Ching*, Mitchell, 54.

10. Isaiah 41:10 (NSRV). As the passage continues, God says, "I will strengthen you. I will help you. I will uphold you [. . .]"

11. Cornel West, *The Cornel West Reader* (New York: Basic Civitas Books, 1999), 554, quoted in *Language*, Nguyen, ed., 248.

12. A feminist critique of this story suggests it marks a turn from matriarchy to patriarchy in Greek culture and the subsequent effort to re-create the life-giving Gaia and mother goddesses as the conniving female that unleashes evil and suffering on the world.

13. W. E. B. Du Bois, *The Souls of Black Folk* (Project Gutenberg ebook, January 29, 2008) eBook #408.

14. Thomas Merton, "Letter to James Forest, February 21, 1965," *The Hidden Ground of Love: The Letters of Thomas Merton on Religious Experience and*

Social Concerns, ed. William H. Shannon (New York: Farrar, Straus & Giroux, 1985), 294–97.

15. Mark Doty, *Heaven's Coast* (New York: HarperCollins, 1996), 218.

16. Václav Havel, "An Orientation of the Heart," *The Impossible Will Take a Little While: A Citizen's Guide to Hope in a Time of Fear*, ed. Paul Rogat Loeb (New York: Basic Books, 2004), 82.

17. Václav Havel, *Letters to Olga* (New York: Henry Holt, 1983), 9.

18. Doty, *Heaven's Coast*, 218.

19. Viktor Frankl, *Man's Search for Meaning* (New York: Pocket Books, 1984), 90.

20. Nicholas D. Kristof, "China's Greatest Dissident Writer: Dead but Still Dangerous," *New York Times*, August 19, 1990, http://www.nytimes.com/books/97/05/11/reviews/21513.html.

21. Exodus 14:15 (NRSV).

22. Martin Luther, *Martin Luther's Works*, 32:24, quoted by Paul Althaus, trans. Robert C. Schultz, *The Theology of Martin Luther* (Minneapolis: Fortress Press, 1966), 245.

23. Emily Dickinson, "Hope Is the Thing with Feathers," *The Poems of Emily Dickinson*, ed. R. W. Franklin (Harvard University Press, 1999), accessed online at: http://www.poetryfoundation.org/poem/171619.

24. Etty Hillesum, *An Interrupted Life and Letters from Westerbork* (New York: Henry Holt, 1996), 95.

25. Ibid, 225.

26. Merton, "Letter to James Forest, February 21, 1965," *Hidden Ground of Love*, 294–97.

Chapter 12: Writing about Redemption

1. Wendell Berry, *The Art of the Commonplace: The Agrarian Essays* (Berkeley, CA: Counterpoint, 2002), 146.

2. *Writer's Almanac*, January 17, 2007, http://writersalmanac.publicradio.org/index.php?date=2007/01/17.

3. Terry Tempest Williams, *Finding Beauty in a Broken World* (New York: Vintage Books, 2009), 6.

4. Quoted by Parker Palmer, "The Heart of Politics: An Interview with Parker Palmer," *Bearings*, 2:1 (Autumn/Winter 2010), 6.

5. Martin Buber quoted by Annie Dillard, *For the Time Being* (New York: Knopf, 1999), 201–2.

6. Naomi Shihab Nye, "Gate A-4," *Honeybee* (New York: Greenwillow Books, 2008), 162–64.

7. Jim Harrison, "Debtors," *Songs of Unreason* (Port Townsend, WA: Copper Canyon Press, 2011), 105.

8. Financial Management Survey, "US Public Debt Per Capita Chart," *YCharts*, http://ycharts.com/indicators/us_per_capita_public_debt.

9. Fatima Mernissi, *Dreams of Trespass: Tales of a Harem Girlhood* (New York: Perseus Books, 1994), 60–61.

10. Anthony De Mello, *The Way to Love: The Last Meditations of Anthony de Mello* (New York: Doubleday Image Books, 1995), 65. The quote continues, "Most people end up being conformists; they adapt to prison life. A few become reformers; they fight for better living conditions in the prison, better lighting, better ventilation. Hardly anyone becomes a rebel, a revolutionary who breaks down the prison walls. You can only be a revolutionary when you see the prison walls in the first place."

11. Martin Buber, *The Way of Man and Ten Rungs* (New York: Citadel Press, 2006), 123.

12. Tim Dlugos, "Ordinary Time," *A Fast Life: The Collected Poems of Tim Dlugos*, ed. David Trinidad (New York: Nightboat Books, 2011), 445–46.

13. Luke 17:33 (NRSV).

14. Ayoub, "The Idea of Redemption," *Mormons and Muslims*, 157–69. http://rsc.byu.edu/archived/mormons-and-muslims/13-idea-redemption-christianity-and-islam. Ayoub writes: "The Qur'an speaks not of ransom by sacrifice even though we do a commemorative sacrifice at the time of the hajj to commemorate the sacrifice of Abraham, but the Qur'an insists that then neither the fat nor the blood of the animals reaches God. What reaches him is our piety or righteousness. So expiation, or *takfir*, of sin must be done by the individual himself, and here, then, redemption is what men and women do with their own sin through repentance and through expiation through prayers, fasts, sharing their wealth with the poor, and so on."

15. John Buehrens and Forrest Church, *A Chosen Faith: An Introduction to Unitarian Universalism*, rev. ed. (Boston: Beacon Press, 1998), 5–6.

16. Ibid.

Chapter 13: Writing about Grace

1. Manning Marable, *The Great Wells of Democracy: the Meaning of Race in American Life* (New York: BasicCivitas, 2002), 16.

2. Rafael Jesús González, "Gracias/Grace," *The Montserrat Review*, 6 (Spring 2003). Nominated for the Hobblestock Peace Poetry Award.

3. Simone Weil, *Gravity and Grace*, Emma Crawford and Marion von der Ruhr, trans. (New York: Routledge, 2002), 10.

4. Augustine, *The Encyclopedia of Religious Quotations*, ed. Frank S. Mead (Westwood, NJ: Fleming H. Revell Co., 1966), 200.

5. Tillich, *The Shaking of the Foundations*, 161–62. The sermon continues, "After such an experience we may not be better than before, and we may not believe more than before. But everything is transformed. In that moment grace conquers sin and reconciliation bridges the gulf of estrangement."

6. Eugene O'Neill, "The Great God Brown," quoted by Robert M. Dowling, *Critical Companion to Eugene O'Neill: A Literary Reference to His Life and Work* (New York: Facts on File, 2006), 198.

7. Jalal al-Din Rumi, *Essential*, 70.

8. Philip Simmons, *Learning to Fall: The Blessings of an Imperfect Life* (New York: Bantam Dell, 2003), 10–11.

9. Thomas Merton, *The New Man* (London: Burnes & Oates, 1976), 29.

10. Arianna Stassinopoulos Huffington, *Picasso: Creator and Destroyer* (New York: Simon and Schuster, 1988), 338, recounted by Charlene Spretnak, *States of Grace: The Recovery of Meaning in the Postmodern Age* (New York: HarperCollins, 1991), 26–27.

11. Frederick Buechner, *The Alphabet of Grace* (New York: Seabury Press, 1970), 7–8.

12. Anne Morrow Lindbergh, *Gift from the Sea* (New York: Pantheon Books, 1977), 23.

13. Martha Heyneman, "Morning Wind in the Leaves," *Parabola* 27:3 (2002), 87. The first part of the quote says: "Although the meaning of the Graces may seem confused to the ordinary mind, it is immediately apparent to the sense of sight, touch, and movement through which we apprehend beauty and harmony in art: unity in diversity; diversity in unity."

14. Sharon D. Welch, *A Feminist Ethic of Risk* (Minneapolis: Augsburg Fortress, 2000), 174.

15. E. Stanley Jones, *The Way: 364 Adventures in Daily Living* (Nashville: Abingdon Press, 1991), 196, quoted in *Encyclopedia of Religious Quotations*, Frank S. Mead, ed. (Westwood, NJ: Revell, 1965), 201.

16. Christopher Bamford, "Donum Dei," *Parabola* 27:3 (2002), 63–70.

17. Matthew 13:33 (NRSV).

18. Catherine Keller, *On the Mystery: Discerning Divinity in Process* (Minneapolis: Fortress Press, 2008), 149.

Chapter 14: Writing about Hospitality

1. Joan Chittister, *Wisdom Distilled from the Daily: Living the Rule of St. Benedict Today* (New York: HarperSanFrancisco, 1991), 130–31.

2. J. P. McEvoy, from a 1920s Buzza wall plaque.

3. According to Lakota artist Arthur Amiotte, the Lakota language has three forms for saying thank you, the greatest of which is a wordless gesture made with the hand as if stroking another's face, and means "I am so thankful, I am stroking your face." "Giveaway for the Gods: An Interview with Arthur Amiotte," *Parabola* 15:4 (1990), 49.

4. Genesis 18:1–15 (NRSV).

5. Helen M. Luke, "The Stranger Within," *Parabola* 15:4 (1990), 17.

6. Lambros Kamperidis, "Philoxenia and Hospitality," *Parabola* 15:4 (1990), 7.

7. Inspired by a meditation by Ellen Dooling Draper, "In the Doorway," *Parabola* 20:2 (1995), 73.

8. Henri M. Nouwen, *Reaching Out: The Three Movements of the Spiritual Life* (Garden City, NY: Doubleday, 1986), 72.

9. Samuel Taylor Coleridge quoted by Madeleine L'Engle, *Walking on Water: Reflections on Faith and Art* (Wheaton, IL: Harold Shaw Publishers, 1980), 111.

10. Ralph Waldo Emerson, *Essays and Poems of Emerson* (New York: Harcourt, Brace & Co., 1921), 80.

11. The phrase "entertained angels unawares" originated in the King James Version of Hebrews 13:1–2, referring to Abraham's welcome of the angels and admonishing early Christian communities to "Let brotherly love continue. Be not forgetful to entertain strangers: for thereby some have entertained angels unawares."

12. Ovid, *Metamorphoses*, trans. Rolfe Humphries (Bloomington, IN: Indiana University Press, 1955), 200-204.

13. Eleazar S. Fernandez, *Burning Center, Porous Borders: The Church in a Globalized World* (Eugene, OR: Wipf & Stock, 2011), 228.

14. D. H. Lawrence, *The Complete Poems of D. H. Lawrence*, ed. David Ellis (Ware, Hertfordshire: Wordsworth Editions, 1994), 195.

15. T. S. Eliot, "Choruses from the Rock," *Selected Poems* (New York: Harcourt, Brace & World, 1964), 109.

16. John Koenig, "Hospitality," *The Encyclopedia of Religion*, ed. in chief Mircea Eliade, vol. 6 (New York: Macmillan, 1987), 471.

17. Samuel H. Miller, *Man the Believer* (Nashville, TN: Abingdon Press, 1968), quoted online at: http://www.spiritualityandpractice.com/practices/practices.php?id =13&g=1#.

18. Hafiz, "Some Fill with Each Good Rain," *The Gift*, 76.

19. Paul Jordan-Smith, "The Hostage and the Parasite," *Parabola* 15:4 (1990), 24–31.

20. Letty Russell, *Just Hospitality: God's Welcome in a World of Difference*, eds. J. Shannon Clarkson and Kate Ott (Louisville, KY: Westminster John Knox, 2009).

21. Denis Huerre, OSB, *Letters to My Brothers and Sisters Living by the Rule of St. Benedict*, trans. Sylvester Houédard, O.S.B. (Collegeville, MN: Liturgical Press 1994), 54.

22. Denis Huerre, Monastic Studies, no. 10 (Pine City, NY: Mount Saviour Monastery, 1974), quoted in *Parabola* 15:4 (1990), 35–36.

Chapter 15: Writing about Reverence

1. "Akdamut," a liturgical poem (*piyyut*) quoted by Schwartz, *Tree of Souls*, 527.

2. W. M. Rankin, "Reverence," *Encyclopedia of Religion and Ethics*, ed. James Hastings (New York: Charles Scribner's Sons, 1919), 20:754.

3. May Sarton, "Beyond the Question," *A Grain of Mustard Seed: New Poems* (New York: Norton, 1971), 69.

4. Peter Mayer, "Holy Now," *Million Year Mind*, recorded 1999, compact disc.

5. Jane Kenyon, "Briefly It Enters, and Briefly Speaks," *Jane Kenyon: Collected Poems* (St. Paul, MN: Graywolf, 2005), 138.

6. Paul Woodruff, *Reverence: Renewing a Forgotten Virtue* (New York: Oxford University Press, 2002), 133.

7. Rankin, "Reverence," 752.

8. Schwartz, *Tree of Souls*, 25–26.

9. Barbara Hamilton-Holway, *Spirit of Life* curriculum (Boston: Unitarian Universalist Association, revised 2008), Workshop 1, Handout 3. List compiled from the Unitarian Universalist Association hymnbook, *Singing the Living Tradition* (Boston: Beacon Press, 1993).

10. Elizabeth Barrett Browning, *Aurora Leigh and Other Poems* (New York: Penguin, 1995), 232.

11. Ibid.

12. Albert Schweitzer, *Out of My Life and Thought: An Autobiography*, quoted by John Webster and Ty F. Webster, *Reverence for All Life* (Sparta, WI: Prell Books, 2005), 11–12.

13. Dr. Edwin A. Schick, professor emeritus, Wartburg Theological Seminary, Dubuque, Iowa, quoted by Webster and Webster, *Reverence for All Life*, 20.

14. Barbara Brown Taylor, *An Altar in The World: A Geography of Faith* (New York: HarperOne, 2009), 15.

15. C. Alexander Simpkins and Annellen M. Simpkins, *Simple Zen: A Guide to Living Moment by Moment* (Boston, MA: Tuttle Publishing, 1999), 99.

16. University of West Florida, "Chado: The Way of Tea," *Japan House*, http://uwf.edu/japanhouse/chado.cfm.

17. Margaret Fuller, *Life Without and Life Within*, 20, quoted by Frederick Augustus Braun, *Margaret Fuller and Goethe: The Development of a Remarkable Personality, Her Religion and Philosophy, and Her Relation to Emerson, J. F. Clarke and Transcendentalism* (New York: Henry Holt and Co., 1910), 171.

18. Woodruff, *Reverence*, 35.

19. *The Analects of Confucious*, quoted by Woodruff, *Reverence*, 41.

20. Thich Nhat Hanh, "Love Poem," *Call Me by My True Names: The Collected Poems of Thich Nhat Hanh* (Berkeley, CA: Parallax Press, 1999), 153.

21. Wangari Maathai, interviewed by Krista Tibbett, *Speaking of Faith*, April 24, 2008; Transcript online at: http://www.onbeing.org/program/planting-future/transcript/2357.

22. John Muir, *My First Summer in the Sierra* (Boston: Houghton Mifflin, 1911), 211.

23. Woodruff, *Reverence*, 142.

24. Based on Woodruff's recounting of Herodotus' tale, Woodruff, *Reverence*, 81–83.

25. Walt Whitman, "Song of the Open Road," *Leaves of Grass* (New York: Penguin Signet Classic, 1980), 137.

26. Laurel Hallman, *Living by Heart* (Dallas, TX: Living By Heart, 2003), 74. The workbook describes a larger spiritual practice of memorizing poetry.

27. Harry Scholefield, *You Book I,* quoted by Hallman, Living by Heart, 74.

28. Ibid.

29. Ibid.

Appendix A

1. Pat Schneider, *Writing Alone and with Others* (New York: Oxford University Press, 2003).
2. Tim O'Brien, *The Things They Carried* (New York: Houghton Mifflin, 1990; first Mariner edition, 2009), 171.
3. Schneider, *Writing*, 187.
4. Lu Chi, *Wen Fu*, 35.

CONTRIBUTORS

Thank you to all the poets and writers who have generously granted their permission to share their beautiful work in these pages. While I was often unable to include whole poems here, it is my hope that the excerpts will provide enough of a taste that readers will seek out the longer works. In my experience, nothing awakens the soul quite like a good line of poetry that moves between the spoken and unspoken in a delightful dance of images and rhythm.

A special thanks to Neil Mikesell and to *all* of you who have shared your stories and writing with me. In some cases, I have changed names and the details of your stories to respect confidentiality; and in many cases, I have not been able to include your stories in these pages. But all of the stories and words you have passed on to me as participants in these writing sessions have helped me understand more deeply the transformative power of words and how we arrange and exchange them.

Some of my own writing in this book first appeared, in different versions and variations, as parts of sermons I have delivered from several pulpits and in the publications of Unity Church-Unitarian and Wisdom Ways Center for Spirituality, both in St. Paul, Minnesota.

"Laughter"   Excerpt reprinted by permission from Daniel Ladin-
                              sky. Copyright © 1999 by Daniel Ladinsky from
                              the Penguin publication, *The Gift: Poems by Hafiz The
                              Great Sufi Master.*

"What Is the Root"   Excerpt reprinted by permission from Daniel Ladin-
                              sky. Copyright © 1999 by Daniel Ladinsky from
                              the Penguin publication, *The Gift: Poems by Hafiz The
                              Great Sufi Master.*

"VII"   Excerpt reprinted by permission of Counterpoint.
                              Copyright © 1998 by Wendell Berry from *A Tim-
                              bered Choir.*

"old man"   Reprinted by permission from Neil Mikesell. Copy-
                              right © 2011 by Neil Mikesell from *Cairns*, 3 (Fall
                              2011).

"Nine Gates"   Excerpt reprinted by permission of Northwestern
                              University Press. Copyright © 2010 by Sam Hamill
                              from *Measured by Stone.* Published by Curbstone
                              Press.

"Origin of Poem"   Excerpt reprinted by permission of The Permissions
                              Company, Inc., on behalf of New Rivers Press, www
                              .newriverspress.com. Copyright © 1997 by Heid
                              Ellen Erdrich from *Fishing for Myth.*

from *Shaking the Tree: New and Selected Poems* published by Fithian Press.

"The Thing Is"   Reprinted by permission of the Permission Company, Inc., on behalf of BOA Editions Ltd., www.boaeditions .org. Copyright © 2002 by Ellen Bass from *Mules of Love*.

"All Love Is Immigrant"   Reprinted by permission from Ed Bok Lee. Copyright © 2011 by Ed Bok Lee from *Whorled* published by CoffeeHouse Press.

"Hope"   Excerpt reprinted by permission from Louisiana State University Press. Copyright © 1996 by Lisel Mueller from *Alive Together: New and Selected Poems*.

"Ordinary Time"   Excerpt reprinted by permission of The Permissions Company, Inc., on behalf of Nightboat Books, www .nightboat.org. Copyright © 2011 by the Estate of Tim Dlugos from *A Fast Life: The Collected Poems of Tim Dlugos*, edited by David Trinidad.

"Gracias/Grace"   Reprinted by permission from Rafael Jesús González. Copyright © 2003 by Rafael Jesús González from *The Montserrat Review*, 6 (Spring 2003); nominated for the Hobblestock Peace Poetry Award.

"Bismillah"   Excerpt reprinted by permission of Coleman Barks. Copyright © 2004 by Coleman Barks from *The Essential Rumi*. Published by HarperCollins. Translations by Coleman Barks.

"Some Fill With Each Good Rain"   Excerpt reprinted by permission from Daniel Ladinsky. Copyright © 1999 by Daniel Ladinsky from the Penguin publication, *The Gift: Poems by Hafiz The Great Sufi Master*.

Imagine...

I magine you have been given a small gift, attractively wrapped. You were told to open it when you had some time to spare, so on this day, you have made a little clearing free of activities and commitments. You're in comfortable surroundings, relaxed and unhurried. With curiosity and pleasant but modest anticipation, you sit down with the gift and unwrap it.

Inside, you find two things: a pen and a simple notebook with just the kind of pages and binding you prefer for writing. The book is blank except for a half sentence written on the first page in handwriting surprisingly like your own. You remember a voice of encouragement saying, *Begin writing whenever you are ready and follow wherever it leads.*

The half sentence reads:

If I turn my ear inward and listen to a whispered truth within, what I hear on this day…

You pick up the pen.